the ALBERTA FIELD FORCE *of* 1885

Jack Dunn

Jack Dunn

Calgary, Alberta 1994

Publisher: Jack Dunn
6404 Norfolk Drive N.W.
Calgary, Alberta, Canada T2K 5K2

ISBN 0-9698596-0-0

Canadian Cataloguing in Publication Data

Dunn, Jack F.
The Alberta Field Force of 1885

Includes index.
ISBN 0-9698596-0-0

1. Canada. Canadian Army. Alberta Field Force. 2. Riel Rebellion, 1885. 3. Northwest Territories – History – 1870-1905.* 4. Strange, T. Bland, 1831-1925. I. Title.

FC3215.D86 1994 971.05'4 C94-910634-8
F1060.9.D86 1994

Design:

Gail Pocock, Bulldog Communications
#3, 830 - 19 Ave. S.W., Calgary, Alberta, Canada T2T 0H5

Printing:

Hignell Printing Limited
488 Burnell St., Winnipeg, Manitoba, Canada R3G 2B4

Printed and bound in Canada

To my wife, Maureen

thank you for your love
and encouragement

Table of Contents

PREFACE

The Alberta Field Force of 1885 outlines the contribution of the far western attacking column, the Alberta Field Force, to the suppression of the North-West Rebellion. The narrative follows colorful Thomas Bland Strange and his amateur troops as they march northward to confront the Cree band under Big Bear. This text adds to western Canadian history, as it is the most detailed study of the Field Force and of events occurring in the District of Alberta during the rebellion. Many documents quoted herein are published for the first time. One weakness, though, relates to the lack of primary Indian accounts. Almost all information concerning the natives derives from white sources – an obvious shortcoming in presenting the Indian point of view.

The study maintains that:

1. The Alberta Field Force, although essential to the area, was only marginally important to the ultimate outcome of the insurrection. On May 11 General Middleton had requested more troops for Batoche. In response, the Minister of Militia mobilized another 1100 men that same day.[1] Canada was not going to let several hundred rebels imperil the great concept of a nation "from sea to sea."

2. The Indian danger to western settlement has been greatly exaggerated. Population statistics reveal the minority status of Indians on the western plains, a fact not generally recognized. Moreover, the Indians were disunited, poorly armed, and incapable of sustained warfare against fortified centres. Many westerners scoffed at the supposed Indian warrior numbers and the alleged Indian bravery.

3. Time or indifference has distorted history. The North-West Rebellion had given Canada its first opportunity for independent military action. Here was a chance for the young nation to prove itself. In 1885 the young soldiers were the pride of the land, clear evidence of Canada's growing nationalism. On the centennial of the rebellion Canada issued a commemorative stamp which depicted Gabriel Dumont overlooking a field of soldiers attacking Batoche – a recognition of the rebel leader that would have been unthinkable in 1885. And the Collins Dictionary of Canadian History, while including references to Frog Lake and Big Bear, omits Thomas Strange.[2] In 1885 everyone in western Canada knew of Gunner Jingo. Had he not "saved Alberta"?[3]

Acknowledgements

It is with gratitude that I acknowledge the generous assistance provided in completing this project.

Many helpful archivists, through personal contact or by correspondence, contributed to the foundation of this book. Institutions providing especially valuable resources were the Glenbow-Alberta Archives, University of Calgary and the National Archives of Canada. Further information was obtained from the Provincial Archives of Alberta, Public Archives of British Columbia, Saskatchewan Archives, Public Archives of Manitoba, Metropolitan Toronto Library, and the Calgary Public Library.

The Social Science Federation of Canada provided four reviews with insightful comments and the Canadian Plains Research Center suggested new perspectives for my study.

I want to thank the following individuals. Donald B. Smith, Professor of History at the University of Calgary, for his direction and help on my thesis which formed the basis of this text. My friend, Art Depatie, for creating the maps. Doreen Norquist typed the original manuscript. Hugh Dempsey found time to read and offer information on the study. Shirley Onn edited the manuscript. Terry Davies carefully proofread the text.

Gail Pocock of Bulldog Communications, designed, coordinated and finalized the publication of *the Alberta Field Force of 1885*. I admire her artistry, persistence, and mastery of the endless details associated with a publication. Gail's expertise was invaluable.

Most of all, I want to thank my family for their continuing interest and enthusiasm for my historical research.

Jack Dunn

Calgary, Alberta
June, 1994

CHAPTER 1

the North-West Rebellion

Photo on Previous Page :

Major General Frederick Dobson Middleton

CHAPTER 1

the North-West Rebellion

"I am delighted at the prospect of being able to take part in defending our country."

– *Walter Stewart, Diary, March 30, 1885*

In late March 1885, a military uprising challenged Canada's western hegemony. Near the tiny hamlet of Duck Lake, Saskatchewan, a brief skirmish between an advancing government column and a Métis force initiated an unequal conflict between fewer than one thousand poorly-equipped insurgents and the resources and technology of 4,500,000 Canadians. The shootings were the violent culmination of long-standing Métis grievances against the government; at stake for Ottawa was the great concept of a nation "from sea to sea."

The Saskatchewan crisis had important military implications for the young nation. In 1871 Britain had withdrawn its garrisons from Canada. This meant that for the first time Canada would independently confront a military threat. Here was an opportunity for the eighteen-year-old Dominion to prove itself.

Great excitement prevailed throughout the country. In eastern Canada, both English- and French-speaking Canadians responded patriotically to the news of an insurrection. Recruits raced to militia drill sheds and special recruiting centres to enlist. A letter from one young soldier in the Halifax Provisional Battalion expressed the confident sentiment:

> All the young men of Canada who have a spark of manly feeling in their nature are coming forward to show that they are true Canadians and not miserable skulking cowards . . . we are going to the North-West in order to show the world that Canada is a power and not a stripling. [1]

Troop movements began almost at once. Enthusiastic crowds thronged to cheer the westward departure of the men. One soldier leaving Ottawa recalled finding it "difficult making our way to the train, due to the immense crowd of people assembled to give us a royal send off." [2] At this moment of euphoria and national solidarity it was inconceivable that, within months, this campaign would fragment the very foundation of the young nation.

Major General Frederick Dobson Middleton

Frederick Dobson Middleton was Commander-in-Chief of Canada's Militia. He was responsible for co-ordinating the military strategy against the insurgents. It was under his direction that three military contingents were assigned to Alberta.

The initial excitement overlooked fundamental weaknesses in the Canadian military. First, an annual budget of under one million dollars restricted effectiveness. Second, the permanent force had only 750 men. These troops were supported by a militia of 37,000 soldiers, organized in twelve districts. However, these reserve units were hardly more than social clubs given to several weeks' training each summer. At his first inspection of the troops arriving in Saskatchewan, an astounded General F.D. Middleton found "that many of them had never fired a rifle, some had never fired any weapon at all."[3]

On the western plains, the news of an insurrection caused many settlements to immediately form a volunteer Home Guard. In the crisis, communities of strangers "suddenly became one household."[4] Wild rumors circulated. A telegram (March 30) sent to Ottawa from the Dominion Land Agent in Calgary reveals the exaggerated hysteria:

> Citizens excited to rashness. Female Indians driven from town at point of pistol. People's actions frightened children in neighborhood. Firearms discharged nightly in street. Mayor mixed and incapable. Patrol small force necessary to control citizens, otherwise may provoke Indians to hostility.[5]

The hostile mood of Calgarians alarmed nearby Indian encampments. The natives approached a settler, F. W. Firth (who spoke their language), and expressed fear of leaving their tents after dark. In a letter to his mother in the Maritimes, Firth attempted to explain the confusing situation. He wrote: "the Indians thought the whites were going to make a raid on them, and the whites thought the same of them."[6]

At this moment in late March and early April, the rebels on the South Saskatchewan held the upper hand. The violence appeared to be spreading. Within days of the outbreak of hostilities, the Assiniboines (Stoneys) at Eagle Hills (150 kilometres west of Duck Lake) had risen, killing their farm instructor and a settler. These Stoneys then joined neighbouring Poundmaker's band to encircle Battleford. Even more startling news came from Frog Lake, 180 kilometres northeast of Battleford. On April 2, Cree Indians under Big Bear murdered nine whites. Eleven days later this band appeared at Fort Pitt and in a brief skirmish killed a Mountie. The following day representatives from the fort and the Indians negotiated a controversial agreement: twenty-three Mounted Policemen were permitted to escape by scow to Battleford; the remaining forty civilians voluntarily accepted the perils of captivity with this truculent band. How far would this violence spread? Was Canada to have its version of an inflamed and bloody American West? Only nine years earlier the Sioux and the Cheyenne had annihilated five companies of the

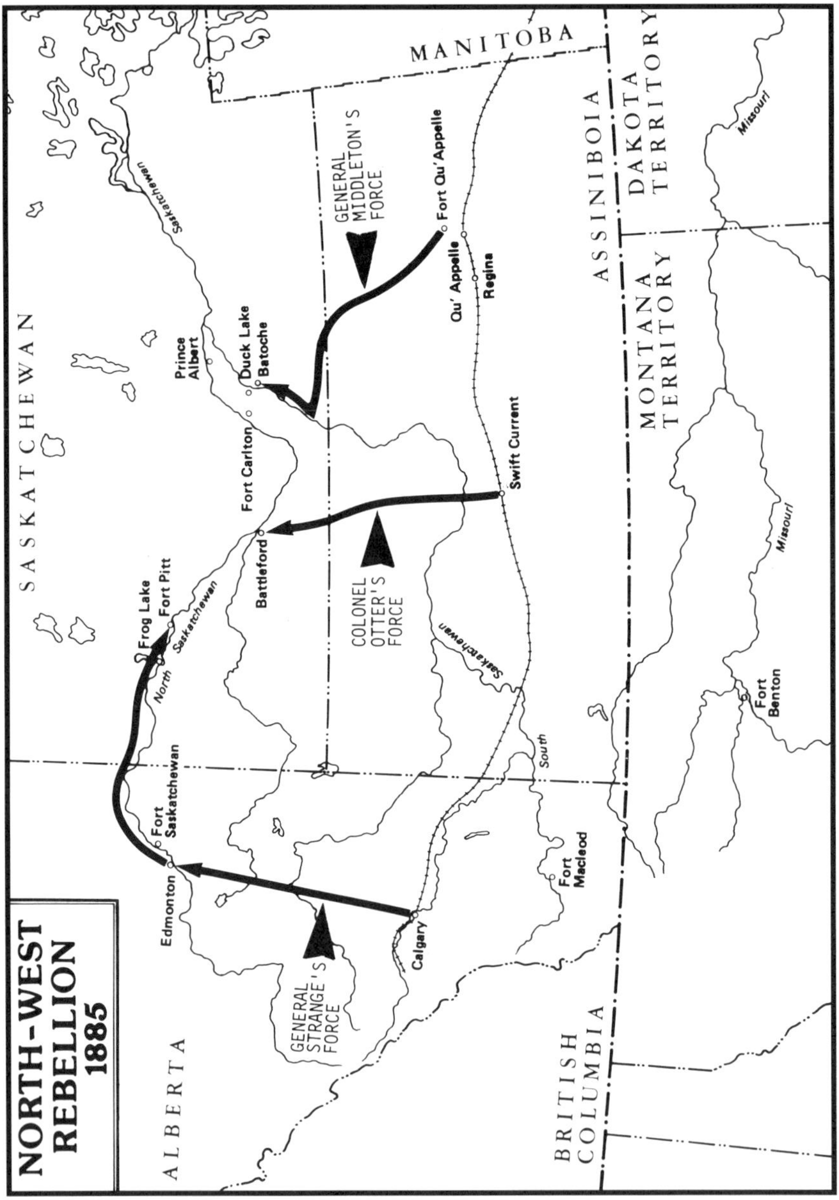
NORTH-WEST
REBELLION
1885
ALBERTA
SASKATCHEWAN
MANITOBA
ASSINIBOIA
DAKOTA
TERRITORY
MONTANA
TERRITORY
BRITISH
COLUMBIA
GENERAL
MIDDLETON'S
FORCE
COLONEL
OTTER'S
FORCE
GENERAL
STRANGE'S
FORCE
Fort Qu'Appelle
Qu' Appelle
Regina
Duck Lake
Batoche
Prince
Albert
Fort Carlton
Swift Current
Battleford
Frog Lake
Fort Pitt
Fort
Saskatchewan
Edmonton
Calgary
Fort
Macleod
Fort
Benton
Saskatchewan
North
Saskatchewan
South
Missouri

7th Cavalry, under General Custer, at the Battle of the Little Big Horn. Would all of the 25,000 destitute and angry Canadian Plains Indians join the rebellion?

Prime Minister John A. Macdonald informed Major General Frederick Dobson Middleton, Commander-in-Chief of Canada's Militia, three days after the clash at Duck Lake that the nation's immediate priority was "to localize the insurrection."[7] In this regard, one of the first directives was to neutralize the Blackfoot Confederacy in present-day southern Alberta, then the District of Alberta. In terms of population and strategy, this region appeared vulnerable. Whites were outnumbered two to one by the Indian population of 6,400; moreover both the telegraph line and the transcontinental railway crossed the Blackfoot and Stoney reserves. The precarious situation impelled the settlers to prepare for all eventualities.

Thomas Bland Strange, a retired Imperial career officer ranching near Calgary, stepped forward to organize local defences. His leadership led to the formation of the third military column – the Alberta Field Force – to march against the rebel forces in Saskatchewan. The contribution of General Strange and his troops to the suppression of the North-West Rebellion is the subject of this book.

Major General Frederick Middleton's revised strategy authorized a three-pronged military offensive northward from the Canadian Pacific Railway against each of the three areas of insurgency. He himself would proceed against Batoche while Colonel William Otter would march to relieve Battleford. The orders for Strange's far western column (using Calgary as its base) were to "over-awe the Indians in the district" and then march to Edmonton.[8] From this strategic centre, the Alberta Field Force was to proceed eastward along the North Saskatchewan River into the Indian-controlled Frog Lake – Fort Pitt area. Here, Cree Indians under Big Bear held forty white hostages. Middleton's plan involved a joint assault against the Indians using the Field Force and troops from Battleford.

The Alberta Field Force was not at the centre of the action. Louis Riel was the key figure in the rebellion, and his operational base was at Batoche. General Middleton directed the attack against Batoche, on which hinged the entire contest. Newspaper correspondents detailed the campaign against Riel to an enthralled national audience. They reported the inglorious attack by a fortified river steamboat; the military astuteness of the legendary Métis "Captain of the Plains" – Gabriel Dumont; the American A. L. Howard and his amazing gatling gun, sent by express from Hartford, Connecticut, and capable of firing 1,200 rounds a minute; and Canada's

Colonel Arthur Williams whose troops bravely swept over the rifle pits, winning the victory. Batoche's capitulation on May 12, 1885, and the capture of Riel three days later ensured the certain defeat of the rebellion.

In the newspapers of 1885, second to Middleton's exploits are those of Otter's Battleford Column. Again considerable drama unfolded as a "Flying Column" marched 300 kilometres across empty prairie to relieve Battleford where for twenty days nearly six hundred whites had remained virtually incarcerated. No sooner had Otter completed this mission than he overstepped his authority and attacked Poundmaker's camp at Cut Knife Hill. The battle became a rout: eight soldiers died, fourteen were wounded, and only the failure of the Indians in attacking the disorganized retreat prevented a total disaster. Further interest ensued near Battleford when the Indians captured a wagon supply train, and again on May 26 with Poundmaker's ceremonial surrender to General Middleton.

The Alberta Field Force's containment of Indians on Alberta reserves lacks the interest generated by the exciting military actions in Saskatchewan. In seventy days of campaigning, the Field Force skirmished no more than six hours. Six casualties (all wounded) in General Strange's expedition hardly compare with the Main Column's twenty-one deaths and eighty-eight wounded. Furthermore, the timing of the actions diminished the Field Force's importance. It was the last column to advance northward and, although the troops were not aware of the fact, their major battle at Frenchman's Butte occurred two weeks after the fall of Batoche and two days after Poundmaker's surrender to Middleton. Then in the final month of the campaign, Strange's troops became only one of four columns haphazardly pursuing Big Bear's evasive band. When contrasted with the two Saskatchewan campaigns, the press allotted far less space to the "third column."

The Alberta Field Force existed for approximately three months. Led by Thomas Bland Strange's energetic command, all military assignments were fulfilled admirably and without any loss of life from military engagements. The campaign was incredibly arduous. Geography foiled communications and complicated the movement of supplies. Some of the soldiers marched over 2,200 kilometres, greater than the air distance from Vancouver to Winnipeg. The visual presence of the government troops over most of present-day southern and central Alberta, and parts of northwestern Saskatchewan, greatly affected the attitude and actions of the Indians. The prompt dispatch of the 700-member contingent did, as intended, convince many of the young warriors at Battle River and in the Edmonton area to stay on their reserves. Along the Edmonton trail, Indians watched incredulously as soldiers marched past, bayonets ready, while a band played martial music. The marching columns were impressive sights.

Father Albert Lacombe, returning to Calgary from Edmonton, met the second echelon moving northward. "The redcoats coming across the prairie made a picture," he informed the *Herald*, "that he would not readily forget. The sun glinted on the bayonets and trappings and the men swinging along with long elastic strides seemed the picture of health and confidence."[9] At Frenchman's Butte and Loon Lake the troops initiated aggressive attacks, clearly demonstrating Ottawa's power. Men had arrived bent on killing Indians. The attacks stunned the rebelling Cree band. The Indians saw a retreat northward into an inhospitable muskeg and swamp region as their only alternative.

Without the Alberta Field Force, quite possibly the suppression of the insurrection would have been more difficult, costly, and time-consuming. Indian unrest was extremely acute in the spring of 1885 in large portions of present-day Alberta. The formation of the Field Force defused the tense situation. A balanced account of the North-West campaign must not overlook the deterrent role performed by General Strange's column.

CHAPTER 2

the Indian Danger in Southern Alberta

Photo on Previous Page :

Chiefs of the Blackfoot Confederacy

CHAPTER 2

the Indian Danger in Southern Alberta

"They attribute all their evils to the whites."

– *Father Cochin*

In early March 1885 the white settlers in Saskatchewan anticipated armed conflict with the Métis. As John Donkin, a Mounted Police trooper stationed in Regina, later recalled: "We in the rank and file used to talk in quite a familiar way, in the barrackroom, of the coming rebellion as a matter of course. We even had the date fixed."[1] Inspector Francis Dickens at Fort Pitt wrote in his diary March 23: "Rumours abroad to the effect that the halfbreeds are in arms against the Government."[2] The very day before the outbreak, on March 25, the *Fort Benton River Press* in Montana Territory had carried a note "Saskatchewan Special: The half-breed population here is on the verge of an incipient rebellion."[3]

Troop movements prior to the March 26 conflict at Duck Lake indicate the government's awareness of impending hostilities. "Riel and his Friends are on the move, and so are the police,"[4] observed the *Saskatchewan Herald* on March 13. Commissioner A.G. Irvine rode northward from Regina with ninety-two Mounted Policemen on March 18 to reinforce Fort Carlton, located approximately thirty-five kilometres west of Riel's base at Batoche. And General F.D. Middleton, was westward bound on American railways as the crisis escalated. He arrived in Winnipeg at 7 a.m. on March 27, and by 6 p.m. that same day departed by train with 260 men of the 90th Rifles of Winnipeg for Troy Station (Fort Qu'Appelle, Assiniboia District).

The Métis victory at Duck Lake caused great concern in Calgary. The expected news, that the whites had been confronted, had arrived with the unexpected – they had been routed by Riel's followers. The departure from Calgary two days before, on March 24, of Police Superintendent W. M. Herchmer and thirty Mounties for Regina left only six policemen in the town. Apprehensive citizens at once feared that local Indians might join the victorious Métis. It was no secret that the three tribes of over 5,000 natives in the Blackfoot Nation and the nearly 500 Sarcees were destitute, disillusioned, and bitter toward the white man. Their transition in the eight years after making a treaty with the white man, from a free nomadic life style to the restricted confines of a reserve, had proved a bewildering and unbelievable experience.

In the twenty-year period predating the North-West Rebellion, terrible epidemics had decimated the prairie Indian population. In 1865 scarlet fever and measles ravaged the Saskatchewan area, killing an estimated 1,200 Indians.[5] A terrible smallpox epidemic occurred in 1867-70, killing, in Reverend George McDougall's estimation, perhaps one-quarter of the Canadian Plains Indians, including 675 Blackfoot, 1,080 Peigans, 630 Bloods, and 200 Sarcees.[6] One account listed the Indian and Métis deaths at 3,544.[7] Some settlements were unable to cope with the deaths. William Butler, in his book *The Great Lone Land*, graphically described how the wolves boldly devoured the unburied corpses left outside Fort Pitt.[8] At the Catholic centre of St. Albert 320 of the town's 800 residents died. The tragedy was unreal. Such mortality compared only to a plague of medieval times. Horrified families fled to the isolation of the plains, only to starve. Travellers reported not sighting a single buffalo between Fort Carlton and Edmonton. In some small groups, no one survived the winter.

For the survivors of the terrible diseases, there remained the debauchery of the whiskey traders, who began in the late 1860s to cross into present-day southern Alberta from Montana Territory. In his reconnaissance of the Indian territories for the Dominion Government, P. Robertson-Ross reported that in the winter of 1871 eighty-eight Blackfoot had been murdered in drunken brawls.[9] Two years later in the Cypress Hills, American wolfers brutally massacred thirty Assiniboines (Stoneys). Clearly, the Canadian Government had to control the lawlessness in western Canada. Order came with the arrival of the North-West Mounted Police in 1874.

Before large-scale white settlement could take place, the Canadian Government recognized that the "North West" had to first be ceded by its aboriginal occupants. At Blackfoot Crossing in the fall of 1877 Treaty Seven, the last of the numbered treaties by the Canadian Government on the Plains, was signed with the five tribal groups of present-day southern Alberta. For annual cash guarantees and promises of assistance in adapting to a new way of life, the Indians acceded to the unfamiliar concept of a reservation.

The negotiations had been successfully concluded, but had they been fully understood? The tribes received almost $60,000 in cash. Some unscrupulous traders immediately cheated the Indians of their new wealth. Many natives did not understand the different denominational values on the money and the police "frequently found that the Indians had been given the labels off fruit jars or cans as money."[10] This misunderstanding of rudimentary monetary values illustrates the wide differences between the negotiating parties. For example, the Indians had no concept of private land ownership. The apportionment of one section of land for each reserve family of five was a meaningless statistic for the native population in September 1877.

Language difficulties caused further problems as all terms and speeches needed interpretation. In the case of the Stoneys, the translation involved two other languages, English and Cree. Father Constantine Scollen, who had served Alberta's Indians since 1862 insisted that the lack of competent interpreters, along with the "dullness of the Indian mind," contributed to the Indians' failure to understand Treaty Seven.[11] Since neither party had adequate knowledge of the other's customs and law, additional problems surfaced. White legal interpretation emphasized written documentation and precedent; the Indians of southern Alberta relied upon oral statements. Father Albert Lacombe commented after the rebellion that "Indians are mere children in matters of this kind. They don't attach the importance to a paper fixing a treaty as we do to the *Winnipeg Daily Times*."[12] Also, the whites incorrectly believed that the Plains chiefs acted as autocratic spokesmen for their tribes, just as David Laird and James Macleod spoke for the Government of Canada. Therefore, the chief best known to the Mounted Police, Crowfoot, one of the two Blackfoot head chiefs, received an elevated status. In reality, however, two Bloods, Red Crow and Rainy Chief, held higher authority in the Confederacy and possessed greater followings.[13]

Why did the Indians sign the document? Certainly the cash grant served immediate needs and won initial native interest in the Treaty. The Indians were destitute, "clothed in rags, without horses and without guns."[14] Father Scollen and his Methodist counterpart John McDougall convinced their followers to accept the pact. Most important of all, the Mounted Police represented the white society and the Forces' prestige still remained very high. The Indians, concluded Father Scollen, signed the treaty as a provision for food and clothing in times of need and because previously they "had always been kindly dealt with by authorities and did not wish to offend them."[15]

In 1877 large herds of buffalo still roamed the Canadian prairies. Trader Louis Goulet recalled that following one day of hunting, Sitting Bull's newly-arrived band traded him "six or seven hundred tongues."[16] Yet incredibly, within two years, the immense buffalo herds were gone. With the disappearance of the great shaggy beasts came terrible suffering. When Indian Commissioner Edgar Dewdney visited Blackfoot Crossing in July 1879, he found the Indians "after eating almost all their dogs, reduced to gophers and mice."[17] Strong young men were so weak that they could barely walk. Father Scollen, the priest with the band, declared never having seen the tribe so depressed and helpless.

About four thousand Canadian Plains Indians, in total desperation, journeyed in late 1879 to the "northern range," a herd estimated at over one million buffalo in Montana Territory. Hunting the buffalo were rival Indian tribes and thousands of white skinners. The American Indians saw the influx of Canadian Indians as a threat to their own meagre existence. One Crow woman, watching 2,000 Crees arrive from the north, wanted the soldiers "to drive them back to their bush swamps rather than allow them to kill buffalo and other game belonging to our people."[18] The *Montana Press* also despised the incursion of British Indians – the so-called "bone pickers." The Blackfoot Chief Crowfoot, for example, was described by the *Fort Benton Record* as "the leader of murderers . . . a red butcher."[19] And the Montana ranching community loathed the Canadian Indians. One rancher wrote:

> Added to the trouble with our own Indians was that with the British Treaty Indians . . . Each autumn after their annual payments at Forts Macleod and Walsh, these tribes swoop down upon us . . . robbing ranches, frightening women, stealing horses and subsisting on our cattle.[20]

In answer to American protests, Prime Minister John A. Macdonald stated that "you might as well try to check a flight of locusts."[21]

A statement by the appointed Lieutenant-Governor of the North-West Territories gives an honest rationale of the government's motives. Edgar Dewdney reported:

> I advised them strongly to go and gave them some provisions to take off. They continued to follow the Buffalo further and further south until they reached the main herd and there they remained. . . . I considered their remaining away saved the Government $100,000 at least.[22]

Inspector L.N.F. Crozier's report from Fort Walsh substantiates the fact that Canadian authorities were determined to rid their posts of loitering Indians. Crozier recorded making "every possible effort to induce them to leave for the buffalo country before the season became too far advanced."[23]

Inordinate hunting quickly wiped out the great buffalo herds in Montana Territory, forcing the return to Canada of the destitute Plains Indians. It was estimated that between 1879 and 1881 at least a thousand Canadian Blackfoot died.[24] Police Sergeant Frank Fitzpatrick encountered one small band of thirty Indians which he described "as a delegation from a grave-yard."[25] When he threw biscuits to the starving natives the "men jumped on the children to take away from them the few biscuits they were able to gather in the scramble."[26] Fitzpatrick found it necessary to distribute the remaining biscuits at gunpoint. Near Calgary, the starving Blackfoot returned on foot, their horses eaten or sold. Cecil Denny left this account of their misery:

> It was pitiable to see parties of the less impoverished bringing their weakened fellows, some mere skeletons, to Fort Calgary for food. Some even ate grass along the road. I have seen them when a steer was shot, rush on the animal with their knives before it had ceased kicking, cut away the flesh and maddened by hunger, devour it raw. [27]

Obviously the Plains Indians had to accept the agrarian future which government authorities hoped would lead to Indian self-sufficiency. A difficult adjustment to the equipment, the new varieties of plant life, and to domestic animals lay ahead. This new life style conflicted with the traditional division of labour whereby the females performed the menial tasks while the male worked not with his hands but providing game and engaging in warfare. The Indian tendency to view things in the short run, such as using the fences each winter for firewood, exasperated the Indian agents.

Many Indians made a sincere attempt to enter an agrarian lifestyle. When Indian Agent Cecil Denny arrived on the Blackfoot reserve in 1882 he "found that the Indians were anxious to go to work, but as yet had no tools."[28] The delayed and inadequate supplies of oxen and implements continued as an on-going problem on many prairie reserves. Distribution and market difficulties limited all produce to the reserve. Unforeseen problems arose. Denny noted that vicious dogs and Indian indifference prohibited cattle raising on the Blood and Blackfoot reserves – yet the Stoneys and Peigans managed their cattle fairly well. Some young Indian men still were involved in intertribal horse stealing pursuits.

The main deterrent to native farming was the harsh prairie geography and climate. The Indian introduction to farming predated the development of quick ripening crops, innovative cultivation and harvest practices, and irrigation networks. Even experienced white farmers had made little headway in the region.

The Indian agents and farming instructors were political appointees. Those men recruited in eastern Canada often had no knowledge of Indians, certainly not the native languages. Some recruits were regarded as incompetent. A difficult workload and inadequate pay discouraged the Indian supervisors. In 1881, for example, the agent on the Blood reserve received a salary of only thirty-five dollars a month for supervising almost 3000 Indians and a staff of eight. The working conditions, isolation, and a lack of amenities resulted in a high turnover of instructors.

The annual reports of the Indian agents between 1882 and 1884 suggest that only marginal progress had been achieved.[29] In 1884 the amount of land plowed and fenced in all the reserves under Treaty Seven totaled

Sarcee Indians on Reserve, near Calgary, c. 1887

The confines of a reserve with rationing had replaced the traditional hunting lifestyle that existed only a few years earlier.

1,458 acres from which 39,631 bushels of roots (mainly potatoes and turnips) and 2,313 bushels of grain were produced.[30] This could hardly provide sustenance for 6,000 Indians. The thrust of white primary educational values upon Indian children placed in denominational settings also met with failure. The resident teachers, described as indefatigable in their efforts, could not surmount the difficulties posed by a foreign curriculum and the reluctance of the natives to accept new values. At the Dunbow Industrial School near the junction of the Bow and Highwood rivers, Father Lacombe failed miserably in providing useful vocational skills for his charges. The frustrated priest declared his pupils unmanageable, reluctant to attend, and handicapped by interfering parents.[31] The native parents identified the schools with diseases and family disintegration.

Among the five Treaty Seven tribes in 1885, only one, the Stoneys, remained relatively well-off. This foothills tribe of slightly over 600 members owned a herd of cattle, cut lumber, freighted for the railway, and, most important of all, could still trap fur-bearing animals and hunt game in the foothills and mountains. Relatively unaffected by the disappearance of the buffalo, they maintained the highest level of self-sufficiency. The Indian Affairs Department regarded the tribe as "the most industrious in this portion of the territories."[32] The *Calgary Herald* reported in May 1884 that the government had cut rations at Morley as the Stoneys were "far enough advanced in civilization to support themselves."[33] Still, life among the Stoneys was far from ideal. On February 12, 1885, the *Calgary Herald* carried a report that twelve Stoneys arrived at the North-West Cattle Company ranch, "gaunt with famine."[34]

At the nadir of adjustment were the Sarcees, the smallest of the Treaty Seven tribes, numbering only 420 members. In 1881 the band left Blackfoot Crossing to relocate their reserve southwest of Calgary. Government officials blamed the proximity of Calgary for the band's slow progress. The town attracted the natives and subverted progress on the reserve. The Indian agent's report in 1885 depicted the Sarcees as dirty, improvident, and indolent. The women were described as "utterly depraved."[35]

Numerically the tribes of the Blackfoot Confederacy were far more important than the Stoneys and the Sarcees combined. Originally the Bloods, the largest Blackfoot tribe in Treaty Seven, chose to take their reserve at Blackfoot Crossing, but then reconsidered and moved closer to their ancestral hunting territory near the American border and next to the Peigans at present-day Brocket. In the first years on this reserve, the Bloods suffered terrible human losses. Statistics for 1884 reveal that from a population of 2,278, only eight births were recorded while eighty-two adults and forty-four children died![36] This death rate was an astonishing 5.5 per cent of the tribe's population. If it continued, the tribe faced extinction. A missionary stationed with the Blood Indians observed:

> Five years ago the Bloods were a rich nation. Every Indian had a horse, and some their bands of horses. Now a mounted Indian is an exception, and the tribe is getting poorer and poorer . . . in fact, the Bloods have lost heart and spirit.[37]

Faced with the danger that the North-West Rebellion might escalate to include southern Alberta, it was fortunate for the whites that the Bloods had long-standing grievances with the Crees.[38] For a century the two tribes had clashed, as the Crees expanded westward from present-day Manitoba. In 1885, the Bloods were prepared to help the government cause. One chief, Bull Shield, asked the agent on the Blood reserve to "give us ammunition and grub and we'll show you how soon we can set the Crees afoot and lick them!"[39] Another Blood chief, Red Crow, told the police to "give the word and they would be ready at any time to fight the Crees."[40]

Lieutenant-Governor Edgar Dewdney supported the recruitment of southern Alberta Indians. Three days after the Duck Lake battle, on March 29, he unsuccessfully proposed the formation of an Indian scout troop (which would remain in Alberta) hoping that this news would demoralize Cree and Métis insurgents in Saskatchewan. On a second occasion, May 1, Dewdney requested that Cecil Denny, special appointed Indian agent in Alberta, organize a Blackfoot force to drive out a small band of Crees in the Cypress Hills. Denny rejected this initiative, stating that once the Indians set out it "would be impossible to keep track of them."[41] In the final analysis, General Middleton's campaign strategy opposed the use of native forces, based on his experience in New Zealand where Maoris recruits "got too much on their own hook, and if you punished one of them the rest got mad or sulky or worthless."[42]

Throughout April, persistent rumours surfaced that American Indians had crossed into Canada. The Peigan tribe was split by the International Boundary: 1,000 Peigans lived in Canada; another 3,000 tribal members lived just across the border. The American segment was, according to one newspaper, "in a very sorry plight with a number of them dead of actual starvation."[43] Would these American Indians remain on their reservations? White residents in southern Alberta were very concerned that their entry into Canada would seriously jeopardize the preservation of peace north of the border.

All reports proved false, although if the *Fort Benton Press* can be gauged as a reliable source of opinion, most residents of Montana Territory would have welcomed the departure of area Indians. "There are too many Indians in town," stated a typical news item. "They are becoming a first class nuisance and steps should be taken to keep them away."[44] But the newspaper gave no credence to stories purporting the northward movement of American Indians:

> The startling reports which are reaching us from the little hamlet of Calgary on the Bow River, that the American Indians are crossing the line to take part in the Riel rumpus, will be news to nearly all of the people of northern Montana.[45]

Police Captain W.D. Antrobus, in a letter from Fort Macleod, likewise rejected the idea of American Indian movements. He wrote: "As to American Indians coming over I do not think it likely they will be allowed to, as the American Government has the boundary pretty well guarded."[46]

Throughout the North-West Rebellion, Americans on the northern frontier facilitated Canadian military efforts. The United States supplied canned food, two gatling guns and permitted some troop movement on American railways. At Fort Assiniboine, Montana Territory, troop reinforcements kept a wary eye on Indian movements toward the border. C.E. Conrad, a trader at Fort Benton, even volunteered to help Canadian authorities by keeping a "detective in the Gros Ventres and Peigan camps to report movements."[47] In 1885, the last thing wanted in troubled Montana Territory was increasing Indian unrest.

In southern Alberta the Indians looked at life with little satisfaction. Few comforts were possible from an annual annuity of five dollars for each Indian. In all, the cost of providing relief payments for those Indians

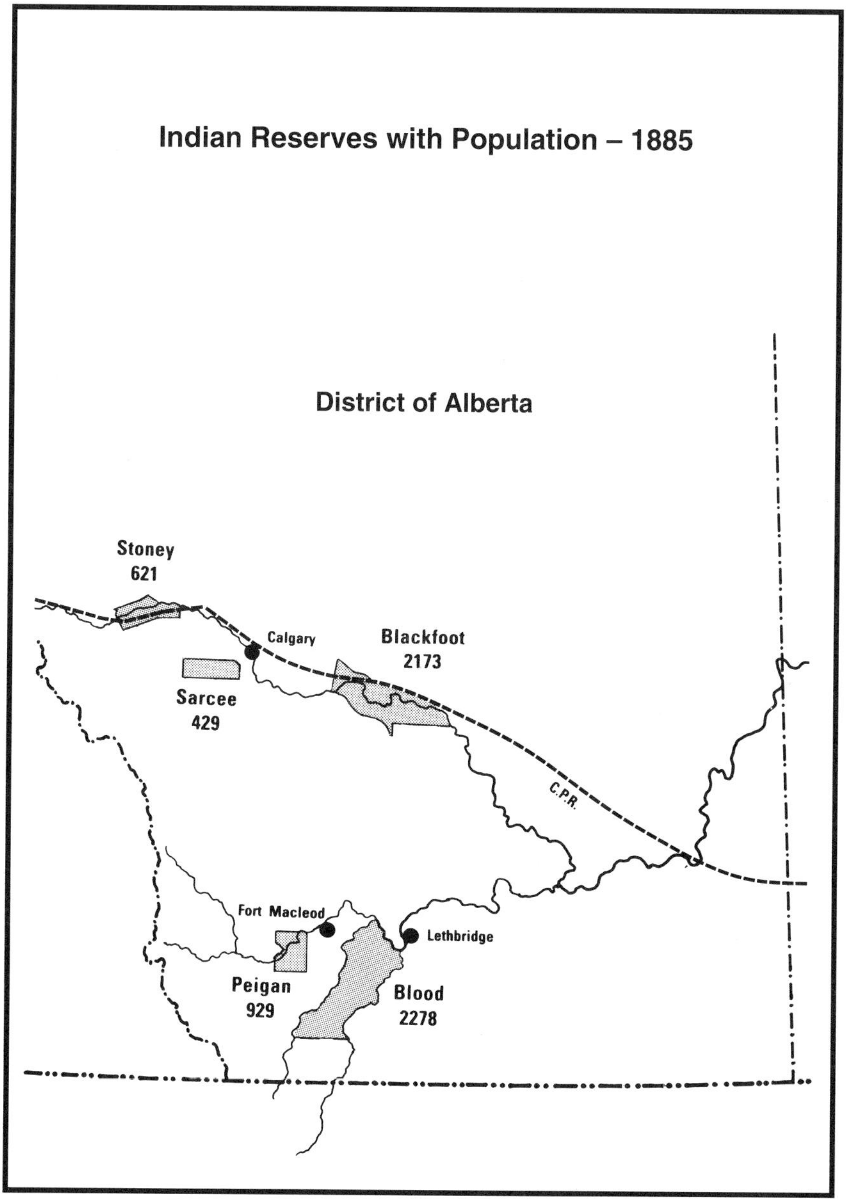
Indian Reserves with Population – 1885
District of Alberta
Stoney
621
Calgary
Blackfoot
2173
Sarcee
429
C.P.R.
Fort Macleod
Lethbridge
Peigan
929
Blood
2278

under Treaty Seven was $455,342 in 1885.[48] Some members of the Federal Parliament regarded this as a lavish expenditure considering the total federal spending was less than thirty-five million dollars. Also, it was a time when there was a reluctance by government to support charities and welfare, leaving these services to churches and the family. Moreover, daily rations of one pound each of beef and flour per Indian appeared satisfactory.

On the reserve, Agent Denny saw the rations "as little enough . . . they have nothing else whatever to live on."[49] The Indians were disillusioned and frequently complained about the substitution of bacon for beef, the substandard flour, the lack of clothing, and the ill-treatment received from abusive white distributors. Chief Crowfoot's assertion that "some of the white men treat the Indians like dogs"[50] is substantiated in a report by the Department of Indian Affairs, which describes the government agents as "a rough class of men . . . who had the habit of abusing the Indians."[51]

The insurrection in Saskatchewan challenged white hegemony over the Canadian prairies. The Indians contrasted their degrading poverty, misery, tragic death rate, and living restrictions with the unfettered lifestyle of only fifteen years earlier. They recalled few whites then and millions of buffalo. A Roman Catholic priest, Father Louis Cochin, serving Cree Indians on Poundmaker's reserve, spoke for all Indians in the three Provisional Districts when he wrote: "They attribute all their evils to the whites."[52]

Among the Indian tribes in southern Alberta, the most serious potential problems existed on the Blackfoot Reserve at Gleichen. Since their return to Canada, this tribe had done little to accept a new way of life. Instead, the 2,000 Indians congregated indolently around the agency where "a pretty wild lot" of young men led the discontent.[53]

In the early 1880s two serious confrontations, the Bull Elk and the Bear's Head episodes, challenged the authority of the Mounted Police and fractured Police-Indian relations. In January 1882, a purchase misunderstanding resulted in a government employee accusing Bull Elk, a minor Blackfoot chief, of stealing a butchered steer's head. In turn, the Indian fired two shots in the direction of the warehouse. Four Mounted Policemen under Inspector Dickens soon arrested Bull Elk but a mob with axes and knives obstructed the police efforts to march Bull Elk to the police post. Even though Dickens held a drawn revolver to guard the rear, one policeman found it necessary to fire three shots to summon help from the police detachment.

While Bull Elk was held inside the police post, 700 milling Indians effectively isolated the other government buildings. John D. Lauder thought "anything might happen" when he saw an Indian pointing a rifle inside a trooper's mouth while other warriors disarmed the policeman's companions.[54] The situation was explosive.

Chiefs of the Blackfoot Confederacy, 1884

Ottawa had arranged for leading Blackfoot chiefs to visit Winnipeg in 1884. The city of 20,000 was visual proof of the power and resources of the white newcomer. Resistance to the government took on a new meaning. From left to right: *Eagle Tail, (Peigan); Three Bulls and Crowfoot, (Blackfoot); Red Crow, (Blood).*

Realizing that the Police held an untenable position, Inspector Dickens requested intervention by the Blackfoot leaders. Support for the police, however, was not forthcoming. Upon his arrival Chief Crowfoot berated the Indian Department's unfair treatment of his people and adamantly refused to allow Bull Elk to be taken off the reserve. Dickens had little choice but to release Bull Elk to Crowfoot's care – news that set off unrestrained yelling and a wild discharge of firearms. Once the Indians returned to their camp Dickens dispatched a messenger to get assistance from Fort Macleod. The remaining twelve man garrison began strengthening the post.

Four days later Superintendent L.N.F. Crozier arrived at the reserve with twenty Mounties. After additional defence preparations, he considered the police post unassailable and entered into forceful negotiations with the Indians. Crozier had Bull Elk taken again into custody and escorted to Fort Macleod where the Indian received a fourteen-day sentence for using a weapon in a threatening manner. A former Mountie observed that the incident "was the first serious resistance shown toward the police since they have been in the country."[55] The whole affair was, in the words of Colonel Macleod, "a very nasty business."[56]

A second unsettling incident at Blackfoot Crossing occurred in the spring of 1884 when Bear's Head, an alleged Métis agent, was arrested under a charge of disturbing the peace. Bear's Head, however, escaped custody by slipping his handcuffs and leaping from the train transporting him to Calgary. He returned to the Indian camp, where the tribe's annual religious ceremony, the Sun Dance, was in progress.

Several days later Inspector Sam Steele and two constables arrested Bear's Head at gunpoint in Chief Crowfoot's tepee. A gathering of Indians became extremely defiant and threatening, but Steele succeeded in removing Bear's Head from the camp. Four days later Bear's Head was acquitted of all charges. To the Indians, the case represented police harassment of a welcomed guest.

In early April 1885, the course of action that the Indians would follow remained uncertain. But with only seventy-five Mounties remaining in all of the District of Alberta, the whites took no chances. Farms were abandoned and Home Guards quickly organized in Calgary, Fort Macleod and High River.

Lieutenant-Governor Edgar Dewdney offered Cecil Denny, a former Mountie of the original march west in 1874 and a former Indian agent, charge of the Indians under Treaty Seven. Denny, whose resignation in 1884 as an Indian agent stemmed from frustration over inept bureaucratic administration, accepted once a proviso acknowledged his supreme authority in all dealings with the five tribes. The new agent immediately conferred with the Blood tribe, giving them an account of events in Saskatchewan and advising the tribe to remain quiet on their reserve. A doubling of rations, hastily bought from I.G. Baker and Company, alleviated the Indian complaints over inadequate food allowances. Several days later Denny detected even greater agitation and dissatisfaction on the Blackfoot Reserve. He found the Indians friendly "but considerably perplexed at the behavior of the whites."[57] Denny told the *Herald* reporter: "They see us arming, they see troops coming into the country, and they see cold looks. . . naturally they think the whites are against them."[58] Denny increased the Blackfoot ration allotments and decided to make this reserve his headquarters.

In his new capacity, Denny antagonized many Calgarians when he asserted that "if any trouble arises it will be solely due to provocation offered by whites."[59] His criticism of General Strange's order authorizing sentries to shoot on sight Indians running off horses further upset the white community. In Denny's words, Strange placed the country in the hands of cowboys "who would shoot an Indian on sight, without waiting to see if he were running off horses or not."[60] Further difficulties arose between the two men following the drowning of thirteen horses from the Military Colonisation Ranche. Strange accused the Indians of a deliberate and malicious act. His ranch foreman, Jim Christie, agreed. Anyone familiar with Indians, wrote Christie in a letter to the *Herald*, knew they routinely obtained unbroken horses by forcing them into the mire.[61] In the same media, Denny countered the allegations suggesting instead that "the horses probably went into the muddy lake to drink, and got sucked down, and then piled upon each other."[62]

Father Lacombe, director of the St. Joseph Industrial School (Dunbow School) east of High River, acted as a second important intermediary between the whites and Indians. One essential assignment for the fifty-nine-year-old Oblate missionary involved a meeting between Lieutenant -Governor Dewdney and the Blackfoot tribe on April 11, two weeks after Duck Lake. A special train took the government authorities to Gleichen where an enthusiastic reception awaited them.

This "pow-wow," according to the *Calgary Herald*, with its many speeches and frequent handshaking, was a great success.[63] A telegram professing the loyalty of the Blackfoot was relayed to Ottawa where on April 13 John A. Macdonald related its contents to the House of Commons. The concluding comment that "the talk was all good – not one bad word"[64] suggested that few problems existed on the reserve. The young clerk who issued the ration allotment, though, would have disagreed. He noted that up to the time of the rebellion rations had always been picked up by the women, but "during this particular time the male Indians did it, each bringing his rifle and a belt or two of cartridges with him."[65]

The efforts of Denny, Lacombe, and Dewdney had bought the government badly needed time. The logistics of organizing a military force in southern Alberta required several weeks, and in the meanwhile the Indians had to be appeased and satisfied. The distribution of additional rations no doubt won the support of most Indians. General Strange quite accurately telegrammed the Prime Minister at the beginning of the rebellion that "the Indians will probably remain quiet as long as they are well fed."[66]

It took approximately three weeks following the opening of hostilities before the Alberta Field Force became a viable unit. During this critical period, Home Guards patrolled the barricaded streets of Calgary and Fort Macleod, and in outlying farms the settlers prepared their own defences. Most of the settlers in the immediate vicinity of Calgary remained on their farms, no doubt with a wary eye on the situation. Near High River, Lulu Short, aged eleven, kept a diary of events, mostly a count of the number of eggs she collected from the hencoop. She also recorded that the family kept a buckboard and horses ready and slept with their clothes on.[67] Farther north, looting and aggressive acts on the reserves near present-day Ponoka caused the entire Red Deer Crossing community to

Father Lacombe with Blackfoot Chiefs, Crowfoot (L) and Three Bulls (R)

With his understanding and experience of natives, Lacombe served as an intermediary between whites and Indians during the rebellion. An important assignment involved arranging a meeting between Lieutenant Governor Edgar Dewdney and the Blackfoot tribe at Gleichen that concluded with the Blackfoot professing loyalty to Ottawa.

seek refuge in Calgary. At Fort Macleod, Superintendent John Cotton organized the defences. His men erected makeshift barricades and strung wire around the police post. With one exception, all women and children were escorted to Calgary.

The absence of rail or telegraph communications increased the sense of urgency concerning events in the rebellion. In one instance, Sergeant S.H. Horner, aboard "Caesar," rode 165 kilometres from Fort Macleod to Calgary in one day. To ensure adequate communications, Superintendent Cotton placed a line of couriers at twenty-kilometre intervals to relay messages to and from Calgary. This service proved astonishingly effective with Fort Macleod, on one occasion, receiving a message sent from Montreal within twelve hours.[68] To further ensure quick and secure communications both telegraph and rail construction began from Medicine Hat to Fort Macleod.

On April 18, twenty members of the Fort Macleod police detachment departed with the nine-pounder gun to join the Alberta Field Force. The police were replaced by members of the Winnipeg Light Infantry and later two companies of the 9th Quebec Battalion. At no time did the soldiers encounter any dangers.

Minor incidents, though, magnified the area's anxiety and uneasiness. When a local rancher rode into the Blood camp, he noticed few men. This news caused concern at Fort Macleod. Where were the Indian warriors? However, nothing resulted from this scare. Some whites disliked what they referred to as "sauciness" by the Indians. John Innis remembered parties of Indians riding near his ranch house and shouting threats of boiling in oil, tearing of limb from limb, and subjecting Innis to other well-known forms of Indian torture.[69]

At Fort Macleod, the premier social event each year was the New Year's Dance. In often hazardous weather, the Mounted Police rode hundreds of kilometres with invitations to isolated area residents. Everyone anticipated a special evening, renewing acquaintances and celebrating. For December 31, 1884, the invitation list was altered. One policeman remembered: "There were a lot of white ladies in the country who objected to dance with squaws, so a cut was made."[70] Three months later, such offending attitudes were not in the best interests of the whites.

The tense situation in southern Alberta increased the white awareness of the Indians' disposition. Hugh S. Cayley, editor of the *Herald*, witnessed a renewed sense of native independence and pride:

> I strolled one evening, alone, along the railway embankment, and met a half-dozen Sarcee Indians walking swiftly by. They walked like free men – so different from their old slouching appearance. The old spirit of the Indian brave had entered into them, and they walked like warriors.[71]

It appears that disharmony existed between the young militant element anxious to win honour in war, and those elders advocating neutrality, although there is no documented evidence of tribal council meetings. Police Captain Antrobus noted on April 27 that the younger Indians "would like to go to war, and I do not think they would be particular as to whether the enemy would be the Crees, half-breeds or whites."[72] For the natives, their remarkable system of communication, the so-called "Moccasin Telegraph," perpetuated the state of excitement with almost instant news of events hundreds of kilometres away.[73]

The role played by Crowfoot has been popularized as that of an aquiline-featured chief sagaciously guiding the Blackfeet on the correct course.[74] In fact, the Annuity List for 1885 numbers his band at only thirty-five men of all ages.[75] Moreover, some observations expressed in 1885 suggest that the chief took advantage of a troubled situation for his own purposes. The *Fort Macleod Gazette*, for example, stated that his "loyalty was by luck rather than good management."[76] And the son-in-law of Red Crow declared that "the old fox's loyalty existed entirely on his lips."[77] Father Lacombe's correspondence stated that the Blackfoot "have been quiet and have made loyal promises purely out of self-interest in order to get more out of the Department."[78]

One important reason for southern Alberta Indian neutrality related to an event the previous summer. Lieutenant-Governor Dewdney, concerned over the troublesome Bear's Head incident in 1884, arranged a train trip to Regina and Winnipeg for Crowfoot and Three Bulls of the Blackfoot, Red Crow of the Bloods, and Eagle Tail of the Peigans. With 20,000 people the city of Winnipeg demonstrated visual proof of the power of the whites. The *Calgary Herald* commented that Crowfoot came back "greatly impressed with the power of the whites, and said they could produce as many soldiers as blades of grass."[79] Defiance to white encroachment took on new meaning.

Were the Indian dangers to the region overrated? Isolated farms certainly were vulnerable, but Fort Macleod or Calgary could not be taken. The Indians were poorly armed, had no artillery or munitions, and had never attacked or laid siege to a fortified settlement. Rather than warfare emphasizing sustained operations and attrition, the Prairie Indians traditionally pursued a strategy of "limited warfare" – usually seasonal – as a means of securing place and area resources. The annihilation of an enemy was a rarity. It is one thing to run off horses. Attacking barricaded streets manned by defenders is an entirely different matter. Moreover, troops would reach the region within days.

Further, the Indian warrior element was surprisingly small. One estimate numbered the Sarcees with perhaps fifty warriors. The Annuity Lists number the entire Blackfoot male numbers at 305 men; the Bloods at 290 men.

In a letter to the Herald, settler John Glenn maintained:

> if all the tribes in the North West were in revolt at once, an attack of Indians not exceeding 500 men – these men being scattered over about 100,000 square miles of territory whilst we can muster three times that number.[80]

John Glenn's contention appears correct. The total white population in southern Alberta (3300), although outnumbered by the Indians 2 to 1, held a preponderance of males in the 20-50 category – a characteristic of a frontier society. The census for the North-West Territories in 1885 documents this fact. While the census does not distinguish by race, male and female numbers in the 1-19 age category are almost equal (665-627). However, the 20-29 age grouping has males outnumbering females almost 4 to 1 (1123-287).[81] This disproportionate ratio certainly reflects the availability of young white men in the region – men capable of bearing arms.

Most western men experienced with Indians scoffed at the alarms and openly stated that there was no Indian threat or even danger to a determined community. These men regarded the Indians, when faced by resolute opposition, as inept in warfare.[82] Likewise, General Strange regarded the Indians as second-rate warriors contending, in his autobiography, that "the noble red man is not fond of fighting in the open and never attacks a large settlement, or at a disadvantage."[83] General Middleton agreed: "Indians are not fond of attacking even slightly protected positions on open ground."[84] Strange, however, conceded that although "the feeling of alarm was much exaggerated, it could not be otherwise, owing to the utter absence of arms among the settlers."[85]

CHAPTER 3

Gunner Jingo

Photo on Previous Page :

General Thomas Bland Strange

CHAPTER 3

Gunner Jingo

"We do not want to fight, but by Jingo! If we do, we have the men, we have the guns, and have the money too."

– *1878 parody*

As the disquieting news from Saskatchewan increased, many residents in Calgary prepared for possible troubles. On March 20, six days prior to the skirmish at Duck Lake, the Castle Mountain Billiard Hall served as a meeting place for a gathering of thirty men. The group appointed General Thomas Strange as chairman. In this capacity, Strange spoke "of the present emergency and of the necessity of forming a volunteer corps of mounted cavalry."[1]

When the news of hostilities reached Calgary, unfounded reports quickly circulated. One rumor had Blackfoot Indians moving in numbers towards the town. In response, the men prepared for an attack. The women and children, recalled one observer later, "were crowded into the old Windsor hotel and the primitive building barricaded to withstand a siege."[2] During the supposed crisis "some of the leading citizens were much the worse for liquor."[3] One witness declared in a letter to the *Toronto Globe* that Calgary was in far greater danger from its "hopelessly intoxicated guardians than she is ever likely to be from Indians."[4]

At a second hurriedly-called town meeting in the Masonic Hall on March 28 Strange, who had already cabled Ottawa to announce his availability for service, again accepted the chair.* Since no regular troops served in the North-West Territories, Strange outlined defence strategy and asked for recruits for a Home Guard. One hundred and four men volunteered immediately and Major James Walker, a former Mountie of the march west in 1874, accepted the responsibility of directing this defence force. Strange then returned to his ranch adjacent to the Blackfoot Reserve to loophole the buildings. After leaving six hired men to defend his ranch

*Apparently Thomas Strange played a prominent role at public meetings in Calgary. In February 1884 he chaired a meeting which advocated public ownership of future waterworks, bridges, and local transportation. That same year, following a brutal murder, Strange conducted a meeting to entertain the idea of forming a vigilante committee to address such crimes.

and livestock, he returned with his wife to Calgary. Although still not officially appointed to any military capacity, the former general, from his headquarters in the police barracks, energetically organized a military corps.

The first men signed were forty cowboys, who were quickly organized as the Alberta Mounted Rifles under Major George Hatton, an ex-military officer and Strange's former ranch foreman at Gleichen. Economic circumstances, coupled with a sense of adventure, triggered the cowboys' eager response to Strange's call for recruits. Trooper Joseph Hicks' motives for enlisting were simple:

> In 1885, my companions and I had just come down from the north to spend our winter wages on a spree, but upon our arrival in Calgary we learned that the Indians were on the warpath and the Army was asking for recruits, so we joined up.[5]

The majority of these men, Strange recalled, "were out of a job; unfortunately the long winter had obliged many of them to sell their horses and saddles, though most of them had stuck to their Winchesters and six-shooters."[6]

Some citizens implored Strange not to enlist "rowdies," citing their unstable nature and lack of discipline. But Strange recognized these men as capable of making valuable contributions to his Field Force. They were experienced riders and most knew Indian customs. He justified his decision: "From start to finish they never gave me the slightest trouble, and were the best-behaved men in the Force, always to the front, yet never grumbling."[7] A number of the men were Americans who, in Strange's words, took the oath of allegiance to Her Majesty "without flinching."[8] Sam Steele, commander of the scouts, endorsed Strange's selection of cowboys. He wrote: "The cowboy has no superior in the world, and in spite of his free life he takes to the order of military experience as if he were born to it."[9]

The cowboy corps proved dedicated and loyal, although most of the men, according to Scout E.A. Hayes, "never saluted an officer from the time they left Calgary until we returned."[10] Yet, Hayes remembered the men "never forgot that Major Steele was our commanding officer."[11] Using this core of men and with unofficial sanction from Ottawa, Strange continued through early April to organize the district's forces into combat readiness.

Born in India in 1831 where his father's regiment was stationed, Thomas Bland Strange was the proud heir to a military lineage which dated back to the Normans. A biography in 1888 outlined the distinguished military record of his Scottish forebears, noting that "for five generations every male in this family has served in the army or navy, and the majority of them have died in service."[12] Following the completion of his education at Edinburgh Academy and the Royal Military Academy at

Blood Indians at Fort Calgary, 1878

In early March 1885 the departure of the Mounted Police to Saskatchewan left the dilapidated fort almost unmanned, heightening local tensions once the news of a revolt arrived.

Woolwich, Strange began his career in 1851 as a 2nd Lieutenant in the Royal Artillery. Subsequently he served two and one-half years in Gibraltar, followed by two years in the West Indies. Unhappily for the ardent young soldier, these routine postings lacked the excitement of British military actions in Crimea. Then in 1857, at age twenty-six, Strange returned to the land of his birth.

India influenced and molded the young officer immensely. He relearned Hindustani, which maids taught him, before he learned English. In India, he married Elinor Taylor, the widow of a British officer. There was no time for a honeymoon; instead the couple left with the army on a 700-kilometre march. The diverse geography and climate of India taxed the resolve of the British soldiers. It also provided exceptional recreational adventures. While on leave, Strange enjoyed climbing magnificent mountains and hunting ibexes and bears.

In this intriguing land the wealth and splendor of historic civilizations reposed beside the omnipresent poverty, filth, and sickness. There were sacred animals, a rigid caste system and remarkable sights. Strange marvelled as submerged elephants crossed rivers with only the tips of their trunks visible; he learned to shoot savage dogs while galloping on horseback, knowing the pack would stop to eat the wounded animal. "Never," observed Strange, "did he find an enemy more formidable than the incorrigible pariah dogs." [13]

Most importantly for the young British officer, India was a land of war – the Indian Mutiny. Strange fought in thirteen fierce engagements. Four military dispatches cited his bravery.[14] Gunpowder explosions singed his body, a bullet grazed his head, a second hit his turban. In India, Strange met and fought with General Middleton.

The Indian Mutiny introduced Strange to the madness of war. During one attack on horseback, he ran his sword through a foot soldier preparing to shoot him. In hand-to-hand combat, sepoys shot an adversary as Strange gripped the man's throat. Strange watched unbridled comrades, "drunk with blood and plunder and thirst for vengeance," [15] rob the dead. He heard the piteous moans of the dying; he held a dying comrade tormented by the agonizing convulsions of cholera.

The Siege of Lucknow was, in Strange's words, "an orgie of blood and plunder." [16] The rotting bodies of the slain were everywhere in the narrow lanes of the city while distended corpses floated down the river. After one battle, Strange rode through a moonlit field of dead. In the eerie light, the arms of a corpse suddenly stretched out – yet Strange knew the man was dead. He dismounted and walked toward the dead man. A vulture, "too gorged to fly, its bald head besmeared with blood," [17] hopped away. This explained the macabre sight: the bird had torn the tendons, causing the frightening contractions. Strange shot the vulture – but it was useless. Nearby, a host of predators awaited for the repast.

After almost seven years in India, Strange's next posting returned him to England for a further six years. In 1871, the departure of the British garrisons brought Strange to Canada. The young Canadian nation had organized two artillery schools: "A" at Kingston, under G.A. French (later the first commissioner of the Northwest Mounted Police), and "B" at Quebec, under Strange. Thus Strange concluded the final ten years of his military career commanding "this Gibraltar of America." [18] In his rather self-congratulatory manner, he described himself in his autobiography as the military father of "B" Battery Canadian Artillery, and "Commandant of the Citadel of Quebec." [19]

In his military capacity, Strange edited the *Canadian Military Review* and published several related articles. Without question, he made a significant contribution to Canadian military development. Early in the North-West Rebellion one newspaper commented: "the efficiency of the batteries now at the front is largely owing to the fact that the Government had adopted the more important recommendations, which, as inspector of artillery, he has seen fit to make." [20] An article, written in the *Canadian Defence Quarterly* in 1924, asserted that "Strange established a standard of efficiency in the Canadian Artillery from which it has never looked back." [21] The writer cited Strange as "the Father of the Canadian Artillery." [22]

Strange enjoyed his years in Quebec. He discovered the mixture of French and English that lent a delightful charm to the society of Quebec. His prominent military position entitled Strange and his wife to enjoy social intercourse with privileged Canadian society. At one New Year's celebration, which also marked the centennial of the American General Richard Montgomery's ill-fated attack on Quebec City, Thomas Bland Strange "organized one of the most unique balls imaginable."[23] On this occasion, he cemented Canadian patriotism by reminding all Quebeckers how their united forefathers had bravely repelled the American invasion.

Strange had a positive relationship with his French-Canadian military subordinates, and spoke admiringly of their qualities. If called upon, however, he lived up to his reputation of "Gunner Jingo." When a mob threatened the Quebec Parliament, Strange marched his soldiers, with bayonets prepared, against the rioters who scattered before the advance. Strange wrote: "I halted the rear section of eight men and opened fire. Half-a-dozen men and a cab horse dropped. Most . . . rose and limped off, but (their leader) remained on the pavement and a little red stream trickled into the gutter, a suitable receptacle "[24]

Mostly, though, Quebec provided Strange with happy memories. In a nostalgic reminiscence of the St. Lawrence in the beauty of a golden autumn, Strange wrote in his autobiography: "There is but one Quebec in the whole wide world."[25] His experience in Quebec, as well his fluency in French, served him well in the rebellion as the two French-speaking regiments sent to the prairies came under Strange's authority. Middleton foresaw a possible problem if these units campaigned in Saskatchewan. He explained to the Minister of the Militia, Adolphe Caron: "I sent them west as I did not think it wise to bring them where so many French half-breeds were to be met."[26] To Strange, Middleton telegraphed: "you may think me very selfish sending you all the French Battalions . . . if anyone can handle them you can."[27]

In 1881, after thirty years' continuous military service, Strange was obliged to retire from the British Imperial Army. The crusty officer expressed displeasure over this turn of events, commenting that a soldier at forty "is considered too old to lead 100 men, but an octogenarian is not too old to run or ruin an Empire."[28] And as his later life would prove, an octogenarian did not have to idle: at age eighty-seven Strange, forever active, remarried.

In his early fifties, Strange rejected the sedentary rewards of retirement. He thrived on challenge and hard work. One example of his perseverance came when his young cowboys gave up on a wild, young bronco as incorrigible. Within one week Strange was seen riding "Sunbeam" quietly around the ranch. The news of an insurgent revolt provided Thomas Bland

General Thomas Bland Strange – Gunner Jingo

After thirty years military service Strange had begun a new career raising livestock east of Calgary. News of a rebellion presented a military challenge. Acting on his own initiative, he organized and dominated the Field Force.

Strange with yet another test, another challenge in a life that thrived on adventure. Here again was a military campaign that would require enterprise and fortitude. Here again was a challenge.

Strange was confident of himself and his ability. He liked appellations. At Military College he was "Long Tom"; the Blackfoot in Gleichen called him the "white chief with one eye open"; and not wearing a uniform but only a buckskin shirt and everyday clothes led eastern troops to call Strange the "Buckskin Brigadier". Strange referred to himself as "Gunner Jingo," after the term which expresses an aggressive foreign policy. He titled his autobiography, written in 1896, "Gunner Jingo's Jubilee."

In 1885, the "Buckskin Brigadier" was raising livestock on his 70,000-acre Military Colonisation Ranche Company adjacent to the Blackfoot Reserve at Gleichen, 100 kilometres east of Calgary. His introduction to the potential of Canada's prairies had come several years earlier while on a military assignment to inspect Pacific Coast defences at Victoria. With capital raised from shareholders in eastern Canada and India, Strange had vigorously launched himself into a second career on land leased for one cent per acre per annum. He was determined to succeed. His initial attempt at ranching in Alberta with an Australian partner, however, failed, partly because of government regulations. Requiring a new application for a charter, Strange arranged to travel overland with two young Mounties to the railhead. En route, a sudden blizzard immobilized the trio. Luckily the chance arrival of a survey party also travelling east saved them from death.

Undaunted by this near disaster, Strange, with his son Alec, returned the following year (1882). From the railway terminus, he drove a buckboard 500 kilometres westward across open prairie to his ranch. The journey took one month and was, in Strange's view, the hardest march the seasoned military campaigner ever made. Once his ranch base was established, Strange travelled to Montana where he purchased three stallions and 100 mares. The 250-kilometre return northward was difficult, with many sleepless nights spent continually circling the skittish animals. In the next two years livestock drives from Idaho and Montana increased the size of his herds.[29] During a visit to Calgary in October 1884, Strange informed the *Herald* that he had 700 cattle and 300 horses on his range.[30]

Strange located his ranch headquarters near the Bow River. In winter, the frozen river served as a highway to Calgary and, when free flowing, as an artery for timber cut in the mountains and floated to the ranch. Soon the ranch, which he named "Namaka," featured a pleasant two-storied home. A garden, flower beds, an English tea room with a piano, made the residence a far cry from the mud-floor shack he had occupied

General Thomas Bland Strange

during his first year in Alberta. Strangmuir, as it was called, served as the home for Strange and his wife Elinor, their two sons and three daughters, an Irish cook, and a lady cousin.

With the completion of the railway, access to Calgary improved, but not without adding problems: the sparks from the smoke stacks caused numerous, destructive prairie grass fires. In the fall of 1883, there was hardly a blade of grass between Blackfoot Crossing (near Strange's ranch) and Calgary. Strange wrote to the governing North West Council asking for the placement of gratings over boiler chimneys. In another letter, to the *Herald*, Strange complained of the "scandalous robbery of her Majesty's mails" [31] between Calgary and Medicine Hat, in particular the disappearance of his weekly edition of the local newspaper.

With the nearby Blackfoot Strange maintained a condescending relationship, applying the principles of the British class system. As a chief, Crowfoot could freely enter and drink gallons of tea, while "uncomely squaws" [32] were left outside to peer through the windows. When losses occurred to his livestock, though, Strange was uncompromising and no one escaped his wrath. One witness recalled Strange telling Crowfoot "in very plain Saxon what would happen if any of his men came around the ranch while he was away." [33] Nevertheless, livestock thefts continued to be a never-ending grievance. One complaint by Alberta ranchers was that the "troublesome" Indians ran off horses "with the view of getting rewards for bringing them back."[34] On one occasion, Strange accompanied two Mounted Policemen to the Blackfoot camp where he identified eight stolen horses. When one culprit was handcuffed, the incident became ugly and the police party departed only after facing hostile Indians brandishing drawn knives.

In response to livestock losses, Strange severely condemned both the Indians and the lax judiciary. He claimed in his autobiography to never recall hearing of an Indian being punished by civil authorities until the rebellion. The usual verdict, he wrote sarcastically, was "not guilty, but don't do it again."[35] He objected to such "leniency" for with "all savages it has no meaning but cowardice, and is followed by contempt."[36] Authorities, in Strange's opinion, must handle Indians forcefully. "Nothing," he telegrammed, "is gained by being afraid of Indians."[37] After all, the "Indians of the prairies had no tangible grounds of complaint beyond their natural dislike to seeing white men occupy their country."[38]

Strange held beliefs towards "less advanced" people that reflected the British Imperialist world which enveloped him. Was not his nation's dominance over vast lands evidence of its superiority? The empire, too, was magnanimous – in Strange's words "more generous to conquered races than any nation on the pages of history."[39] Only under British leadership would the Empire's colonial subjects achieve success. He reminds his readers that "the redoubtable Ghoorka [*sic*] Infantry, under their officers, were a useless and undisciplined mob. What the little Ghoorka becomes under the British officer goes without saying."[40]

Strange considered his fellow Englishmen an elevated race. His writings show prejudice against non-whites. For example, he foresaw West Indian negroes, because of their rapid reproduction, giving political "superiority to an inferior race."[41] When relating his fist fight with one negro, Strange describes his black opponent as having "a certain lion-look ferocity," not "the loose lips of the common banjo variety of nigger."[42] Added to the ardent imperialist's catalogue of dislikes were Catholics, Jews, the Irish, and "Yankees." During the campaign, Strange's "sahib" attitude towards Indians caused considerable concern in Ottawa.

To the veteran campaigner of India, the Minister of Militia's telegram on March 29 (three days after Duck Lake) must have reverberated like a predawn bugle call. Adolphe Caron's message read: "Can you get a corps? Would like to see you at the front again. Trust you as ever. Arms and ammunition will be sent up upon a telegram from you."[43] Strange reacted instantly. He hitched up his fastest team to a buckboard and raced for Gleichen station, twenty kilometres away, where he wired that his services were at the disposal of the government.

On April 9, General Middleton, already advancing with his column toward Batoche, formally appointed the enthusiastic volunteer as commander of military operations in Alberta. This directive acknowledged Strange's military skills and his leadership in securing the region's defences. As well, it reflected Strange's "connections" with key government officials. As stated, Strange had fought with Middleton in India, and while living in Quebec had become well-acquainted with both the Minister of Militia and Defence, Adolphe Caron, and Prime Minister John A. Macdonald. This familiarity is reflected in his telegram of April 4 to "My dear Sir John,"[44] whereby Strange outlined the desperate situation in Alberta, and indicated his willingness to help. Now Gunner Jingo commanded, as he proudly wrote, "a country larger than England and Wales."[45]

In March 1885, Strange was fifty-four. A full beard and a height of six feet two inches (188 cm) gave Strange an imposing figure.[46] A reporter from Winnipeg described the general as "a giant in height [and] is as cool as a cucumber."[47] The *Toronto Globe* called Strange "a man of marked will power, a disciplinarian, and yet one whose commands are not unkindly enforced."[48] And R. G. MacBeth, in the Winnipeg Light Infantry observed:

> Major-General Strange was a man of splendid appearance, bearing his years lightly. In manner he was bluff and curt enough, but he had withal a strong emotional nature and an underlying reverence for things sacred that made him a strong character – the kind of man every soldier likes to follow. He was an intense Imperialist and an ardent advocate of the federation of the Empire.[49]

For one young boy, the arrival of the Field Force in Edmonton was an exciting moment. How could he ever forget Gunner Jingo?

> Strange was a tall man with a ferocious black beard. He rode at the head of his column wearing artillery trousers (with broad red stripe) tucked into long jack boots, a dark blue frock coat and a black felt hat with the brim pinned up on the left side; a sword hung from his sword-belt.[50]

The observer, W.A. "Billy" Griesbach, "decided, then and there, at the age of seven, that the only thing worth-while was to be a general."[51] This event may have triggered a distinguished military career. Forty years later Griesbach commanded a division of the Canadian Expeditionary Force in France and, during World War II, served as Inspector-General (Army) Western Canada, 1940-1943.

Although undoubtedly Strange's military credentials were sound enough for operations in Alberta, an element of "eccentricity" surfaces in written references regarding his character. General Middleton, in an assessment of Strange to the Duke of Cambridge on May 6, 1885, noted that Strange was "a little odd, and does funny things."[52] In another reference, Middleton bluntly informed Caron:

> Afraid Strange will cause trouble. I always thought it a dangerous experiment giving him command. He is a good fellow but he is what you call in this country a "crank" and with a little religion in it which is dangerous.[53]

Subordinates, too, observed erratic behavior in their commander. One young officer acknowledged that Strange was a splendid type of British soldier but "somewhat eccentric in certain ways."[54] Strange's disheveled appearance reinforced this reputation for eccentricity. A young trooper in the Winnipeg 90th recalled in his diary:

> June 28 - Saw General Strange today and was surprised. He looks like a farmer that might be driving oxen. Wears a slouch hat and a sash.[55]

The appointment of Thomas Bland Strange to the military command of southern Alberta was not without the its detractors. Some Albertans, reported the *Manitoba Daily Free Press* on April 20, wanted Colonel Macleod to "have command rather than General Strange."[56] In an earlier article, the newspaper supported Sam Steele's arrival in Calgary, "as General Strange . . . has made himself so obnoxious that townspeople and settlers refuse to enlist under him."[57] Another criticism appeared in the *Macleod Gazette*:

> It is said that General Strange has not made himself at all popular among the people of Calgary and vicinity . . . due to favoritism in appointing his own son to his staff and to the fact that he has been trying to force unbroken horses from his ranch on the troops.[58]

As the campaign progressed, added uncertainties concerning Strange developed. Two policies increasingly disturbed his superiors. There was, first, his autocratic behavior with the Indians encountered and, second, his liberal promotion of subordinates. In May, General Middleton and Minister of Militia Caron engaged in secret communications to remove Strange of his command. However, the mobility of the Field Force thwarted their intrigue and the controversial General Strange remained in charge of the Alberta Field Force until the end of the campaign.

Thomas Bland Strange preferred an independent command. He had, remembered one comrade, "no use for red tape."[59] Strange was by nature expedient, independent, and pragmatic. An anecdote by a newly-hired ranch "flunky," Lachlin McKinnon, provides this insight into Strange's character. McKinnon related that one of his first assignments involved plowing a garden. The youth, unhappy with his results – "in Ontario I would have been the laughing stock of the whole neighborhood"[60] – approached his new employer to express his dismay. But Gunner Jingo, upon inspection, told McKinnon that he had never seen such straight furrows – not that it mattered, as the potatoes "would grow anyway."[61]

CHAPTER 4

the Canadian Denver

Photo on Previous Page *:*

George Murdoch (far right), Mayor of Calgary, 1883

CHAPTER 4

the Canadian Denver

"From first to last, the aim and desire of the Alberta settler and citizen appears to be how they can best fleece the government."

– Edmonton Bulletin

General Strange made Calgary his headquarters, the base from which he would organize the Alberta Field Force. In 1885, the town consisted of an assortment of ramshackle tar-paper structures clustered near the railway station. In all, 248 buildings (of which 107 served as dwelling houses) comprised the community.[1] Five hotels and six boarding houses provided temporary residence, and hinted at the large number of transients in the town. A weekly newspaper, *The Herald*, provided the area with news. During the rebellion, bulletins placed in the store front became a gathering point for interested crowds of local residents. The sandstone image associated with early Calgary was still a year away – a building precaution after the great fire of 1886.

The railway's decision in 1883 to locate a station near the police post at the confluence of the Bow and Elbow rivers assured Calgary of economic dominance over the southern portion of the District of Alberta. The newly-incorporated town of under 1,000 residents now served as a focal point for area service, distribution, and commerce. Already the nearby ranching area was enormous: 75,000 head of cattle grazing on 4,000,000 leased acres. The residents of Calgary exhibited an uninhibited sense of optimism. This "boosterism," which most new western centres displayed, manifested itself that March in a ninety-four page booklet, prepared and published by local businessmen. It cited Calgary as the "Canadian Denver,"[2] comparing it with a city of nearly 100,000 inhabitants

This promotion of Calgary and its surrounding area by self-serving businessmen is understandable. Few visitors would deny that the town had a truly picturesque setting. No one would question the booklet's glowing optimism about regional mineral and agrarian potential. However, for the brochure to claim that "blizzards are unknown" either reveals a selective memory or borders on fraudulence.[3] Two winters earlier the

Calgary, 1885

View of Calgary from the Elbow River in 1885. The 700 residents occupied some 250 buildings strung along the newly-completed rail line.

Cochrane ranch alone lost 8,000 cattle in blizzards. Carcasses filled the coulees and the Indians "made very good wages for some time skinning the animals at twenty-five cents each." [4]

Mayor George Murdoch, the local harness maker, and his four councillors faced all the problems of a small growing centre.[5] During the first half of 1885, the town's agenda included the digging of numerous wells to provide better fire protection, hiring a dog poundkeeper, finding land for a cemetery, constructing a new Town Hall (estimated to cost $750), and soliciting federal financial assistance for a bridge across the Bow River. The entire municipal budget was only $6,000. With relief for the poor budgeted at $20, the five elected officials were not faced with today's burgeoning social costs. They, too, could rely upon community spirit for minimizing expenses. One item on the April 29 agenda included awarding five dollars to Louis Beaupré for being "the first in furnishing water at the recent fire." [6]

Prohibition legislation throughout the North-West Territories supposedly made Calgary a "dry town." Criminal statistics in 1885 support Strange's contention that in Calgary "the evils of drunkenness were greater than in any community which it has been my lot to live."[7] Of the eighty-seven cases before Calgary courts that year, no fewer than fifty-three involved liquor. The usual penalty for drunk and disorderly conduct was $20 or one month in jail; importing alcohol resulted in a $200 fine or six months' hard labour.[8] The police regarded the enforcement of this unpopular law as an onerous and unrewarding assignment. When the local police detachment departed on March 24 for Regina, an Indian told a hardware merchant: "Police gone, plenty whisky now." [9]

Still a feature of the young town was the cowboy. These rough men typified the surrounding hinterland – raw, unfettered, and untutored. Soldier R.G. MacBeth wrote of "the straggling shacktown's" frontier character:

> Calgary . . . seemed that year the very paradise of cowboys, horsemen and scouts, for the place was full of the great rough, good-hearted fellows, fairly bristling with arms. Belts of cartridges round the waist and slashed across the chest held supplies for the Winchester rifle and Colt's revolver; great leather leggings, called 'schaps', bowie-knives here and there about the person, huge jingling spurs, immense grey hats turned up at one side, 'the cavalry swagger', and somewhat ferocious language were the prevailing characteristics. These men were magnificent riders, more at home in the saddle than on carpets, and as they had the run of the town the sight of a number of them, with their wild horses at full speed along the principal streets, was quite common.[10]

The wild riders fascinated the eastern troops. In a letter to his father in Quebec City a soldier stated: "There are a lot of cowboys around the place, they are mounted on Indian ponies, and it is something beautiful to see

George Murdoch, Mayor of Calgary, 1883

Calgary's first mayor, George Murdoch(far right), a harness maker by trade, is seen here in 1883 at his log cabin. Murdoch was an ardent town booster.

them riding their ponies and shooting at bottles and breaking them every time. They are the most reckless set of fellows that can be imagined and are still far worse than we, down east, imagine them to be."[11]

Another feature of Calgary, though unwanted, was the omnipresent Indian. Most Calgarians regarded their presence as "generally a nuisance."[12] The proximity of the reserves was considered both "annoying to the white population and injurious to the Indians."[13] In July 1884, the editor of the *Herald* noted 100 lodges in the vicinity of the town and asked "how long is this sort of thing to continue?"[14] Efforts by the police compelling the Indians to remain on their reserves always failed. Within a few days the Indians would reappear. The *Herald* warned of the potential trouble: "If these Indians and their dogs are not kept on their reserves there is liable to be trouble with them presently in Calgary."[15] In another article, the paper advised residents against giving the Indians any assistance (such as money for chores), thereby discouraging their visits to the town.[16] Even when the Indians showed initiative, as when they shipped a rail car of potatoes to Calgary for sale, the white ridicule continued. Wrote the editor of the *Herald*: "to each sack of potatoes were one or two squaws, three or four papooses, and six dogs."[17]

A Toronto newspaper criticized Albertan attitudes which branded an Indian as "cruel, lazy, filthy, steals whenever he can, and won't work while the government feeds him in his idleness."[18] In turn, many settlers

Stephen Avenue Calgary, 1885

In Calgary the rebellion gave the depressed economy a welcome boost. Local merchants escalated prices enormously, in some cases even doubling the cost.

felt that outsiders misunderstood the Indian situation on the western plains. One former Ontarian defended frontier prejudices as a necessary protection against the Indian insults, begging, and stealing. Experience with the Indians, the writer maintained, quickly effaced "the general eastern notion regarding them." [19]

The rebellion had an immediate impact on the town. First, with three major units attached to the Alberta Field Force the army population exceeded, for a period, the town's population. The influx of soldiers, in one observer's eyes, gave Calgary "the appearance of a garrison town." [20] That 500 of the men were French-speaking is a fact not generally recognized in the city's history. Second, the economic impact of the rebellion was an enormous boost to a depressed economy. The town's operating expenses were a mere pittance compared to the money generated by the campaign. The pay and allowances for the Winnipeg Light Infantry is recorded as $32,000; the 65th Battalion, Montreal, $23,500; the 9th Battalion, Quebec City, $18,000; and the local Rocky Mountain Rangers and Steele's Scouts, over $42,000.[21]

The extensive spending ranged from government purchases in the Calgary Hudson's Bay store of $10,700, all the way down to $4 to the Lamoureaux Brothers for bullet moulds and $2 to an Indian guide "for information." Total transport costs for freight between Calgary and Edmonton amounted

Stephen Avenue, Calgary, 1885

Stephen Avenue, looking east toward the police barracks. The main avenue clearly reveals the small town's raw character.

to over $36,000. The demand for teamsters brought a going rate of $8 to $12 daily for drivers and teams. Some transport companies received large sums: J. Lineham $7,250 and J. McGuire $5,100.

Everyone appeared to benefit from the massive government expenditure. The list is extensive and varied. J. Sinclair received $1,650 for oats, Miss Armstrong $10 for fifty scarves, even the mayor himself, a harness maker, received $26 for "leather work." The foregoing monetary statistics become relevant when based upon 1885 costs, as advertised in the *Herald*. Meat was priced usually between 10-16 cents per pound; coffee, 18 cents a pound; bread, 4 cents a pound; potatoes, one dollar a bushel; meals, fifty cents; boots, four to ten dollars; a coffin, sixteen dollars; overalls, $1.25; a hotel room, one dollar daily. For Calgary the rebellion had a silver lining, providing a depressed economy with a welcome boost. Merchants "took advantage" of the situation and inflated prices. A soldier from Quebec observed: "Horses that sold at $60 on our arrival here are now worth from $120 to $130 . . . flour has gone up $5 a sack in four days, and the Calgary merchants are circulating the wildest rumours of Middleton's defeat and utter rout in hope of preventing our departure."[22] One day prior to the column's movement to Edmonton on April 20, 1885, General Strange expressed his annoyance at the mercenary interests prevalent in Calgary. To an old friend he wrote:

> I march tomorrow . . . I have had a terrible time fighting the greed and selfishness of the people here . . . of all the cowardly rascals I ever deat [*sic*] with the Calgary people are the worst. No patriotism nothing but trying to cheat the government into paying enormous sums in transport.[23]

Throughout the North-West Territories the Canadian government faced massive "ripoffs." Early in the campaign General Middleton had wired the Minister of Militia: "Everyone seems to think the Government fair prey."[24] Likewise, Edward A. Whitehead, Chief Transportation Officer in Winnipeg, telegrammed Ottawa: "It looks to me as if everybody must take advantage of this unfortunate rebellion to make all they can."[25] The soldiers, at Calgary and elsewhere on the Canadian prairies, became economic victims of the very people they had come to help. Alex Laidlaw, serving in the artillery with Middleton, recorded:

> The settlers were determined to make hay while the sun shone. We were charged exorbitant prices for everything – $1.25 for a dozen eggs, $.40 for a pound of bread, $1.00 for a pound of butter, and $.50 for a quart of milk – pretty good considering that a private's pay was $.50 per diem.[26]

One letter, written less than one month after marching from Calgary, clearly expressed the resentment felt by the men. The recruit wrote: "everywhere we have been, notwithstanding that the settlers, storekeepers, and

Calgary Train Station, 1884

The C.P.R.'s decision to locate the railway station at Calgary elevated the town to become the focal point for area service, distribution and commerce.

merchants, and others clamoured for protection they have shown a desire and a willingness to rob their protectors not credible to themselves."[27] No doubt, the greed of the resident population dampened much of the enthusiasm of the recruits for their historic campaign.

This mercenary preoccupation of local merchants placed Calgary in an unfavorable light. Several eastern newspapers even questioned the loyalty of the town. One unsigned letter to the *Toronto Week* derided Calgarians: "The majority of the inhabitants of this place [are] an ignorant set of rebels, scarcely knowing under what government they are living."[28]

Local "boosters," realizing the impact of a negative image upon future investment and immigration, supported expressions of loyalty by Calgarians. The unfortunate death of one member of the Quebec 9th Battalion first served this purpose. Private Théophile Marois had taken ill on the journey west and died from "inflammation of the lungs" at Swift Current. His remains were forwarded to Calgary for interment on May 5 – sadly far away from his wife and four children in Montreal, who were left almost destitute.[29] For the military funeral and burial, Mayor Murdoch urged the attendance of all citizens. The local people all attempted to promote a positive image about the region. In one example of many, the *Herald* described the enthusiastic reception given on May 24 in the skating rink by town residents for "our French cousins", as "striking proof of the unity of Canada."[30]

In spite of efforts to ameliorate Calgary's negative image, evidence indicates that concern for economic gain remained uppermost in the town. As one soldier observed, "from first to last, the aim and desire of the Alberta settler and citizen appears to be how he can best fleece the government."[31]

Chapter 5

Organizing the Field Force

Photo on Previous Page *:*

Lieutenant Governor Edgar Dewdney

CHAPTER 5

Organizing the Field Force

"Many of the men had never fired a shot until they joined my Force."

– *Thomas B. Strange*

Although Strange had been given a relatively independent hand in logistics and local organization, he remained nominally subordinate to the dictates of three senior officials. The first of these, Middleton as Commander-in-Chief of Canada's Militia, directed the strategy and overall campaign. At fifty-nine, Middleton was a forty-two-year veteran of the British army. His most active campaigning occurred in 1846 against the Maoris in New Zealand and during the Indian Mutiny in 1857-58, where he received two citations for the coveted Victoria Cross. His decision to use only Canadian soldiers in this campaign was an important first for the young nation. Canada responded with an outburst of pride and nationalism.

Edgar Dewdney, a friend and appointee of John A. Macdonald, acted as the government's liaison in the Territories.[1] Since the North-West Council, a legislative framework of six appointed and eight elected members, did not meet until the fall, Lieutenant-Governor Dewdney was able to assume much greater power than normally permitted. His main task involved assisting in the containment of hostilities and redressing the popular discontent with the government. Dewdney also served in the capacity of Indian Commissioner for the Territories, and in this regard worked to mollify ill-feelings. Perhaps arranging a meeting with the Blackfoot at Gleichen was his most important decision during the rebellion. Dewdney proved zealous in providing Ottawa with "intelligence," even to the point of sending a spy to Montana after the rebellion to observe American attitudes and report on Canadian Indian refugees.[2]

Strange's third superior was Adolphe Caron, Canada's Minister of Militia and Defence. The forty-two-year-old lawyer representing Quebec City in the House of Commons supervised the complicated logistics of the campaign and acted as government spokesman in the House. It was a arduous assignment, with up to 165 telegrams to read each day and a task involving enormous political patronage. In spite of his lack of military

Lieutenant Governor Edgar Dewdney

Lieutenant Governor Edgar Dewdney was a friend and appointee of John A. Macdonald. He acted as the government's liaison in the North-West Territories.

training, Caron proved to be a tireless and capable master of detail, whether distributing 10,000 free cigars for "the boys," buying 10,000 rifles from England, or sending a routine congratulatory note.

During the first three weeks in April Strange worked hard to resolve the logistical problems of his campaign. The Field Force required weapons, lodging, and suitable horses. The organizational details were endless – an ambulance corps and supplies, officers' baggage to organize, the needed saddlery delayed by customs in Winnipeg. Strange discovered the ammunition for the Snider rifles was eleven years old. Was it safe? The raw troops required "incessant" drill and inspection. The few settlements in the region plagued Strange with calls for assistance.

Unlike the two Saskatchewan columns, much more improvisation and reliance on local resources was necessary. Advertisements in the weekly *Herald* and posted notices provided for some needs. The flood of telegrams added to the confusion and difficulties. One telegram ordered Strange to report with his force to Qu'Appelle; another ordered an advance to Edmonton – even before one soldier had arrived from the east. Those telegrams sent to Gleichen were unfailingly brought to his ranch by Indian couriers "if paid half in advance and the remainder upon delivery."[3]

The delays and inadequate supplies proved troublesome. Strange resolved the problem with an old ruse, the threat to resign. He telegrammed Caron: "If you decline to furnish arms and equipment, please let me know at once and authorize payment of expenses already incurred and I will disband the corps."[4] "This action," wrote Strange in his autobiography, "had the desired result; it fetched them all round."[5] Middleton's April 9 telegram in cipher, when translated, placed Strange in command of the district, directing him "to take what steps you consider necessary."[6]

Local interference by some citizens, led by Mayor George Murdoch, exacerbated the difficult problems of logistics. Strange and Murdoch disagreed over priorities. Mayor Murdoch, in a reference to Strange, stated, "The interest of other parties is to protect cattle, ours people."[7] In one example where he overstepped his authority, the mayor requested arms and ammunition be sent directly to Town Council. The Minister of Militia curtly informed Murdoch that he must "apply to General for arms."[8] Council felt that Strange, by his highly successful recruitment programs, had jeopardized the safety of the town. Who would be left to defend Calgary? In reply, Strange coldly commented that "in the multitude of town councillors was no wisdom found."[9] Strange sought local support by posting a public notice requesting "the cordial cooperation of all ranks of loyal citizens."[10]

A second problem involved nearby Fish Creek settlers upset with the government's delay in recognizing their land claims. They organized a meeting on April 5 out of which developed the fifty-member Alberta

Settlers Rights Union. Their action came at an inappropriate time for Strange. He observed: "They expressed strong Western terms against the Government and threatened a White Rebellion in addition to a Red one."[11] Strange, however, refused to allow local problems to interfere with the organization of his column. With his characteristic energy and determination he continued his preparation for the campaign.

Willing recruits lightened the burden of his job. "Everywhere I went I found old soldiers,"[12] Strange wrote in his autobiography. From his small nucleus of forty cowboys, the Field Force quickly expanded. Soon included were some prominent missionaries. These men knew the country, spoke Cree, and had years of experience with the Indians. The Methodist, John McDougall, rode ahead of the first column on the Edmonton march, scouting for possible trouble. At Battle River he conferred with the Indians and advised them of an approaching government force. In Edmonton, McDougall contacted the area Indians and arranged for the construction of scows to facilitate the eastward movement, in which he also participated. Strange acknowledged McDougall's help in a letter to senior church officials: "During the whole of the march he was ever at my side ready to inform me of the character of the country in my immediate vicinity, and translate information from half-breed and Indian scouts."[13] Father Albert Lacombe likewise served the Field Force energetically. The Oblate priest met the incoming Montreal contingent at Medicine Hat and traversed the Edmonton route in advance of the soldiers. On May 1, after travelling on horseback 650 kilometres in ten days, the fifty-eight-year-old priest could justly write that he was "fatigué."[14]

George McKay, an Anglican clergyman, on Strange's orders conferred with Crowfoot early in the rebellion.[15] McKay carefully assessed the Indian chief's attitude, not forgetting in his conversation to number the whites in eastern Canada "as countless as blades of grass."[16] He then rode from Fort Macleod to join the Field Force at Blindman River. "I was travelling light," wrote McKay, some sixty-one years later, "my Bible and Prayer Book rode along in my saddle bag with my extra cartridges."[17] Major Sam Steele remembered McKay as "brave as a lion an excellent horseman, a good shot and speaking Cree fluently, just the man for the cavalry."[18]

A fourth participating missionary, W. P. MacKenzie from Fort Macleod, served throughout the march as chaplain. His services and those of the other missionaries received substantial remuneration. McDougall presented the government with a bill for $435, MacKenzie for $271, and Father Lacombe received $1,000.[19]

Unlike General Middleton, who ordered Commissioner Irvine's Mounted Police detachment to remain in Prince Albert, and then rewarded them with the derisive title of "gophers," Strange included two units of the Mounted Police in the Alberta Field Force. One of Mayor Murdoch's first

Sam Steele and detachment, Beavermouth British Columbia

Steele answered the call to organize a scouting troop – appropriately named Steele's Scouts. The mounted men served as the vanguard of the northward march.

frantic telegrams had requested Major Steele's police detachment move from the "End of Track" site in the interior of British Columbia to Calgary. Labour riots, however, delayed the twenty-five Mounties from reaching Calgary until April 10. They organized into a scouting troop, appropriately named Steele's Scouts, and served as the Field Force's vanguard throughout the campaign. Steele added Hatton's Alberta Mounted Rifles and Oswald's Scouts to his command.

Sam Steele played a prominent role in the Field Force. Wrote one trooper, "He was afraid of nothing and any man in the troop would do his utmost for him."[20] A second soldier recalled Steele's "colossal stature, powerful figure and grim though kindly soldierly bearing."[21] Near the end of the campaign, Strange acknowledged the contribution of the thirty-six-year-old Mounted Policeman. To a friend in Quebec he wrote:

> Things are drawing to a close . . . I look back and think why were we not destroyed 100 times over? Why? Simply because I was fortunate in having a most splendid body of Scout cowboy cavalry – under Steele, a rare combination of caution and daring.[22]

Even Middleton conceded that "Steele and men were useful to Strange and they did excellent service with me."[23]

Two days after the arrival of Steele's police detachment the first major contingent, the Mount Royal Rifles, reached Calgary. These 340 men (the 65th unit), under Lieutenant-Colonel J. Alderic Ouimet, a Conservative member of Parliament, had departed for the west with great expectations. In Montreal, ten thousand residents had given "the boys" a rousing sendoff and as their special train passed through the settled parts of Quebec and Ontario, thousands of well-wishers lined the tracks.

All eastern units moving to the front had to march about 150 kilometres across four uncompleted sections – the gaps – in the rail line north of Lake Superior. The first march was almost seventy kilometres. For the Montreal contingent this journey began as a pleasant experience. The moonlit night, the mild temperature, and the excitement of adventure encouraged the men to sing from their horse-drawn sleighs, making the dense woods resound with the ring of their voices. In a few hours, however, the arrival of a cold blinding snowstorm presaged the misery ahead. For the remainder of the gaps, the 65th either tramped through deep snow or rode slow-moving platform cars. On the rail sections, the men placed their baggage as a windbreak and huddled together for warmth. Even so, wrote one soldier, the biting cold wind made "la situation de soldats intolerable."[24] At one stop, work crews engaged in a profitable business selling whiskey to the soldiers at twenty-five cents a glass.

Two bizarre incidents marred the difficult trek. One private, named Boucher, "desiring to rid himself of life,"[25] threw himself under a rail car. Quick action by train members left the soldier alive, though with a badly mangled foot. Another soldier, Henry Flanagan, suffering from *delirium tremens*, was placed under guard after unsuccessfully attempting to stab Lieutenant Gabriel Des Georges.

For the weary contingent, the arrival in Port Arthur was an uplifting experience. Even at 6 a.m., six thousand residents turned out to give the 65th a memorable welcome. After a short stay in the city, a travelling correspondent described Port Arthur as a place where "popular enthusiasm knew no bounds."[26]

In Winnipeg, waiting crowds greeted the 65th's arrival. After breakfast the soldiers were free to visit and purchase souvenirs. An observer noted "the boys from Montreal fraternized with their comrades-at-arms and were cheered in every street corner."[27] Upon departure, a buzz of excitement engulfed the Winnipeg station. Colonel Ouimet spoke to the 2,000 assembled citizens, and vocalists from the battalion favored the crowd with a few songs. As the train moved slowly westward, it appeared that spectators filled every door and window near the track. For the Montreal men, the six-hour stay in this city of 20,000 was a warm welcome to western Canada.

The 65th reached Calgary at noon on April 12. The eight companies of soldiers, happy that their ten-day journey of 3800 kilometres was over, arrived waving their hats and cheering. General Strange was waiting at the station. It was an exciting moment. This was the first body of troops

Troops Travelling West

A C.P.R. car provides rest for soldiers en route to Saskatchewan. Even with the 150 kilometres of "gaps" in the rail line north of Lake Superior eastern troops reached the prairies within ten days.

to arrive – 340 men assigned to a small town of fewer than 1,000 residents. "Calgary was," in the words of the local press, "all agog Sunday morning last awaiting to see the arrival of the 65th, of Montreal . . . to the Amphitheatre City."[28]

Upon arrival, Ouimet surprisingly asked to return east. His reasons were related to attending to supplies, Parliamentary duties, and illness. This unexpected request by the Member of Parliament led to a series of telegrams between Strange and puzzled superiors.[29] Ouimet's return by rail partly through the United States, increased the mystery. A visit to the Minister of Militia's residence at 6:30 a.m. was, in the words of one newspaper, "irregular and suspicious."[30] The *Toronto News* caused a stormy controversy by stating that French-Canadian troops were mutinous and drunken, unwilling to fight and that this had necessitated Ouimet's return East to ask the government to disband his useless battalion.[31]

Meanwhile, Ouimet remained evasive. On April 30, eighteen days after the arrival of the 65th in Alberta, Ouimet was back in Calgary. By this time his battalion was preparing to move downstream from Edmonton under his able successor, Georges Hughes. Ouimet started for Edmonton, supposedly became ill and returned to Calgary. At last on May 9, he left for Edmonton where he served as commander of the district until the end of the rebellion.

The exemplary response by the rank and file of the 65th countered the embarrassment caused by Lieutenant-Colonel Ouimet's questionable actions. Captain Edouard Bauset sent the following account to Montreal newspapers:

> The health and spirits of the privates are excellent, they have borne infinitely better than any other battalion the hardships of the journey, and have everywhere been praised on account of their good and irreproachable conduct and mirth. Discipline is perfect, and all the battalion is doing honor to its name.[32]

Moreover, the Mount Royal Rifles added a new spark to the somewhat lacklustre town life. Every night, Calgarians heard lively French tunes coming from the campsite near the confluence of the Bow and Elbow rivers, and during the day visitors observed recruits drilling from sunup until dark. General Strange found "the officers and men were cheerful and active, as French-Canadian soldiers always are."[33]

A second unit, the 294-member 92nd Winnipeg Light Infantry, reached Calgary five days after the Montreal battalion. A blinding snowstorm greeted their arrival, obscuring view of the town and fort. Local residents assured the wide-eyed soldiers that such weather in Calgary on April 17 was "quite exceptional."[34]

The 92nd was a volunteer unit responding to retired Colonel William Osborne Smith's call for a Provisional Force. Although the contingent was raised in a few days, delays relating to supplies and to the military status of Osborne Smith kept the unit in Winnipeg until April 10. During this time, the restless men drilled three times daily, using the old Board of Trade building for headquarters.

Between 1872 and 1877, Osborne Smith had served as military commander over the new province of Manitoba. Restoring the rank Smith held at retirement meant Smith would outrank some officers holding senior positions. The uncertain status of Smith developed into a topical issue. On March 30 John Norquay, premier of Manitoba, telegrammed Ottawa: "Smith embarrassed in consequence of not being gazetted."[35] Apparently the question of rank was resolved and the Winnipeg Light Infantry – "with much rejoicing" – received word to report to Alberta.[36]

As with all departing units, local residents gave the men an enthusiastic sendoff. After an address by Lieutenant-Governor Aikins, the soldiers followed a fife and drum band to the railway station. The *Manitoba Daily Free Press* described the parade:

> Along Kennedy street and down Portage avenue marched the gallant corps, keeping time to the familiar strains of "The Girl I Left Behind Me." Main street was lined with spectators, and persons appeared at almost every window in the various buildings, all anxious to secure a farewell glimpse of the departing volunteers The depot platform was packed with citizens and friends of the soldiers.[37]

Lieutenant Colonel J. Alderic Ouimet of the Mount Royal Rifles

Lieutenant Colonel J. Alderic Ouimet commanded the 65th Mount Royal Rifles. Upon his arrival in Calgary, Ouimet surprisingly asked to return east. His evasiveness movements in the following weeks created a stormy controversy that questioned French Canada's willingness to fight.

At 5:30 p.m., after final farewells and the presentation of a pound of tobacco to each soldier by Mr. Tees, of Tuckett & Company, the "train steamed away to the land of the setting sun."[38]

Initially three of the seven companies were assigned to garrison duty. One company replaced Inspector Bowen Perry's police at Fort Macleod while two other units guarded the rail line east of Calgary. The Qu'Appelle *Vidette* suggested an ulterior motive for one posting: "The men are annoyed because General Strange detained one of their companies at Gleichen, presumably to look after his ranch."[39] Later, the Quebec City battalion replaced the three garrison detachments, allowing the Winnipeg men to march northward. Unhappily, for those soldiers wanting action, by the time they reached the main column the skirmishes with the Indians had taken place.

A second police unit arrived in Calgary from Fort Macleod on April 21. This troop of twenty-one Mounted Policemen under Inspector Perry brought the only artillery piece available, a nine-pounder, along with 150 shells. Strange, who had just departed for Edmonton, left written orders for Perry to command the second column on the march northward.

The 9th Battalion of Quebec City constituted the third military unit in the Alberta Field Force. Like their French-speaking counterparts in the 65th, the 232 men of the 9th Voltigeurs had a Conservative parliamentarian, Lieutenant-Colonel Guillaume Amyot, in command. Recruitment difficulties, relating to academic concerns from Laval University about students serving in the battalion, initially delayed the 9th's departure. As a French Canadian it was extremely important to the Minister of Militia that his province's effort remain beyond question. Accordingly, Caron wired Amyot on April 1, "I am anxious that you show how rapidly a Quebec regiment can move. Hurry up!"[40] The French-speaking Montreal battalion received similar urging the same day. "Why do you delay so long in leaving?" Caron wired Ouimet.[41]

Caron's prodding telegram spurred the Voltigeurs into leaving Quebec City the following day. Torch-bearing men on snowshoes escorted the troops through immense crowds of enthusiastic well-wishers. The departure was described by George Beauregard as "très-difficile" because of the farewells and encouragement, and it was only "après mill obstacle surmontés" that they reached the station.[42] Arthur Potvin's diary recorded that the excitement of their departure continued far into the night: "La soirée se passe gaiment, chansons, discours, etc. Mais le plus malheureux, on ne pu dormir de toute la nuit."[43]

Upon reaching the four gaps north of Lake Superior, the Voltigeurs encountered, like the 65th days earlier, severe weather conditions. It was, wrote one, as "froid de Sibérie."[44] On one thirty-kilometre march over the frozen ice of Lake Superior, the glare of sun on snow caused the men's "pauvres yeux souffrent horiblement."[45] Most of the completed rail sections

Lieutenant Colonel Osborne Smith

had an unballasted railbed which necessitated slow and careful travel. The soldiers rode on benchless platform cars and were, remembered Beauregard, crowded "comme des harengs."[46] Each stop required the wearisome task of transferring the baggage.

In spite of the adverse elements, George Beauregard remembered the men enthusiastically sang a song – "Au Nord-Ouest nous allons" – composed by one of their comrades, M. Charles DeGuise.[47] Still, at the end of the final gap, the sight of a waiting troop train lit by a blazing bonfire caused the troops to break rank and rush forward for warmth and comfort. At last the gaps were crossed. Little did the 9th Battalion realize that this would be their most difficult campaigning in the great Canadian northwest.

On April 12, the 9th Battalion set up camp in Winnipeg. Although the large number of French-speaking residents came as a pleasant surprise for the soldiers, the charms of the small city soon wore off and the men clamoured for action. Eight days of waiting and watching other units move west increased the dissatisfaction. Arthur Potvin's diary relates: "Tous les soldats murmuraient dans les rangs."[48] His diary's entry – "même routine" – for April 21, nineteen days after leaving Quebec City, tersely documents the boredom.[49] That day Colonel Amyot telegrammed his displeasure to the Minister of Militia: "Our loyalty is suspected because we remain here so long. Many other reasons as health, discipline, and sobriety make our removal urgent."[50] In response, Caron suggested help, provided Amyot "keep quiet and not let out I am interfering."[51] Amyot, however, could not restrain his frustration and two days later telegrammed: "We are humiliated. Please send us to Calgary."[52] That evening, orders arrived granting the battalion its wish. The order to depart "fut salué d'acclamations enthousiates," wrote one soldier.[53] And what did the 9th Voltigeurs remember of their stay in Winnipeg? For many of the soldiers living in flooded campgrounds, it was "la boue de Winnipeg restera longtemps gravé dans notre memoire."[54]

The 9th Battalion reached Calgary on April 29. The city's fickle weather (which produced a blizzard only nine days earlier) now was described as hot as "du mois de juillet à Quebec; mais le temps est sec, ce qui est bien preferable."[55] The soldiers enjoyed their surroundings. Near their camp at Fort Calgary, flowed the Bow River where they bathed. Local residents informed the men that the clear, cold rivers in Calgary were good for swimming, having never "been soiled by an Indian's dip."[56] A few paces east of their base was the Elbow River, a smaller but also beautiful mountain stream. One soldier followed the Elbow upstream and ascended a hill for a westward view. He wrote of the sight: "Vue magnifique des Montagnes Rocheuses. Quel panorama splendide! Ces pics gigantesques, dont les sommets couverts de niege semblent toucher le ciel."[57]

Some Voltigeurs quickly were dispatched to garrison Gleichen, Langdon, Crowfoot, and Fort Macleod. They apparently overcame any language barriers and enjoyed good rapport with the assigned communities. Upon their departure for Quebec nine weeks later, the *Herald* wrote: "Residents will be sorry to lose sight of the Quebec boys . . . [who] have been as pleasant and jovial a set as one could wish to meet."[58]

The deployment of his battalion concerned Lieutenant-Colonel Amyot. He foresaw an Indian attack overwhelming each small detachment. Perhaps because of this perceived military weakness, Amyot gave some Indian visitors a display of military precision. The *Herald* wrote of the incident in uncomplimentary words: "The Sarcees have never seen a bayonet exercise before and their eyes protruded at the sight to such an extent that they would have served readily as hat pegs."[59]

Written accounts by Voltigeurs, like those in the *Herald*, generally express negative remarks about the Indians. The French-Canadian soldiers described the natives as indolent and prone to loitering, ugly and repulsive physically, and clothed in blackened rags decorated with bizarre ornaments or feathers.[60] One soldier referred to the papooses as baboons.[61] The native women were, in the view of the soldiers, abused and relegated to the onerous camp tasks. J. Drolet, stationed at Langdon, observed the arrival of one small band. He wrote: "The squaws pitch the camps, raise the teepees,

Militia at Winnipeg on their way to the Rebellion, March 1885

The effective mobilization and transportation of 4000 soldiers to western Canada countered the early rebel successes.

light the fires and do all the heavy work while their lords and masters sit down and quietly enjoy a good pipe."[62] Many soldiers lacked an appreciation of traditional Indian rituals. One account of a "danse du soleil" compared the frenzied dancing to a "cirque satanique."[63]

In their quest for Indian souvenirs and artifacts, the soldiers assessed the Indian character as having an "avidité insatiable . . . Plus on leur donne, plus ils veulent avoir."[64] One letter branded the natives "as a thieving lot at best."[65] Unfortunately, research reveals no documentation of the Indians' observations of the guardian soldiers.

Other than several small parties of soldiers escorting teamsters to Edmonton, the 9th Battalion remained on garrison duty throughout the rebellion. Often this task occupied only two hours each day. After the initial excitement of visiting Indian camps and exploring a prairie covered with buffalo bones, wild flowers, and often overrun by gophers, most soldiers found their spare time monotonous. Those men stationed at Calgary had some added diversions. One diary relates: "Puis après le souper au camp, nous nous mettons en rang, puis nous allons amuser avec les jeune filles de Calgarry [*sic*]."[66] Life in Calgary, though, required contending with skittish townspeople. On one occasion, the sound of an enemy approaching turned out to be I.G. Baker bull teams descending Mission Hill. Another supposed attack happened after a westbound train moved past a practice skirmish by the 9th Battalion, who were using the rail tracks east of the town for earthworks. Within half an hour it "was reported in the town that the car had been attacked by rebels."[67] A correspondent from Winnipeg mocked this incident, noting that the high elevation of Calgary gave the mind "almost eternal space in which to wander."[68]

While companies of eastern troops garrisoned key areas in southern Alberta, a mounted force called the Rocky Mountain Rangers patrolled stretches of the land between High River and Medicine Hat. The 150 western men, organized by Captain John Stewart (a rancher near Pincher Creek) and led by the legendary frontiersman, John "Kootenai" Brown, supplied their own horses and equipment for a daily payment of seventy-five cents and a horse allowance of $2.50.[69]

The Rocky Mountain Rangers lacked any formal military training. "Discipline is quite unknown to them" observed a Fort Macleod druggist.[70] As a travelling troop, they resembled a mob of vigilantes. The *Fort Macleod Gazette* printed this description of a patrol leaving the town:

> as they moved past armed to the teeth with Winchesters, and waist and cross-belts jammed full of cartridges, there was but one opinion expressed regarding them, and that was that they would make it extremely unhealthy for several times their number of rebel half-breeds or Indians, should occasion require.[71]

As expected, the men quickly responded to any threat. When a rider arrived in Medicine Hat claiming that Indians had fired at him, Captain Stewart had sixty mounted Rangers headed toward the source of trouble within three minutes.

In town, the Rocky Mountain Rangers displayed their version of "the wild and wooly west." A soldier from the Halifax Provisional Battalion, stationed in Medicine Hat, wrote his mother that the riders were "all armed to the teeth and go through the town firing revolvers and swearing like fiends."[72] The Rangers challenged the Halifax men – "feet soldiers," they called them – to contests in cricket, baseball, shooting, and tug of war.

On their patrols in southern Alberta, the Rocky Mountain Rangers exchanged long-range shots with Indians on several occasions. Generally, though, their task involved long, monotonous patrols or guarding work parties constructing telegraph and rail links between Medicine Hat and Lethbridge. In spite of this military inactivity, until the force disbanded July 19, the Rocky Mountain Rangers acted with the six garrison bodies as a visual presence of the government's military power in southern Alberta.

In one month's time Strange had accomplished a great deal. Troops from the East had arrived to garrison strategic centres, patrols moved throughout southern Alberta, and the Field Force was organized and training for action. Georges A. Hughes, a veteran of the Pontifical Zouaves,

Rocky Mountain Rangers at Medicine Hat, 1885

This troop of 150 western men, led by legendary frontiersman, Kootenai Brown (far right), patrolled the region between High River and Medicine Hat.

acted as a capable new commander of the 65th. Strange had selected for his personal staff: a friend from India, Captain C.H. Dale, appointed Brigade Major; son, Harry Strange, to act as aide-de-camp; and Surgeon-Major John Pennefather to supervise the medical needs. Enormous supplies of munitions had reached Calgary: 208,000 rounds for the Snider Enfield rifles and 15,000 rounds for the scouts using Winchester rifles – hundreds of rounds for each potential Indian opponent. The rifles had an effective range of up to 600 metres. The region was secure. Samuel Steele wrote in his memoirs that General Strange "had saved Alberta." [73] Now the "Buckskin Brigadier" could advance northward to relieve Edmonton.

It was a remarkable assortment of men who prepared to march north. Strange had moulded policemen, cowboys, missionaries, Manitoba volunteers and two French-speaking units into a force relatively powerful in numbers, if not military experience. Everyone anticipated a great adventure. An esprit de corps helped counter the occasional problems caused by language between the Montreal men and their western comrades. Late in the campaign, a travelling correspondent recorded that in spite of the difficulties posed by language, "the two regiments are on the very best of terms and will long remember each other." [74]

The volunteer composition of the Field Force probably reduced the problems associated with a military body of young men. There were still, of course, many difficulties. As outlined, several bizarre incidents had occurred while crossing the "gaps"; in Calgary during the April 17 blizzard, soldiers were suspected of stealing several gallons of alcohol from the medical stores; and prior to the march to Edmonton three members of the 65th regiment deserted. Possibly the most serious incident occurred in

Calgary when a Mountie threatened to shoot an officer from the Montreal 65th. Strange telegraphed General Middleton for authority for a court-martial, but for reasons unclear, Middleton rejected this request.[75] Some recruits may have had ulterior motives for enlisting. One employer in Montreal informed the Minister of Militia that Thomas Bell had joined the 65th to avoid "being arrested for theft and embezzlement."[76]

For the forthcoming campaign, members of the Field Force, along with the two Saskatchewan columns, faced a unique military directive. General Middleton, acknowledging that "most men in the militia were in the habit of having a certain amount of stimulants daily," nevertheless elected to adhere to the prohibition restrictions legislated in the North-West Territories.[77] Some officers agreed with Middleton's "bold step." Lieutenant J.V. Preston wrote: "Our Battalion had been recruited largely from towns on the Lake Ontario waterfront, from hard-bitten sailors and dockworkers, who, if liquor had been generally available, would sometimes have been trouble."[78] Middleton's prohibition directive, however, proved impossible to enforce; throughout the campaign many soldiers used every opportunity to obtain liquor. In Calgary, for example, Lieutenant Colonel Amyot found it necessary to complain to Police Inspector Tom Dowling about the sale of intoxicants to his troops.

For the coming campaign, each soldier received a felt hat which the men looped at the side. Varying twists of gold cord around the hats distinguished the ranks of officers. Other than this common head apparel, a disparate appearance characterized the Field Force: General Strange dressed in buckskin, scouts and teamsters in western field clothes, the Winnipeg men in scarlet tunics, and the Montreal 65th in green uniforms. The Mounties replaced their scarlet tunics with canvas fatigue dress. The wind and rain quickly disfigured and faded the uniforms and clothing of the men. After one month in the field, W. Wilson described his fellow soldiers "as a tough looking party, and might be taken for anything from horse thieves to dudes in hard luck."[79]

Medical requirements for those men recruited by Strange apparently related only to an ability to ride a horse. Those soldiers who underwent a medical examination experienced a rudimentary routine. One recruit recalled:

> I remember that the medical examination experienced by the Winnipeg soldiers was short and snappy. Upon entering the office of the medical examiner, I was surprised by a stiff blow on the chest. Knocked up against the wall by this foul attack, I, in pained amazement, faced the business-like medico. What would his next move be? But, 'Can you see well?' and 'What is your name?' completed my personal examination.[80]

That most men had held physically demanding jobs, countered the low medical standards. General Strange was provided with robust men in the prime of their lives. He recognized this fact, stating, "the physique of the men, mostly western working men, was far superior to that of a modern British regular regiment."[81] Middleton, too, noted a physical "superiority in the Canadian Militia over our regular soldiers."[82]

Incredibly, for recruits entering a military campaign, most, in the words of General Strange, "had never fired a shot until they joined my force."[83] Further, some recruits entertained fanciful notions about warfare. One Winnipeg soldier anticipated war to be "a holiday excursion on a trail – a prolonged Sunday School picnic."[84] He "visualized the battalion formed in a line, advancing to the strains of the regimental band – the enemy also lined up, with whom we would have hand to hand fighting."[85] Reviewing his military exploits years later, the soldier recalled that he had seen the enemy only once, and then because "like a young fool, I stood erect to locate the source of fire."[86] Many men were unfamiliar with basic military routines. At a reunion in British Columbia, Private Robert D. Bremner recalled with a smile how Corporal David Cranson ordered him to salute Cranson every time they met – a practice that Bremner faithfully followed for days.[87]

General Strange recognized that his force needed more extensive military preparations. Besides himself, only two or three men had experienced actual battle conditions. The men, however, in spite of their lack of military skills, were, in Strange's words, "willing and obedient and anxious to get to the front."[88] Nevertheless, Strange recalled: "Experience from the Indian Mutiny taught me to expect the unexpected."[89] With this in mind, Gunner Jingo declared early in his preparations, "I need not say I had no intention of committing Custer."[90]

CHAPTER 6

the March to Edmonton

Photo on Previous Page :

Samson, Cree Chief at Battle River

CHAPTER 6

the March to Edmonton

"We're making history, eh?"

– *Howard Angus Kennedy*

The Alberta Field Force of nearly a thousand men marched toward Edmonton in three echelons. Strange led the advance group, departing from Calgary on April 20 and arriving in Edmonton ten days later. His group consisted of over 400 men: sixty "Steele's Scouts," 160 men – the right wing – of the 65th Battalion (now under Colonel Hughes), and 175 transport wagons. He was followed on April 23 by Inspector Perry's force of approximately 210: the left wing of the 65th, twenty-four Mounties with a field gun, and sixty-eight teamsters. Perry arrived on May 5. The final column of about 280 men under Osborne Smith left on the 28th and arrived in Edmonton May 10. It included the forty-two Alberta Mounted Rifles under Major Hatton, 180 men of the Winnipeg Light Infantry, and sixty teamsters. Small medical units were attached to each column.[1]

Two precautionary movements preceded Strange's column. On April 15, the Red Deer settlers who had sought refuge in Calgary, now armed with Snider rifles and organized as a Home Guard under Sergeant J. Beatty, returned to their homes. Lieutenant J.A. Corryell with fifteen members of Steele's Scouts acted as their scouting troop. Strange ordered Corryell to fall back if attacked; if unopposed, move to Red Deer Crossing. Despite a sudden spring blizzard (that caused temporary snow-blindness in half his troopers), Corryell's party reached and secured Red Deer. The second precaution taken prior to the march was the reconnoitering of the route by the Reverend John McDougall. The well-known Methodist minister, who in General Strange's words could "ride and shoot as well as speak the truth,"[2] offered his services for this assignment and came with four Stoney scouts, identified by white scarfs to prevent "a mistake" by some trigger-happy Eastern soldier. At the troubled Battle River area McDougall conferred with the Indians, informing them that a large number of armed white men would soon enter the country to punish those who were creating disturbances. Following this warning, the party continued on to Edmonton, from where McDougall relayed dispatches back to the advancing column under Strange.

In 1875 along this trail of 330 kilometres, a Mountie, Jean D'Artique, had found sleep difficult because of the doleful howls of the numerous wolves. Day-time travel had been very slow because of the enormous herds of buffalo.[3] Ten years later, in 1885, much had changed. The buffalo were gone, and the cart trail had become a well-travelled route. Certain geographical features – Lone Pine, McPherson's Coulee, Scarlett's, Pipestone Creek – were familiar stopping places. In July 1883, biweekly mail service had been established between Calgary and Edmonton, and the following month stage coach service began operating between the two points. Leaving Edmonton at 9 a.m. Monday morning, the stage reached Calgary on Friday, and returned on a Monday-to-Friday schedule the following week. The fare, at twenty-five dollars each way, was expensive relative to the wage structure of that day.

The steady stream of freighters, though, had hardly altered the original flora of the land, which Strange had been told "exactly resembles the Siberian steppes."[4] The area between Calgary and Edmonton remained virtually a wilderness, occupied by fewer than 1,000 Cree Indians in the vicinity of Battle River. The surgeon of the Winnipeg Light Infantry, John Pennefather, recorded the attraction and the isolation of the land they travelled in late April:

> For beauty of scenery and extreme fertility it will compare favourably with most parts of the world. We met with one solitary settler's house, with its single inhabitant, a veritable monarch of all he surveyed.[5]

Everyone recognized the potential of this vast plain. At their feet was a land of enormous opportunity. Surgeon Pennefather wrote:

> While marching along I could not help contrasting the happy life of freedom which thousands of the struggling poor of London might here enjoy with the misery and want they are known to suffer from, though dwelling in the centre of the world's civilization.[6]

After their military service had ended, this first-hand observation of the prairies drew some soldiers back to western Canada. One Montreal recruit, Cortlandt Starnes, returned in 1886 to join the Mounted Police. He rose in rank, eventually becoming commissioner to the Royal Canadian Mounted Police from 1923 to 1931.

Of interest, Starne's tenure followed the directorship of A. Bowen Perry, Commissioner of the Police Force from 1900 to 1922. In 1885 the two men marched together, as Perry led the second echelon of the Field Force northward to Edmonton.

Prior to the April 20 departure, Strange addressed his column. It was, he told the men, not the first time that he had experienced the good fortune to command a unit comprising French- and English-speaking soldiers. He spoke to the 65th, in French, of their proud ancestry and their loyalty. The soldiers responded in "acclamations enthousiastes."[7]

The early morning departure took longer than planned. Sam Steele described the start as "like a circus," with the semi-wild horses bucking whenever mounted.[8] Once under way, no doubt everyone in the small town watched a band from the Winnipeg Light Infantry accompany the procession along the streets. On teamster Wheeler Mickle's wagon waved the only battle flag available, a cotton pocket handkerchief printed with the Union Jack. Onlookers could not miss the tall, bearded General Strange, described by one soldier as "our grizzled veteran of the mutiny . . . standing at the head, erect, powerful, serious."[9]

At the main intersection of town, Stephen and McTavish, Strange stopped his charger to warn an Indian spectator of the consequences should trouble occur while he was gone. The *Herald* reported his words:

> Go back to Crowfoot and tell him if he doesn't behave himself I'll clean out him and his whole gang, and Sir John Macdonald, or Dewdney, either, won't be able to save him. He knows I don't lie; go and tell that to Crowfoot.[10]

As always, Gunner Jingo's outspoken and explicit communication avoided any ambiguity.

At the unbridged Bow River, the Field Force suffered an early marching casualty. On the bank of the river, the transport officer was discovered dead drunk. His body, moreover, remained impervious to buckets of cold water. At this moment, an old soldier from the British India campaign seized the mane of Strange's horse and implored Gunner Jingo for one final chance to fight before his days ended. Strange, ever expedient, offered his old comrade the position of transport officer.

The waterways were the greatest obstacle in the movement of men and supplies to Edmonton. At Calgary each column faced the fording of the Bow River. R.G. MacBeth, of the Winnipeg volunteer unit, left a vivid description of the crossing of the wide, swift-flowing river:

> The loaded wagons, with four and six horses or mules driven by skilful though somewhat profane teamsters, the red-coated soldiers, the Mounted Police in scarlet and gold, and the picturesque corps of scouts, all passing through the water together, made a view worthy of being placed on canvas. Occasionally the scene would be spoiled by a mule throwing himself down in the water, but the free use of the black-snake whip, with the freer use of language not to be repeated here overcame the obstinacy of the animal.[11]

After the Bow, each echelon soon faced a second delay at Nose Creek Crossing – a shallow meandering stream with muddy banks which caused much skidding for the teamsters. Because of the delays at these two water crossings, all three marching units made little headway their first day. Strange regarded this as not serious, stating that in military practice "old hands know that it is never advisable to make the first a long march." [12]

With the movement across the Bow River, the Field Force left the telegraph behind. Strange had the autonomy he wanted. He wrote: "Now there was no string holding me, to be jerked day and night. I had cast myself loose at last." [13]

The spring runoff made the rivers subject to sudden change. As there were no bridges, this caused considerable problems. The second column, for example, found the Red Deer River impassable, although only twenty -four hours earlier Strange's troops had forded it with only minor difficulties. Since the second column brought the artillery gun, a ferry had to be constructed. Further problems resulted when the makeshift raft detached from an anchoring rope and carried Inspector Perry and the field piece five kilometres downstream. In all, the second echelon spent four and one-half days at this one crossing.

During the first days of the march, the new land fascinated the Winnipeg volunteers and Quebec militia men. On the western horizon stood snow-clad mountains; the burnt prairie, inundated with wild flowers, was turning a verdant green, and birdlife abounded. This land was beautiful and enchanting, "un pays magnifique." [14] The first column even had the luck to see a mirage, described by police trooper Alexander Dyer: "The Red Deer River, fifty miles away, was laid out before us, the trees and a solitary horseman appearing right before us." [15]

There was a majesty, a spellbinding splendor in this empty land that affected everyone. When one soldier, on night sentry duty, observed the clear heavens and the bright moon lighting an encampment of white tents on a wide prairie, he understood why few men remained unmoved when contemplating the immense universe and its Creator.[16] This was truly the "Great Lone Land" – a marvellous region for a military adventure.

In the prime of life, far from their homes, the soldiers went northward eagerly, with a spirit of purpose. The men realized that they were witnessing a pivotal point in Canadian history, a transient moment before the plow ripped the virgin soil upon which they marched. Howard Kennedy, a newspaper correspondent, recalled riding beside a young Mountie for an hour in dead silence. Suddenly the young man spoke for all young men serving in the campaign with the words: "We're making history, eh?" [17]

But after the initial excitement of marching, many soldiers found the immense countryside monotonous. For the first 120 kilometres there was "toujours la prairie!"[18] One soldier recalled some of his comrades intently scaling a small hill, hoping to view a change of scenery. But, at the summit, the same unending plains unfolded. It was not until they neared the Red Deer River that the columns entered a parkland region which extended throughout their remaining march.

The weather caused considerable problems for both Corryell's advancing unit and Strange's forces. The melting and flooding of every depression in the prairie caused mounted men to sink down "to the saddle-girths, and wagons above the axle trees."[19] The first column recorded temperatures as low as -6°C. "One morning," Strange recalled, "the tents were frozen stiff, the ropes like rods, making them difficult to pack, and the pegs had to be chopped out of the frozen ground with axes."[20] The second echelon enjoyed better weather, even hot temperatures. One soldier wrote: "Le temps était devenu beau. Vers le midi, cependant, la chaleur devint insupportable."[21] Surgeon Pennefather, in the third column under Osborne Smith, described the weather as "most delightful – robins singing, frogs croaking, and ducks quacking in all directions. The men were in excellent spirits, singing gaily, though many trudged along with badly blistered heels."[22] The troops in the third column noticed that "the further north we travelled, the more advanced was all the vegetation."[23] Each spring day, of course, added to the greenery. Modern meteorological research, too, records an annual frost-free period in Edmonton exceeding that of Calgary by eight days.[24]

Grievances usually surfaced because of the weather and the food. For the new recruits, whose daily marching created appetites that "are enormous,"[25] the steady fare of hardtack biscuits quickly became a major source of discontent. General Strange wrote of the food:

> The men complained that a long course of tinned Chicago beef . . . produced only the results of chewing blanket. The entire absence of vegetables, the hard tack washed down by the tannin of boiled tea, caused weakness of physique and irritability of temper.[26]

The soldiers recalled running out of tea and sugar, but never hardtack.

The order placed by General Strange against the shooting of wild game proved unpopular. Charles Daoust, a young French Canadian marching in the second echelon with the 65th, wrote that although game was abundant – ducks innumerable, prairie chickens everywhere, and hares running through their legs – the order remained inflexible.[27] Another unidentified French Canadian soldier commented, "We can kill Indians, we can't shoot game."[28]

Transport Teams, the North-West Rebellion

The Field Force relied on 300 teamsters to convey the needed supplies. At times the marching column extended to three kilometres in length, certainly not a desired military procedure.

Yet, perhaps Strange was correct in forbidding the shooting of wild game, as there were many inexperienced recruits in his ranks and any "indiscriminate discharge of firearms might create a false alarm."[29] The horrendous marksmanship of his men also gave the commander ample cause for caution. A Cree Indian, Joe Bird, recalled the firing skills of the recruits during the daily rifle practice:

> At noon and at night they used to put up a target, the bull's eye of which was 20 inches across on a white square four feet wide. The soldiers used to miss the whole thing at 200 yards.[30]

At the Methodist settlement located at Red Deer Crossing the settlers, escorted northward only a few days earlier by the scouts, were quick to capitalize on the recruits' dissatisfaction with their bland and monotonous diet. When a community director, Leonard Gaetz, saw a distant marching column he raced to his store, knowing "they would need looking after on their arrival."[31] The Red Deer merchants "looked after" the soldiers in a calculating manner. In Surgeon Pennefather's words:

> The few settlers here reaped a rich harvest, selling their bread at a dollar the small loaf, and a compound called homebrewed beer at twenty-five cents a glass. . . . Milk was sold at a dollar a quart, and eggs ten cents apiece. These prices were freely paid by those who luckily had cash, as hard tack and meat fibre called canned beef, had already begun to pall on many.[32]

Apparently, everything had a price, even eleven boards from a fence used by soldiers for firewood. The owner presented Colonel Smith with a bill for $22.[33]

The bland food, the gouging, and the tedious marching all contributed to the sour mood of the men north of Red Deer Crossing. A homesteader observed: "The troops began to arrive in due time, wearied and worn, cursing everything, Indians and all. I told the officers I thought they were worse than the Indians."[34]

For the first one hundred kilometres there were no farms, only treeless prairie. Prairie fires had left this region without a blade of grass or stick of firewood. This necessitated carrying fifteen days of provisions and forage, in addition to all the column's ammunition. Out of all proportion to the protecting force of 160 infantry and sixty cavalry scouts in Strange's echelon, were the 175 wagons and carts. Because of intervening swamps and creeks, this train was, at times, extended over a distance of three kilometres. This disarray in the march certainly contravened prudent military procedure.

On the final half of the march, from Red Deer north to Edmonton, the route was nearly impassable. Progress often was delayed as the men labored in mud and stinking bog helping to push the gun carriage and transport wagons. To expedite the advance, Strange sent a party of six axemen and four scouts ahead of the main column to corduroy swamps, bush muskegs, and build small bridges. The men did excellent work. To Strange, this was not unexpected. "Canadians," he wrote, have "a resourcefulness which comes of life in the forest lumber camps."[35] They can, he added, "build a house or make a toothpick with an axe."[36]

The military inexperience of many of the soldiers required instructions and drill at every opportunity. Strange issued a memo of orders which explained basic military procedures, outlined security precautions, and the order of march. The guidelines included preparing camp, positioning wagons, herding and feeding horses, fire regulations, sentry duties, a system of signalling using bugles, and duties when breaking camp. The energy and enthusiasm of the raw recruits compensated for their inadequate military preparation. Strange observed with satisfaction that the men "were rapidly becoming hard and disciplined soldiers."[37] Likewise, Inspector Perry praised the members of the second column for their courage, spirit, and energy.

The daily marching plan followed a prescribed routine. One soldier recorded: "We do not vary a minute – 4:30 a.m. reveille, 5:10 a.m. tents down, 6:10 a.m. advance . . . we march exactly one hour and a half, and rest for fifteen minutes."[38] For nighttime security, one company (forty men) formed a circle 1.5 kilometres from the camp with each man posted 200 paces apart. A second inner picket defence provided safety nearer the camp and special guards watched over the ammunition supplies. The horses were allowed to graze all night, herded by mounted scouts. The password changed nightly. Usually the word related to geography or history as, for example, Frontenac, Montreal, Quebec, Edmonton.

As the three columns proceeded northward, the Indians remained distant and evasive. From the Reverend John McDougall they knew already of the dispatch of the force. On one occasion near Red Deer Crossing, six Indians appeared and Hatton's Scouts in the third column unsuccessfully pursued them. More often, the Indians remained hidden, carefully watching the long column. General Strange realized this:

> Their signal fires by night and smoke signals by day were constantly visible . . . the Indian also uses his mirror for flashing signals, as we do the heliograph.[39]

The crossing of the Red Deer River brought the troops near the area of Indian settlement. As the men forded the river, distant smoke signals indicated the Indian presence.

At Battle River, almost two-thirds of the distance to Edmonton, the Field Force finally contacted large numbers of Indians. Five bands consisting of almost 800 Indians lived in this vicinity (near present-day Hobbema).

Samson, Battle River Chief

At the beginning of the Battle River unrest, Samson, chief of the largest Cree band, left to consult with the Reverend John McDougall at Morleyville. Samson returned as one of the four Indian scouts hired by the Field Force.

Bobtail, Cree Chief at Battle River

One of the four Cree chiefs at Battle River, Bobtail apparently attempted to prevent the looting. General Strange, however, ignored Bobtail's efforts and treated the Indian chief with disrespect.

Of the five, four were Cree. The largest, Samson's band, had nearly three hundred members, and equalled in size the three smaller ones combined (Bobtail, Ermineskin, and Muddy Bull). The other band, Sharphead's, was Assiniboine, or Stoney, and had nearly two hundred members.[40]

In recent years, severe hardships had beset these Indians. The extermination of the buffalo had caused utter destitution, reducing a proud people to misery and mendicancy. One visitor described Chief Ermineskin's home as a "little mud shanty, destitute of furniture and in the condition of absolute squalor."[41] A letter from the chiefs in January 1883 to John A. Macdonald vividly described their desperate poverty and the indifferent government help – but few improvements had resulted.

Some help came from three area missionaries: Methodists E.B. Glass on Samson's Reserve, John Nelson on Sharphead's Wolf Creek Reserve, and the Reverend Constantine Scollen's Roman Catholic Mission at Battle River. In the Peace Hills (Wetaskiwin) Indian Agent Sam Lucas supervised a government farm station.

Conflicting documentation and inadequate details obscure the exact situation at Battle River early in the rebellion. On about April 9, Chief Bobtail opened a council meeting with a plea for peace.[42] His brother, Ermineskin (a brother-in-law of Poundmaker) repeated the same message, but acknowledged his loss of control over the aggressive young warriors in his band. Of the meeting, the Catholic priest, Scollen, noted: "The young men kept a sullen silence, which I considered rather ominous, and the meeting broke up without further talk."[43]

A tense situation prevailed in the Battle River area. There was an exodus of Indians. Muddy Bull withdrew his band to the northwest, Sharphead moved his tribe west to Battle Lake and Samson left his people to ride to Morleyville for consultation with John McDougall. Samson returned with McDougall as one of his scouts.

Most whites left the area. The Hudson's Bay trader and an independent trader followed the Red Deer settlers to Calgary. However, Indian warriors physically stopped Reverend E.B. Glass and his wife from leaving for Calgary. When the couple took refuge with missionary John Nelson, some young Indian men began to loot their abandoned home. To stop the vandalism, Bobtail posted his wife at the dwelling. She stayed for two days "notwithstanding Indian threats to throw her in the river."[44] When she left the Indians completed their wanton destruction. Mrs. Glass, considering her four years of service to the band, was bitter, calling the Indians "an ungrateful class of people."[45]

In regard to this incident, the Catholic priest Constantine Scollen, suggested that had Mr. Glass "shown pluck enough to face the Indians and stay at his house, he would have saved it."[46] Scollen's negative comment reflected the dispute between Methodist and Catholic missions, with each blaming the rival church for having rebellious Indian followers. The accusations continued openly for several months.[47]

Father Scollen played a pivotal role at Battle River during the turbulent early weeks of the rebellion. For twenty-three years he had served the Indians. He understood their nature and rash acts failed to intimidate him. When some young men returned from looting a store, Scollen "tongue thrashed them until I was tired."[48] The Catholic priest realized that the natives, who thought Riel was about to sweep through the country, were afraid and distrusted the whites who they thought "had received some extraordinary information and were hiding it."[49]

On April 12, Scollen attended a wild council meeting in a large tent. Between the drumming, yelling, and firing of guns the chances of a general massacre, in the opinion of the *Edmonton Bulletin* on April 18, "seemed excellent."[50] Father Scollen recalled that "young scoundrels fired shots over my head, and shouts went forth of No Surrender! Riel! Riel!"[51] Undeterred by the threats, the priest persevered over the uproar. At his urging, Bobtail jumped up and attacked the drummers. This was Scollen's opportunity. He wrote:

> I took the floor at once. This was all I wanted. I knew I could hold them once I got a hearing. I kept them for two hours until I had left nothing unsaid.[52]

Earlier that day a courier had delivered two letters from Dewdney. Once Scollen read their contents an immediate change in the Indian attitude occurred. "I saw," recalled the priest, "that I had broken their spirit."[53] Talk began of restitution. The Indians collected a wagon load of goods to compensate the pillage taken from the Hudson's Bay store.

On his arrival in the area General Strange served warning that he would sternly suppress any troublesome Indian activities. He wrote of his meeting with Chiefs Ermineskin and Bobtail on April 29:

> They were repentant and wanted to shake hands. I declined to receive them, and had them informed that I would shake hands upon my return, provided they behaved themselves in the interim otherwise – I left a blank for their imagination to fill in.[54]

Sam Steele regarded the two chiefs as a "forbidding pair and their bands the most depraved in the north west."[55] In turn, Scollen, from first-hand knowledge, countered the views expressed by the two Field Force officers.

Even though the presence of the military columns had stabilized the Battle River area, Strange was surprised to learn that his Montreal men had failed to impress the Indians "as they did not wear red coats, and talked

Catholic priest, Father Constantine Scollen

At Battle River, Constantine Scollen played a pivotal role in quelling rash acts by young warriors. Two decades of administering western Indians proved helpful in his negotiations.

French like the Half-breeds."[56] Therefore, an ostentatious display by the red-coated Winnipeg Light Infantry in the third echelon was in order. A member of the unit wrote of the march through the Battle River reserves:

> With bayonets fixed and rifles at the slope, with band playing and every weapon exposed to view, we marched through, while the Indians gathered in the woods by the roadside and gazed wonderingly at the spectacle.[57]

Most written accounts give negative impressions of the natives. One newspaper described the Battle River bands as "a sorry lot of vagabonds as ever took treaty money."[58] "The braves," wrote one soldier, "had a dirty, unkempt appearance."[59] Another reference described "the squaws [as] repulsive, hideous looking people."[60] The eastern troops perhaps found the only image of the noble red man in Chief Ermineskin's chequered tunic, so decorated that it was "impossible de compter le nombre de couleurs."[61]

No action was taken at this time against the Indians involved in the April troubles. All five bands resented General Strange's order prohibiting the purchase of munitions. They knew very quickly, however, through the remarkable moccasin telegraph, of events occurring in Saskatchewan. As Osborne Smith's third column was passing through Battle River, Middleton was preparing his attack on Riel's base at Batoche. This information greatly reduced the possibilities of Battle River bands entering open revolt.

As the force marched northward, General Strange secured his lines of communication and supply along the advance. A troop under Lieutenant T.H. Dunne patrolled the route. By the first week in May, regular courier service travelled the Calgary-Edmonton trail with relays established every thirty kilometres.

The construction of three wooden garrisons began following the arrival of the Field Force in Edmonton. The responsibility of building these fortifications rested with the Montrealers in the 65th, and each fort received the name of one of their commanding officers. The most southerly post became Fort Normandeau, located at Red Deer Crossing. J. Bedard Normandeau and twenty soldiers from Company 8 spent six weeks constructing the palisade and they finished their task about the end of June. The fort, located 200 paces south of the river, had as protection wooden pickets and a moat, two metres deep and three metres wide.

The 65th built a second fort at Battle River near present-day Ponoka. After arriving in Edmonton on May 7, Strange instructed Captain John Benjamin Ostell to return with a detachment of twenty-five men to Battle River. The soldiers occupied the old Hudson's Bay post and ran a

Fort Ethier in the Peace Hills

Fort Ethier was one of the three forts built by troops to guard the Calgary-Edmonton trail north of Red Deer. Tiny loopholes for firing are observed on the building front.

defence trench out to prevent the enemy from approaching near enough to fire the house. When not digging trenches, fatigue parties under guard repaired nearby roads. Edward Barnett, the sole remaining homesteader north of Red Deer, observed the efforts of Ostell's rather nervous detachment:

> They dug trenches 8 ft. deep and if they got tired of their job an Indian would appear all dressed up in his war paint which would put new incentive into the trench digging until they had trench works big enough to hold Napoleon's army.[62]

Captain L.J. Ethier and twenty troopers constructed the third garrison in the Peace Hills near present-day Wetaskiwin. An old building on the government farm was loopholed to serve as a fort. Surrounding the log structure was "a small river, Rivière de la Paix, on one side, the Calgary Trail at the front, a big ditch on the right and a fence at the back."[63]

These forts were never tested, but they did serve to guard the supply and communication lines. The soldiers stationed at these garrisons followed an onerous daily routine: "They will not carry away with them the most

View of Fort Edmonton, 1884

Fort Edmonton as viewed from the south bank of the North Saskatchewan River in 1884. When ice free, a ferry conveyed travellers across the river.

pleasant impression of the North-West," aptly commented the *Edmonton Bulletin*, "almost the whole of the time during which they were in garrison was occupied in erecting fortifications."[64] Meanwhile, the main body of the Field Force continued their march into Saskatchewan. Although the men missed the adventure of battle, they recognized a sense of history or mission in their "solitude environnante."[65] When the soldiers departed from Fort Normandeau on June 26 they hoped their fort would remind later onlookers that the 65th had passed here.

The long-awaited approach of the Alberta Field Force excited the residents of Edmonton. The expected arrival was noon, May 1, but many eager residents rode to meet Strange's advancing troops. Later, as the column of soldiers and well-wishers neared the south bank of the North Saskatchewan, townspeople prepared to fire a salvo from an antiquated brass field gun at the fort. There was, however, no ammunition. According to several accounts, no doubt embellished, they discovered that tins of canned salmon had the same diameter as the bore. This solved the problem. A half-breed dwarf, John Collins, directed the firing, but in the excitement of the occasion overloaded the charge of powder. The resulting explosion recoiled the cannon against the fort and propelled the rammer across the river toward the advancing troops, "who probably felt that the salute was being overdone."[66] Witnesses declared that the projectile travelled around the world for, though they searched extensively on the south side of the river, the rammer was never found.

The march to Edmonton had taken each column from ten to fourteen days. This advance toughened the recruits and taught them rudimentary military skills. It was a quick and safe adventure, although trooper Joseph Hicks of Hatton's Scouts remembered that "both men and horses were very tired after making the 200 miles [300 kilometres] to Fort Edmonton."[67] A correspondent recorded:

> The long march from Calgary was a trial, but not more than a dozen rode on the teams, with the exception of those who did picket and guard duty at the camps the night previous. Everybody is terribly sunburnt.[68]

The visual presence of nearly seven hundred soldiers and several hundred teamsters must have presented a strange spectacle to the Indian observers. But it was a clear demonstration of the government's resources and the numbers it could command.

On the final day of Strange's march, Indian scout Joe Bird rode ahead of the column with a dispatch informing the Edmonton garrison of the approach of the Field Force. About twenty kilometres south of Edmonton, Bird encountered a large body of Indians preparing a dance. The Cree scout recalled:

> "Where are the soldiers you went for?" they asked.
> "Today," I said, "you should see them pass."[69]

A little later, when Steele's Scouts arrived at the spot, the Indians were gone.

In assessing campaign strategy, General Middleton's directive to send a column north from Calgary was an effective decision. The mere presence of a military force did much to quickly reduce the prospects of an Indian revolt in the Battle River area. As important, the Field Force ended the isolation of Edmonton.

CHAPTER 7

Holding Northern Alberta

Photo on Previous Page *:*

Buildings at Fort Saskatchewan, c. 1884

CHAPTER 7

Holding Northern Alberta

"This is the most remote settlement in the country and the least protected."

– Edmonton Bulletin

If Fort Edmonton, Fort Saskatchewan, and the St. Albert Mission had fallen into rebel hands, the insurgents would have controlled all of what now is present-day northern Alberta. Of the three, the commercial base at Edmonton was the most important, located at the heart of a transportation network to the west, east, and south. The town itself began at Walter's ferry and extended northeastward beyond the fort (near the vicinity of the present Legislature) for about three kilometres. Five trading establishments, a hotel, several churches, private homes and Indian camps stood scattered along this trail, known as High Street. The dense stands of trees and thick undergrowth increased the settlement's vulnerability in the event of an Indian or Métis attack.

From Fort Edmonton, a trail led twenty kilometres northwest to St. Albert, the most important Métis community west of Batoche. The Roman Catholic Church in 1839 had responded to the destitute conditions of local Métis by constructing a mission seventy-five kilometres west of Fort Edmonton at Devil's Lake, renamed Lac Ste. Anne. In 1861, the Church removed the mission to a more suitable area along the Sturgeon River which was named "St. Albert." Under the guidance of the Roman Catholic Fathers, this new location developed into a thriving religious and farming centre. In 1885 St. Albert, with a population of 800, rivaled Calgary as the largest settlement in the District of Alberta.

This large Métis element at St. Albert, along with a large ethnic French community (36% of the area's white population), made the Roman Catholic Church the dominant Christian faith in the Edmonton area. Over two-thirds of the population were Catholic.[1] In contrast to southern Alberta, where a Métis population of 233 in a population of almost 10,000 was insignificant, Métis numbered approximately twenty percent of the Edmonton area population. Also, with the French Métis and French ethnic population totalling almost sixty percent of the Edmonton area non-Indian population, the French language was a prominent factor in the region. Again, a situation quite unlike southern Alberta.

The third Edmonton area community was Fort Saskatchewan. Located thirty kilometres east of Edmonton, it was a North-West Mounted Police post with a detachment of nineteen Mounties under Inspector Arthur H. Griesbach. Having the police stationed this distance, and on the opposite bank of the river from the valuable stores and supplies, was, in the words of one Edmonton resident, "perfectly useless."[2]

Population statistics for the Edmonton region reveal the potential danger facing the white settlers. The total white population in the three settlements and surrounding farms numbered 1,600 (28%); the Indian population totalled 3,000 (54%); and the Métis 1,000 (18%). As the whites were decidedly outnumbered by the Indians, they realized the importance of gaining the local Métis support. This support, though, could not simply be assumed, for the nearby Métis had many grievances similar to those expressed at Batoche. These included the frustration arising from inconsequential dealings with distant Ottawa, a concern regarding their legal title to river lots, and a future clouded by uncertainty. Aside from these contentious issues, two principal differences distinguished the local Métis population from their Saskatchewan counterparts. First, most of the Edmonton area Métis (unlike those in the Batoche area) were born in the region, and had not served with Riel in 1869-70 or participated in the exodus from Manitoba in the 1870s. Secondly, the small English-speaking "half-breed" settlement on the North Saskatchewan in the Victoria region east of Edmonton identified with white interests.

When telegraphic communication brought news of the Duck Lake conflict, Mounties rode out to notify the area farmers of possible hostilities. The spring thaw increased the difficulties of this task. One policeman, William Parker, after warning all the settlers south of the river, broke through the ice when crossing the North Saskatchewan. The horse resurfaced and Parker continued to Edmonton, so frozen that two men had to pull him out of the saddle.

On account of the uncertain state of affairs, few settlers stayed on their farms. "We all left our homes in great haste, turning the stock loose and taking what little we could carry, thinking we might never return,"[3] recalled one settler. Everyone reached the forts safely, although three families from Beaver Lake, 80 kilometres east of Edmonton, encountered some anxious moments when Indians pursued their plodding ox teams. An old half-breed, John Whitford, whom General Strange later hired as a scout, saved the day by telling the Indians that Mounted Police were coming to meet the settlers. The Indians left to raid the abandoned farms.

Within a week, over 250 whites from the outlying region moved into the three settlements. A Home Guard of thirty-six men under Captain W. Stiff protected Edmonton and another body of forty-four men under Sam Cunningham policed St. Albert. It was, in the words of one correspondent, "a fearfully anxious"[4] time in Edmonton. Settler Henry Long recorded in his diary: "Everyone very excited about the hostile Indians."[5] No one shared the opinion expressed by General Middleton (stated in a telegram to Caron) that "Edmonton has Home Guards and is as safe as Ottawa."[6]

The sudden departure of local Indians increased the fears. The natives used the Hudson's Bay fort as both a trading and social centre. At the nearby tent encampments, convivial gatherings featured gambling, dancing, and tea drinking. The throb of drums always accompanied this social intercourse, so much so that its sound became a "permanent and prominent feature of life in Edmonton."[7] As news of the escalating troubles in Saskatchewan reached Edmonton, concern focused upon the nearby Indians. Could the Cree bands be trusted? Only a few years earlier, people at the fort had witnessed a brutal massacre of a small Blackfeet party by "the very Crees . . . that were so well-known and friendly to their white neighbours."[8]

On March 26, Frank Oliver, publisher of the *Bulletin*, discussed possible Indian dangers with a group of men considered knowledgeable about "the native character." They assured Oliver that the settlement faced little danger as long as the constant drumming continued, as the Indians never entered battle without first moving their families to safety. The following morning a stunned Oliver observed all the tents gone, a sign, in his words, "that a state of war existed."[9] In the days that followed, the distant glow of Indian campfires continually reminded Edmonton observers of their lonely and hazardous existence.

The shortage of adequate weapons concerned area residents. One wrote, "We are without arms and suitable ammunition, and without help are in a critical position."[10] A second correspondent commented that "there are not 100 rifles and guns all told, and the police have only 21 rifles."[11] The fifty-seven rifles at the Hudson's Bay post were described as "of all ages, sizes and kinds."[12] Moreover, as one community member complained, "they refuse to give them to the citizens unless we leave our houses, and go to defend the fort."[13] The *Edmonton Bulletin*, noting the location of the police post thirty kilometres downstream and the disrepair of the local fort, commented that this was "the most remote settlement in the country and the least protected."[14] It also became one of the most isolated during the first week in April with the cutting of the telegraph line.

For the next three weeks, the Edmonton area lacked instant accurate information. The news that did arrive, from travellers or people seeking personal safety, increased the apprehension. On April 7, news came of the nine Frog Lake killings and of the Indian hostilities near Battleford.

Members of the Edmonton Scouts

In Edmonton a number of local scouts joined the Field Force. This group includes: L. Whitford, C.L. Whitford, A.B. Spence and B. Laroque.

This information outraged many settlers as the two priests and several of the victims were well known in the Edmonton area. Then two traders arrived from Saddle Lake with news that four of Big Bear's followers, wearing police uniforms, were inciting the Indians at Whitefish Lake, one hundred kilometres east of Edmonton. On April 13, a scout reported that at Beaver Lake (Beaverhill Lake), east of Edmonton, several Indians had forced a settler to kill and cook a pig for them, then left taking two head of cattle. The same day, Edmonton learned that Alexis, chief of the Stoney Reserve about fifty kilometres directly west of Edmonton, had sacked the area trading post. The rebellion appeared to be spreading with looting everywhere. Would Edmonton be next? As the *Bulletin* pointed out, it was an inviting target: the town's trading establishments held at least $50,000 in merchandise.[15]

Inspector Griesbach detailed scouts from Fort Saskatchewan to scour the countryside. They returned with important intelligence. Fortunately, a number of tribesmen opposed joining the rebellion. The band of Papaschase (Woodpecker) at Two Hills immediately east of Fort Edmonton, for example, showed friendship to the Mounties. Blue Quills at Saddle Lake (120 kilometres northeast) desired peace and Pakan's followers at Whitefish Lake had spurned delegates sent by Big Bear. These bands, no doubt, realized their dependence on the white man for rations and trade goods such as axes, kettles, rifles.

The few Indians contacted in Edmonton appeared sympathetic to Riel. "The Indians we met scowled,"[16] recalled Canon William Newton. Thomas Anderson, a government timber agent, described their attitude as "defiant."[17] Suddenly, minor acts contained added significance. Anxious Edmonton housewives, for instance, expressed indignation and surprise that their former dependable handyman, Grasshopper, now began stealing apple pies!

Following the loss of telegraphic communications, concerned citizens met in Edmonton on April 7 to organize the Committee for Defence. During the proceedings the arrival of M. McKinnon created a stir of excitement. McKinnon, however, in delivering the mail from Calgary, reported an uneventful ride. He was able, though, to give details of Strange's organization and news that munitions had arrived by rail in Calgary.

A second unannounced arrival, that of Police Inspector Griesbach, threw the meeting into an uproar when he refused requests to remove seventy-nine refugee women and children from Fort Saskatchewan. The assembly agreed, however, to send a messenger to Calgary to outline Edmonton's desperate situation. The rider, James Mowatt, being familiar with the Calgary Trail, knew the location of potentially troublesome Indians and also the residences of settlers at which he could exchange horses. Leaving just after midnight, Mowatt reached Red Deer Crossing the following afternoon. Before continuing on his way he urged the few settlers to seek refuge in Calgary. By noon the following day Mowatt arrived in Calgary, ending a remarkable thirty-six hour ride of almost 300 kilometres.

Whites in Alberta rightly applauded Mowatt's skill and endurance. In Edmonton, the *Bulletin* detailed his determined ride in the April 25 edition. A second equally arduous ride from Edmonton to Calgary, however, remains almost unknown. Two days after Mowatt's departure, Cree scout Joe Bird rode the same route. Bird exchanged horses five times, stole one – "in the name of the Queen" – and reached Calgary within thirty hours. The scout recalled that it was two days before he was able to move again.[18]

After Mowatt's urgent departure for Calgary, defence preparations in the Edmonton region began in earnest. Workers at Fort Saskatchewan constructed four bastions, a barrier of spiked poles, and loopholed the walls. Inspector Griesbach hired Métis helpers at fifty cents a day to clear the brush back three hundred paces. The women organized the cooking, loaded shotgun shells, and prepared a large supply of bandages cut from their own raiment. In preparation against a possible siege, hay and wood were stored and a well was dug. The selection of a well site was a riveting moment. Everyone watched as a half-breed scout, Charlie Henderson, ceremoniously moved around the compound with his willow divining rods. Henderson's predicted location proved accurate: at a depth of ten metres an abundant supply of water issued.

At Fort Edmonton, brush clearing commenced and several antiquated cannons were readied for action. Rifle pits were dug, a line of sentries stationed, and steam hoses prepared in case the Indians employed "fire arrows" in an attack. In spite of the efforts and precautions taken by the defenders, one glaring military weakness remained: the compound could be fired upon from nearby elevated ground.

In St. Albert, Bishop Grandin called a general meeting which appointed a delegation to meet any approaching Indians, should that need arise. Even though there were no physical fortifications, refugees (including thirty-six women and children from Edmonton) thought the spiritual centre more "secure" than Fort Edmonton. Fortunately, ample provisions were on hand at all three settlements.

It was a difficult waiting period. Lovisa McDougall, the wife of a merchant, recorded on April 9 her impressions of the situation:

> We are living in the most intense excitement . . . all business and work is suspended here. Every hour in the day you see men passing with guns. They have scouts out all through the country watching and as soon as there is the slightest movement among the Indians they will report and all will go into the fort.[19]

Fear fed upon itself. To quote Thomas Anderson: "Great excitement exists. We do not know the hour the Indians in our midst will rise, and if they do, God only knows the consequences."[20] Even the newly-founded Literary

Buildings at Fort Saskatchewan, c. 1884

Having the police post, Fort Saskatchewan, stationed thirty kilometres downstream from Edmonton weakened area defences. In the words of one Edmonton resident it was "perfectly useless."

Society stopped meeting (either as a reflection of the dangers or the lack of interest, their last topic being: "All art was copied from nature and could only be a miserable imitation of the grand original"). Barking dogs and reports of "prowling Indians" caused great anxiety. Unsettled nerves responded alertly to any disturbance. Anna Laura Robertson remembered, as a nine-year-old, having dinner interrupted by strange noises. The men immediately jumped from the table and raced outside with their weapons. Instead of hostile Indians, noisy Canada geese hurried northward.[21]

Wild rumours added to the tensions. Scarcely a day passed without some such report spreading rapidly, for, as Canon Newton observed, "every new story is somehow or other believed, simply because there is no evidence to the contrary."[22] The most startling story came on the afternoon of April 11: the Indians had attacked Fort Saskatchewan and 1,500 of them were crossing Miner's Flats on their way to besiege Edmonton. Fortunately the editor of the *Bulletin,* Frank Oliver, kept his head, and calmly pointed out in his next edition that although an "unmistakable panic existed in Edmonton town on Saturday afternoon . . . [it] must be universally admitted as well that it was groundless."[23]

By the third week in April, the tense situation showed a marked improvement. Mowatt, the dispatch rider, returned with a companion from Calgary on April 20. They brought *Calgary Herald* "Extras" containing the most up-to-date information on the rebellion, an official notice that the government had appointed a commission to study Métis grievances, and news that a column of soldiers was coming in a few days. Two days later, a messenger, W.B. Young, arrived with a message from Strange to Griesbach announcing the troops' march northward. The appearance of Father Lacombe and John McDougall, Strange's messengers, further indicated that the isolation was about to end. Some of the settlers, feeling there was less danger, now left to prepare their fields for spring planting.

During the final week in April, a terrible disease stunned the small community. Within one week diphtheria tragically claimed the lives of five young children of the Leon Harnois family. The obituary, carried in the *Bulletin* May 2, dramatically illustrates the appalling rate of child mortality that Canadians faced a century ago. As Mrs. Harnois was Father Lacombe's sister, this family calamity probably contributed to the priest's decision not to march with the Field Force eastward from Edmonton into Saskatchewan.

The arrival of the first echelon on May 1 eliminated any real danger to the area. Within ten days, one thousand armed men and teamsters had arrived in Edmonton. Their presence caused the nearby Indians to reconsider their position. The *Bulletin* remarked that the natives' "desire to go on with their farming is marvellous."[24] Soon the return of Indian visitors to the town indicated things were back to normal. The *Bulletin* commented: "the Indians are back around the town and fort again, which looks more like peace than their late marked absence . . . and everything was me-wa-sin (good)."[25] The local population rejected taking punitive measures against the Indians. They preferred, wrote Frank Oliver, "to let bygones to bygones,"[26] – but not to the point of supplying ammunition. Notices posted around the town announced the prohibition of "sale, gift or disposal of fixed ammunition to Indians, under penalty of $200 fine or imprisonment for six months."[27]

Edmonton functioned as a centre from which Strange's troops could assert their presence, regroup, and prepare for the eastward movement downstream into the Frog Lake – Fort Pitt area. The second and third columns arrived on May 5 and 10. The general crisply complimented them, soldier MacBeth later reported, "in characteristic soldier style, with few words, and these shot out with quick emphasis, like the firing of bullets."[28] Seeing flags displayed from tepees surprised soldiers in the third column. The arrival of the Field Force, so awesome in size, had brought the Indians around Edmonton totally into line.

South-West Stockade of Fort Edmonton, 1884

Citizens organizing the defence preparations recognized a glaring weakness: an enemy on nearby elevated land could fire into the fort.

At their camp adjacent to the fort, drill and target practice occupied much of the Field Force's daily routine in Edmonton. One exercise had the troopers gradually bring their horses nearer to the noisy shelling of the field piece. Further training accustomed the horses to remain stationary when troopers fired rifles placed over the backs of the animals. In further preparation for his eastward march, Strange hired some local men as scouts. Sam Steele's three brothers accepted this service. Unknown to the Field Force members as they arduously prepared for their eastward advance, General Middleton's column was attacking Riel at Batoche. In effect, the rebellion was over.

Secure communications remained uppermost in Thomas Bland Strange's mind. By May 6 he had established a courier system between Edmonton and Calgary, using relays stationed every thirty kilometres. A reorganization of the transport was necessary, with some teamsters assigned to the Calgary Trail. The movement of supplies northward was extensive. One trip recorded 228 teams transporting over eleven thousand tons of supplies. Again operational along the route was the weekly Calgary-Edmonton stage.

Red Deer was the principal stopover. Trader Gaetz recalled that "there was a steady traffic of freighters going north and returning; halfbreeds, whites from all over North America, of every calling and profession, professional gamblers and the very riff raff of creation."[29] Travellers passed their time in Red Deer gambling, drinking, playing cards and dancing.

In May, work began on a telegraph line south from Edmonton to Calgary. This emergent project, like the construction of a rail link between Medicine Hat and Lethbridge, clearly demonstrated how in a crisis, monetary difficulties could be surmounted and defensive precautions prioritized.

Edmonton welcomed the soldiers, for they brought much more than armed security. As in Calgary, the Field Force created an immediate boom to the local economy. Government spending alone exceeded $20,000; Walter's ferry received $800; settlers received $8 daily for a team of horses; $5 daily was offered for construction workers on a telegraph line being extended south to Peace Hills. Daoust, a young recruit in the 65th Battalion, noted how money flowed freely: "Lorsque nous y sommes arrivés, l'argent y était des plus rares . . . Notre arrivée a été comme un torrent d'argent qui a envahi le pays."[30] The Hudson's Bay Company, acting as the paymaster for the soldiers in Edmonton, later recouped the money as the men purchased the store's high-priced goods, particularly the food "delicacies."

Prices escalated outrageously. For example, the price of hay jumped from $15 to $75 a ton. The exorbitant prices caused one soldier to complain: "The only conclusion one can arrive at is that the citizens think we are travelling gold mines."[31]

The rebellion passed into history without one shot being fired in the Edmonton district. Firing, that is, at the enemy. On several occasions unwarranted volleys by French-Canadian sentries at Fort Saskatchewan aroused everyone to their battle stations. The enemy, upon inspection, was Inspector Griesbach's cat and, on the second occasion, a nervous horse and foal. Such incidents actually provided humor – a break from the increasingly boring garrison duty. In the end, most Métis supported the government. No doubt the Roman Catholic Church influenced many, reminding them of the enormous power of the Canadian government. The priests deeply felt the loss of their two fellow Oblate fathers at Frog Lake and took every opportunity to condemn the rebels.

The economic gain in freighting and clearing brush also encouraged many Métis to co-operate with the government. As well, every settler had vested interests to protect. In the words of Kate Maloney, just a young girl at the time, they had "no intention of seeing the fruits of their industry pillaged by Indians."[32] The call for volunteers for a Home Guard had met with an enthusiastic response. An even more obvious action supporting Ottawa was the formation of a militia unit named the St. Albert Mounted Rifles. On June 9 thirty volunteers, hired at a daily rate of $2.50, left under Lieutenant G. Des Georges of the 65th for Lac La Biche where Big Bear's emissaries were active. Until their disbandment one month later, the St. Albert Mounted Rifles provided patrol duties and courier service.[33]

Dated from their first arrival, the Field Force remained two weeks in Edmonton. As preparations for the next stage of maneuvers – the movement downstream – were finalized, a delegation of citizens, unhappy over the proposed size of the troop garrison, presented a petition requesting a larger military presence. Strange assessed the military defences as adequate. More importantly, the Field Force's primary responsibility was to move on to the Frog Lake – Fort Pitt area. Therefore, in response to the delegation, Strange succinctly declared, "I cannot cripple this expedition which I am ordered to carry through, by leaving more troops at Edmonton."[34]

Strange assigned two companies of the 65th (about 35 men each) to garrison the Edmonton area. One company was stationed at Fort Edmonton; a second remained at Fort Saskatchewan, where it had been since May 1. One lieutenant in the small Fort Saskatchewan detachment, C.J. Doherty, achieved prominence in later life as Minister of Justice under Borden and Meighen (1911-1921), as Canada's representative at the Versailles Peace Conference, and as a delegate to the League of Nations.

Strange appointed Inspector A.H. Griesbach as district commander. This appointment lasted only a few days. On May 11 the Inspector departed with a police detachment and forty members of the Alberta Mounted Rifles to arrest some suspected Métis sympathizers at Battle River. Upon his return Griesbach found, in his words, "General Strange gone and Colonel Ouimet in command."[35] As outlined, the Conservative Member of Parliament, J. Alderic Ouimet, had been an embarrassment to John A. Macdonald's government. With this posting as district commander, Ouimet accommodated the interests of both the military and the government.

Now that the Indian dangers had diminished, Ouimet's stay was uneventful. One incident, though, attracted national attention. On July 2, in the House of Commons, a member questioned the government whether laws guaranteed freedom of conscience and worship to soldiers as well as citizens.[36] At issue was the arrest of seven soldiers. The men, stationed at Fort Edmonton, had refused to participate in a procession (Corpus Christi Day) to St. Albert on the grounds that they were Protestants. Four men were imprisoned overnight, but one private received eight days' detention in the bastion on a bread and water ration. Ouimet viewed this case as a disciplinary matter, not a restriction of freedom. His telegram to the Minister of Militia stated:

> Conway, the private referred to, enlisted as a Catholic. He, for the first time, pretended, on the occasion in question to be a Protestant. However, he was punished, not for having refused to attend the Catholic service, but for inciting his comrades to mutiny and having used insulting language to his captain.[37]

In any event, the incident now was of minor importance. Two days earlier, on June 30, the steamer *Baroness* had arrived in Edmonton to transfer those soldiers stationed north of Red Deer downstream to Fort Pitt to rejoin the 65th Battalion for their return to Montreal.

CHAPTER 8

Downstream to Frog Lake

Photo on Previous Page :

Victoria Settlement, 1884

CHAPTER 8

Downstream to Frog Lake

". . . no 'good Indians,' i.e., dead ones, were found the next morning."

– *Thomas B. Strange*

On the morning of May 14, the Alberta Field Force left Edmonton. It began its advance down the North Saskatchewan towards Frog Lake and Fort Pitt, a large area of open prairie bordered by northern forest. At this location the force planned to confront the rebellious band led by Big Bear. These Indians were described "as a bad lot, in spite of the missionaries . . . and with no more gratitude than an Irishman."[1] This observer, soldier Henry Brock, continued:

> They say the only thing to do is to get them when they are children, keep them entirely from their relatives and educate them, and then after two or three generations of selection you may get a good strain. This process, however, generally kills them, and it is a question if the American plan is not the best – exterminate them in the beginning.[2]

The untried troops faced a difficult dual assignment. They had to arrest the Indians responsible for crimes, while at the same time making certain that all the hostages were released unharmed.

No longer was the Field Force landbound. Eight scows built or purchased in Edmonton accompanied the eastward thrust. Five of the boats served as infantry transport, one as an artillery carrier, another contained a horse gun team, and a final boat contained equipment that allowed it to function as an impromptu ferry. Barrels of salt pork and sacks of flour, arranged along the gunwales and down the centre of each scow, fortified the crew members from possible rifle fire. The artillery piece, lashed solidly to its scow to control the recoil, acted as a primitive gunboat. The boats transported approximately one-third of the troops and the bulk of the supplies, thereby reducing the dependence upon teamsters. The largest scow, named Big Bear, held sixty men in addition to the quartermaster's stores and ammunition. The remainder of the force marched near the north bank of the river, following the route taken by an advance party of Steele's Scouts that had left six days earlier.

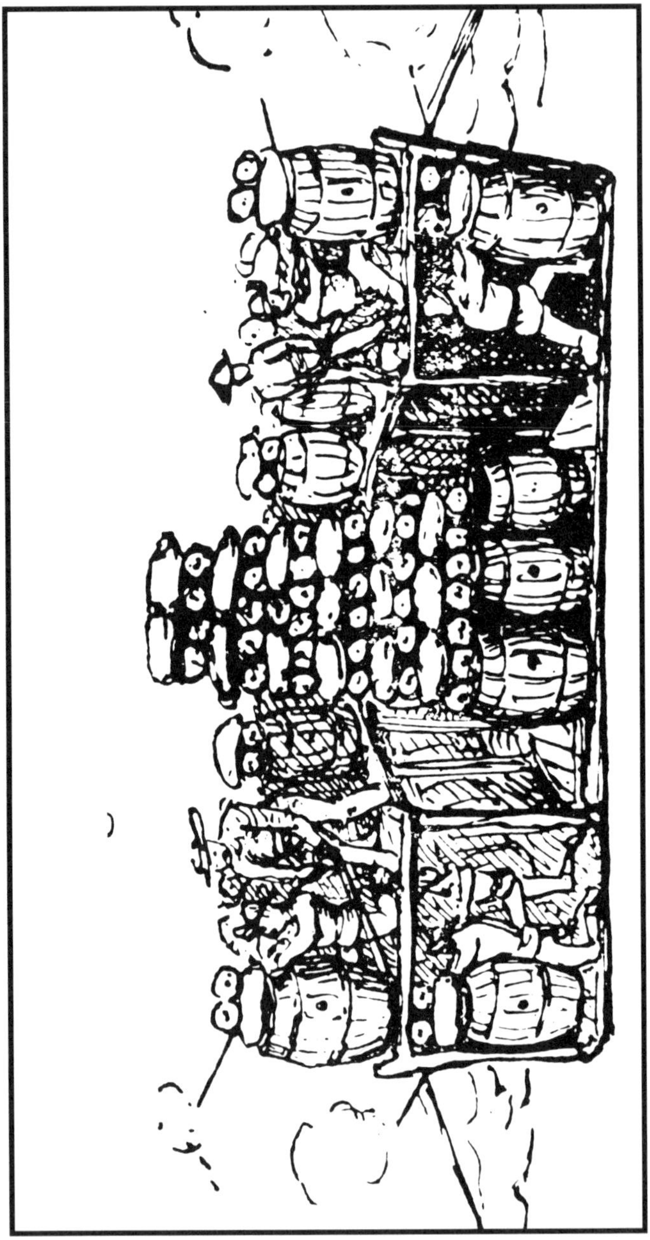

Barricaded Transport Scow

Thomas B. Strange's drawing of one of six barricaded scows transporting infantry and supplies downstream. About one-third of the soldiers were assigned to the scows while the remainder of the men marched near the north bank of the North Saskatchewan River.

A problem developed in finding reliable boatmen. Even before embarking from Edmonton, Strange discharged the first group employed because they failed to bail adequately, causing the boats to flounder. Attempts to hire local Métis boatmen failed. These men knew the river well enough but were afraid that Indian sharpshooters would strafe the boats from the wooded banks. Several men agreed, however, to serve as scouts in canoes that would precede the flotilla. Strange eventually solved his problem by employing a Hudson Bay pilot and an assistant for each boat.

Another difficulty arose with the commander of the Winnipeg Light Infantry, the unit assigned to the scows. Osborne Smith presented an official letter condemning both the safety of the boats and the quality of the ammunition supplied to the troops. In addition, the letter contained a request to test the penetration of flour sacks by rifle bullets. Strange, ever expedient, viewed these demands regretfully as they only "increased the difficulties of the situation and caused delay."[3] Nevertheless, he appointed a Board of Officers to question experienced navigators and boat builders about the construction of the scows .

Osborne Smith's concerns regarding the boats apparently had widespread support. One newspaper correspondent noted that "old hands in these parts, when they look at the scows, shake their heads [and] state that it is simply murder for men to be sent down the river."[4] Even Gunner Jingo, upon inspection, admitted "to an Englishman's eye the boats certainly looked cranky."[5] The explanation given was that because of the river's shifting sand bars, the boats had to be elastic with give-and-take, hence the flimsy appearance and use of wooden pins instead of nails. In any case, time was essential: the boats would have to do. In response to the other two concerns, Strange suggested that the defensive aspect of flour sacks "be relegated to hostile bullets,"[6] and, second, that the troops only fire their suspect ammunition at short range.

To refute "an openly-expressed opinion that the flotilla would never reach its destination without disaster,"[7] Strange and his staff embarked on the boats. A system of bugle signals maintained communication between the marching column and the eight boats. In the event of a determined attack from the Indians, Strange planned a combined response from his forces. If for some reason, however, the land and water units became separated or lost contact, the flotilla's orders were to continue downstream to the Frog Lake destination.

The scenery along the waterway was described as superb. The high, precipitous banks were well-wooded with a variety of trees to the water's edge. At sandbars, signs of gold mining remained evident. Exposed cliffs showed coal outcroppings and were honeycombed with swallows' nests. The banks of the river, observed a Winnipeg newspaper correspondent, swarmed with small, harmless snakes.[8]

Victoria Settlement, 1884

During the rebellion, Indian dangers caused the Victoria settlers to abandon the settlement and seek refuge in the brush. The settlers returned to Fort Victoria once the Field Force arrived.

Scouts in canoes led the advance down the swift, yellow waters. Once under way, the river currents prevented the boats from remaining in close proximity and a three-kilometre distance soon separated the lead from the rear boat. The soldiers, observed Strange, "pulled lustily at the sweeps, cheered by the lively boat songs of the French-Canadian pilots."[9] Clearly this noisy descent would warn any enemy, but Strange recalled:

> I had not the heart to stop them, though they might have attracted the attention of a prowling Indian scout; still it cut both ways, raising the confidence of my men, while it showed the Indians we had no dread of what they could do.[10]

Towards dusk, the men wisely curtailed unnecessary noise.

There were only two settlements along the 500-kilometre water route to Frog Lake. The first, the Mounted Police post at Fort Saskatchewan, was reached the morning of the 15th. After inspecting the facilities, Strange imprisoned two Métis men for suspected correspondence with Riel. One prisoner, after being "facetiously informed by different members of the regiment that he would be shot at daybreak,"[11] confessed to fighting at Fish Creek against Middleton.

Upon hearing that two men were in custody, some members of the half-breed community in Edmonton rode to Fort Saskatchewan, but communication with the prisoners was forbidden. The questionable incarceration of the two Métis remained an issue as Strange suggested to Inspector Griesbach "not to hurry the trial until the present troubles were over."[12] At the conclusion of the rebellion both prisoners launched legal action against Strange.[13]

The flotilla reached the settlement at Victoria, approximately one-third of the projected route downriver, on May 16. The advance troop of Steele's Scouts awaited their arrival. With them was Canon McKay. In his remarkable biography, written in 1946 at age ninety-two, the parson recalled travelling alone along a route littered with the Indians' plunder and waste. When McKay reached Steele's Scouts, he proudly marched three Indians at gunpoint before his horse. The minister had spotted the trio walking along a ridge, decided that he "might just as well have a little skirmish," estimated their speed and direction, cut ahead and waited to arrest the surprised Indians.[14]

Upon their arrival at Victoria, Steele's Scouts had found the tiny community preparing for an Indian attack. For two hours the troopers conducted a futile search of the nearby area without observing any signs of the enemy. Only that evening was the mystery of the anticipated Indian attack resolved. Apparently two young men from the settlement had mistaken the approaching scouts, clad in buckskin, for Indians. As they fled towards Victoria the scouts' calls of "Chesque! Chesque!" (wait! wait! in Cree) only confirmed their fears.[15]

For six weeks warriors from Big Bear's band had made intimidating visits to the settlements at Victoria, Whitefish Lake, and Lac La Biche area. These tactics had achieved limited success. A small band from Beaver River had entered the rebel camp, some Crees from Saddle Lake made a half-hearted assault on Victoria, and at Lac La Biche nine armed Indians had sacked the Hudson's Bay post on the pretext that "they wanted to take the goods and hide them, and save them for the company."[16] Fortunately for the government, though, the Cree bands at Victoria and Whitefish Lake ultimately rejected the strident appeals to join the native uprising.[17]

The Methodist Church exercised a strong influence at Victoria and Whitefish Lake. For thirty years the native preacher, Henry B. Steinhauer, had laboured in this area. Although he had died in 1884, his influence and teachings remained. Originally from Ontario, Steinhauer knew the power of the white Canadians, as did James Seenam, the Whitefish chief. Seenam had travelled to Regina in the summer of 1884 in an attempt to rectify his band's insufficient land allotment. Even if the government's promises "were like clouds, always changing",[18] Seenam was determined to stay out of the fight. After the hostilities the chief, because of his tough resistance to the rebels, received the name Pakannuk, meaning hazel nut. The Victoria settlement adopted the first part of his name and today is called Pakan.

The murder of Louis Cardinal, a suspected emissary of Big Bear, gravely increased the tensions in Victoria and Whitefish Lake. The killer, a Cree Indian named William Stamp, apparently became incensed at the insolent attitude Cardinal displayed at an assembly. By shooting Cardinal, Stamp – now called Cootsoo (manslayer) – jeopardized the safety of Seenam's entire band. Seenam immediately sent horses and cattle as gifts to Cardinal's four brothers, provided a coffin, and promised not to harbour Cootsoo. Then, still fearing reprisals by Big Bear's band, Seenam led his followers into hiding in the nearby wilderness.

The forests offered a refuge for three other frightened groups: the English-speaking half-breeds from Victoria, nuns and children from the Catholic mission at Lac La Biche, and the families of white traders moving to Athabasca Landing en route to Edmonton. One remarkable woman rode with her three young children to Edmonton, a journey lasting twenty-three days.

For the refugees hiding in the wilderness, life quickly became a drab and deprived existence. Their bland diet consisted mainly of salt pork and rabbits they snared. Caution was necessary when lighting fires and guns could not be discharged. Most of all, uncertainty about the course of the uprising maintained the level of fear and apprehension. When two Hudson's Bay traders, Harrison Young and Peter Erasmus, travelled to Edmonton for ammunition, they encountered not a single person in their 600-kilometre journey. From the signs of plunder, the two men believed that the rebellion had swept the entire North West. On their return to Victoria they

John McDougall with Indian Chiefs, 1886

From left to right: *John McDougall, Samson, Pakan or James Seenam, Reverend R.B. Steinhauer, and Jonas Goodstoney.*

encountered Reverend A. McLaughlin (McLachlan), who had been hiding. After helping the missionary organize defences at the settlement, Young left to join his family at Athabasca Landing and Erasmus sought the location of Seenam's band. A gifted woodsman, Erasmus easily located the 150 refugees, led now by his foster son Peter Shirt.

The residents at Whitefish Lake held Peter Shirt in awe because of a disquieting dream that Shirt had related some years earlier.[19] In his strange apocalyptic dream, an old man with flowing locks commanded Peter Shirt to look east. Dark and threatening clouds appeared over the Saskatchewan River, along with a figure Shirt recognized as Big Bear. Then the venerable figure commanded Shirt to look west. A picture of a little valley near Victoria appeared, alive with tents and red-coated soldiers. Deeply perplexed, Shirt asked the old man in his dream for a sign portending the coming of these events. In answer, Shirt was told it would be the death of a white horse. In 1884, Peter Shirt gained possession of a white horse. He found the animal dead in April, 1885 – the very moment two riders arrived announcing the tragic killings at Frog Lake.

Peter Shirt's dream was to have startling significance. After Erasmus' return from Edmonton, the Whitefish band moved to a location fifteen kilometres north of Victoria. From here Shirt, Erasmus and Chief Seenam left to observe the Victoria mission. The men approached the settlement with great care. From a hill they gazed down at Victoria. Before them lay a military camp – as the dream had foretold.

The Field Force remained at Victoria for five days, from May 16 to May 20. The soldiers spent the time perfecting drill routines, fishing in nearby lakes, and constructing anchors for the boats. During the stopover, a Home Guard under the Reverend McLaughlan was organized, the delapidated Hudson's Bay fort was repaired, and half a company of the 65th (about twenty men) was detailed as a garrison. With almost one-half of the 65th Mount Royal Rifles from Montreal deployed in this capacity, Strange was criticized for depleting the strength of his striking body. In turn, he insisted that a secure supply and communications line was an essential military precaution.

All communications with the Field Force followed the line of advance taken from Calgary. The distance and rugged geography of the route inevitably delayed information. For example, a letter from Middleton describing the April 24 skirmish at Fish Creek did not reach the Field Force until May 21. Meanwhile, Middleton had captured Batoche and taken Louis Riel prisoner. Further, Strange was improperly informed on the overall field strategy. In one instance, he understood that Amyot's 9th Voltigeurs would reinforce his troops once a Montreal unit took over their garrison duty in southern Alberta – something that never occurred. To open communication with General Middleton via the North Saskatchewan route, Strange sent two scouts downstream by canoe on May 21, the day after the Field Force left Victoria.

On his second day in Victoria, Strange held a "Pow Wow" with Chief Seenam. John McDougall acted as interpreter. Strange asked for Indian scouts, but Seenam remained noncommittal and requested time to consult his band. The chief returned on May 20 with a negative answer. Even though the Indians probably already knew (through their effective prairie communications) that Batoche had fallen a week earlier, they were reluctant to act against other Cree bands.[20]

Also at this time Chief Seenam brought William Stamp (Cootsoo), the killer of Louis Cardinal, into camp. Strange greeted Stamp with praise, presented him with a plug of tobacco, and promised him a guarantee of non-prosecution. After the rebellion, William Stamp received four head of cattle for "a most marked case of loyalty."[21]

Sam Bull, a young Indian boy visiting Victoria with the hope of seeing his first steamboat, provides one of the few native accounts of the North-West Rebellion. His version counters the "official" record alleging that Cardinal was a Big Bear agent. First, wrote Bull, Stamp held a grudge against Cardinal, "a friendly man who had never caused anyone trouble, and used the troubles as an excuse to kill him."[22] Second, the interpreter Peter Erasmus made a false statement to General Strange that "the murdered man had been a rebel so the accused was released."[23]

While at Victoria, Gunner Jingo dealt with the camp correspondents, "the curse of modern armies,"[24] in a calculating manner. He enjoyed deceiving the reporters about his plans, so much so that one denounced the general "as a madman who did not know his mind for twenty-four hours."[25] The reporter from the *Manitoba Free Press* wrote that Strange's dilatory and contradictory behavior aroused "the most open expressions of contempt for him by all [giving] . . . some foundation that he is slightly insane."[26] What Strange planned was the switching of the land and water units, with the green-uniformed Montreal men being assigned to the boats while the scarlet-coated Winnipeg Light Infantry marched. This meant that, most likely the Indians initially would face soldiers in red tunics, a special symbol on the Canadian prairies for authority. Only at the moment of departure were the assigned positions revealed.

Although the scows relieved the problem of blistered feet, the boats took on water. Despite pumping, twice the horse barge sank. The numerous sandbars and rapids made the downstream route difficult. One evening the gunboat steersman mistook a light for a rendezvous point and directed the boat toward the dangerous Vermilion Rapids. The boat was saved when Reverend John McDougall impulsively took command and had everyone jumping to do his bidding. Afterwards, McDougall was embarrassed by his forwardness and only felt better when everyone agreed that he was "the right man at the right place."[27]

Steele's Scouts left Victoria three days before the main column. The one hundred mounted men reconnoitered, prepared the trail, selected the campsites, and picked up any supplies of potatoes and grain left by the pillaging Indians. The main marching column followed a set routine: bugles only at reveille, spread out if attacked, follow sentry regulations, and wagons in a circle (with the tents just outside this ring) at night. Mounted scouts, usually about 500 paces ahead and to the left and right, formed a defensive shield for the main column of wagons and infantry. The ammunition wagons and "MacLeod" guns occupied the centre forward position of the string of wagons. A guard of scouts and police followed the rear wagons. As promised, the teamsters received weapons before leaving Victoria. Those wagons depleted of supplies continued with the column as troop transports. All along the advance, the muddy trail became increasingly difficult for the rear wagons. At times the column extended to three kilometres in length, not a desired military procedure.

The route was well-wooded, with many creeks, sloughs, and lakes, all high from the spring runoff. The countryside was beautiful, vast and empty, with rich, fertile soil that awaited only the plow. The rigors of each daily march preoccupied the thoughts of the men. Quartermaster Sergeant George Bliss wrote in his diary May 21: "Houses along the line of march vacant and provisions gone. Camped after 31 miles [54 kilometres] heavy march."[28]

Inclement weather prevailed throughout the ten-day advance. R.G. MacBeth, in the Winnipeg Light Infantry, wrote:

> During these days the rain fell almost incessantly; it was a case of marching in the mud by day and sleeping in our wet clothes by night. To make matters worse, we were on half rations.[29]

Only on the afternoon before reaching Frog Lake did a warm sun appear.

On the last day of the march to Frog Lake a soldier recalled awakening "from our cheerless bivouacs on the muddy ground"[30] to face another day. This morning, however, was special – May 24, the Queen's birthday. Everywhere in Canada, the militia organized celebrations. However, as the men of the Alberta Field Force stood in the driving rain there seemed little to celebrate. In a brief address, Strange reminded his troops that they had marched well and that they would stick to Big Bear's trail as long as the "grub" lasted. He continued in words "that came like bullets from a Winchester":[31]

> This is the Queen's birthday; we have no time to celebrate and can't have fireworks, but let us hope we soon will have fireworks with the enemy. Boys, three cheers for the Queen; God bless her![32]

A spontaneous shout erupted from the troops. One soldier considered this moment – men rain-drenched at daybreak, in a wilderness far from home – as a high point in the campaign. Strange concluded: "Boys, this also is Sunday, but we have no time for service today; we must push on the march."[33] John McDougall led the troops in a hymn and another day of marching began. This day they would bivouac two kilometres from Frog Lake.

Looking back, the soldiers regarded their journey from Edmonton to Frog Lake as often miserable, and generally uneventful. There was little "fun" – "we always spoke of a brush with the Indians as 'fun'," wrote one volunteer.[34] Any excitement usually resulted from mistakes. Mud and language difficulties caused one mishap. At each swollen stream the advance teams cut up the soft banks making the crossing progressively more slippery. Sometimes it was necessary to hitch extra teams to the rear wagons, but a quicker method was to attach a long rope to the wagon's tongue and have fifteen to twenty men help the horses pull. During one delay an officer in the Montreal regiment, unable to get some help from some mounted men, called in French for the rear guard to help extricate the wagons. The rear guard misinterpreted the request as an attack at the front. Consequently, they thundered through the entire column, "leaving everyone splashed with mud."[35] All ranks prepared for battle and listened for the reports of carbines. All was quiet. Soon the rear guard rode sheepishly back to their position.

On another occasion, an Indian night attack on the scows turned out, upon investigation, to "be young poplars waving in the wind."[36] A third incident occurred at the end of a day when a wide-eyed, bootless, bare-back rider charged into camp shouting that Indians had chased him. A force of weary mounted men immediately set out after the Indians. Soon they sighted some horses and prepared for action. However, the trail led away from a reserve and the tracks indicated that the horses were shod. Only then did the scouts realize that they had been tracking their own advance guard! The exhausted riders turned their lathered horses back toward the main column, knowing full well that they would be the sport of the camp that night. Their only consolation, trooper Milton Williams recalled, "was a universal cursing of the baldheaded old idiot and a wish that he was dead."[37]

The Field Force encountered Indians on two occasions. Near Saddle Lake a bullet pierced the hat of a soldier on a scow, and the 65th landed to search for the sniper. Their firing, however, proved ineffective, as the next morning Strange recorded derisively that he failed to find any "good Indians, i.e., dead ones."[38] On the second occasion, during an attempt to steal horses, an Indian shot at one of the guards. The gunfire put the entire camp into a state of frenzy for some time. Then as the excitement died down, a hundred convoy mules began to bray wildly. Joseph Hicks remembered that "no person slept any more that night."[39]

The march downstream to Frog Lake had ended unrest in the region, allowing the return of settlers and missionaries to their tasks. Moreover, the military movement demonstrated Ottawa's power and ability to dispatch armed columns to all corners of the North-West. The visual presence of armed soldiers greatly impressed the Indians. When a small patrol of Hatton's Scouts (delayed in Edmonton) rode through the Sucker Lake Indian Reserve, fifty kilometres east of Victoria, a picture of Queen Victoria attached to an arch constructed of evergreens attracted their attention. The chief insisted on shaking each trooper's hand, and stated that although some of his followers had joined the rebels, he hoped the soldiers would "kill all of them."[40]

One month had passed since the third column left Calgary. The men had crossed 700 kilometres of rugged wilderness. Now their most important objective was at hand: soon they would face Big Bear.

CHAPTER 9

Prisoners in the Indian Camp

Photo on Previous Page :

William B. Cameron and Horse Child – son of Big Bear, 1885

CHAPTER 9

Prisoners in the Indian Camp

"The war drums and the dance which they kept going most of the day and all night, with an occasional volley of rifle fire, kept us in a continuous state of nervousness and fear."

– *W.J. McLean*

The Indian camp, referred to as that of Big Bear, contained 520 members at the beginning of 1885.[1] The band, made up of both Wood Cree and Plains Cree members, had camped that winter near the Frog Lake agency. Conditions had been harsh. Indian agent Thomas Quinn reported in February that the band had only twenty miserable dying horses and that there was little nearby game. The desperate conditions, aggravated by abusive white officials demanding a work-for-rations policy, sustained the long-standing Indian grievances. By early spring, an angry mood gripped the camp.

Upon learning of Louis Riel's victory over the police at Duck Lake, the Cree band chose a violent course of action. On April 2, warriors brutally murdered nine white men at the nearby Frog Lake settlement. Ten days later they forced the surrender of Fort Pitt, located sixty kilometres southeast of Frog Lake. The Fort Pitt negotiations allowed the twenty-man police detachment to escape downstream, while forty-four civilians voluntarily became hostages in the Cree camp. With the pillage of the trading post, most of the pressing needs of the Cree band were met. On May 1, accompanied by their priest, Father Laurent Legoff, fifteen Chipewyan families from the Beaver River settlement joined the Cree camp. This decision appears to have been a reluctant response to intimidating visits by Cree warriors. Father Legoff recalled that "his flock" departed on the seventy-kilometre journey to the rebel camp "blèmes de peur et d'emotion."[2]

When the large war party left Frog Lake for Fort Pitt, the Frog Lake hostages contemplated terrible consequences. Six days later, the sight of forty-four unharmed prisoners among the returning warriors aroused exhilarant emotions. "It was a relief to see white people again," remembered Theresa Gowanlock.[3] W. B. Cameron added: "We now had other prisoners to share our troubles and we felt better. . . . misery always did love company."[4]

Big Bear's Encampment at Maple Creek, 1883

Later that year the Canadian government closed Fort Walsh and moved the Cypress Hills Indians north of the rail line, with Big Bear's band assigned to the Battleford area.

The hostage population now numbered twenty-seven whites and perhaps sixty Métis. White captives taken at Frog Lake included the wives of two of the murdered men, Theresa Gowanlock and Theresa Delaney, trader James K. Simpson, and clerks William Cameron, Henry Halpin and Stanley Simpson. Twenty-one whites had surrendered at Fort Pitt. Hudson's Bay factor W.J. McLean, his wife and nine children formed a large nucleus in this group. Others included farm instructor George Mann, his wife and three small children, Reverend Charles Quinney and his wife, and three single men – Malcolm McDonald, John Fitzpatrick, and Robert Hodson.

The sixty half-breed prisoners, a less well-defined group, had their situation helped by an understanding of the semi-nomadic Indian lifestyle, a knowledge of Cree, and certain assistance from relatives in the Indian camp.* And although captivity was never ideal for the Métis, it was, in Louis Goulet's words, "comfortable enough."[5] Some whites contended that many Métis could hardly be classed as true hostages, but were "for the most part, willing captives, who shared in the plunder, and were allowed to carry arms."[6] Several Métis men later fought against the soldiers.

The hostages faced their greatest dangers at the beginning of the captivity. Farm instructor Mann recalled, upon his capture, being told that "every white man would be killed in seven days."[7] Reverend Quinney's diary for April 20 graphically describes the volatile situation:

> Breakfasted with Long Indian on nothing but beef and bread. Soon after Miserable Man came up and charged me with wanting to shoot him at Fort Pitt, and I was now more than ever afraid of him. I wanted to shake hands with him, but he refused. I had to get him some tea, but Mr. McLean having very little I went to Mamso, who took up his revolver and threatened to shoot me. He changed his mind, however, and instead of giving me lead handed me some tea for his brother warrior.[8]

Quinney's diary reflects the view held by most whites that their captors were capricious and often unpredictable. The Indians had refused Father Legoff's request to bury the two murdered Oblate priests, yet "les infidéles" never interfered with his daily mass. Moreover, after one service which emphasized the "Christian love of all men," the largest collection came from the Plains Cree – the very warriors who had butchered Legoff's two

*Some of the Métis included: trader James K. Simpson and his wife Catharine; Hudson's Bay Company interpreter François Dufresne, his wife and three children; Glader (Gladu), his wife and child; Henri Dufresne; Edward Francis Dufresne; Otto Dufresne; John Perry; Isadore Moyen, his wife and four children; John Pritchard, his wife and eight children; Alfred Schmidt (Rabasca), his wife and four children; Huzil, his wife and child; Abraham Moots, his wife and six children; Isadore Pambrun, his wife and three children; Joseph Auger, his wife and child; Pierre Blondin; Andre Dreneau; Peter Saint-Luc; Gregoire de l'Aunais (Gregoire Donaire); Henry Quinn; Andre Nault; Etienne Moran; Louis Goulet; Jean-Baptiste Poirier, his wife and three children; Louis Patenaude; Benjamin Patenaude; François Mallieu; Charles Gouin; Baptiste Desnoyers.

Cree Band Members Trading at Fort Pitt, 1884

From left to right: *Four Sky Thunder, Sky Bird, Motoose (seated), Napases, Big Bear, Angus McKay, Mr. Dufresne, L. Goulet, Stanley Simpson, Mr. Rowley (seated), Alex M. Donald (in back), R.B. Sleigh, Mr. Edmund.*

colleagues at Frog Lake. Was it not strange that Little Poplar, camped across the river from Fort Pitt, was the first to warn the garrison of the Indian approach?[9] Later, he was a leading spokesman against the whites.

One account described the Indians as "vicious, treacherous, and superstitious."[10] The young men were especially belligerent and their cruel taunts shocked. Theresa Gowanlock was told, "That's right, cry plenty. We have killed your husbands and we will soon have you."[11] Those prisoners taken at Frog Lake had witnessed grisly murders. During the killings Louis Goulet had rushed to aid Father Marchand. He recalled his horror: "When we lifted him his head fell back and his brain ran into one of my boots."[12] The women, Gowanlock and Delaney, were walking with their husbands when Indians shot the two men. When the Fort Pitt hostages entered the Frog Lake settlement, a corpse "propped up against a tree with a pipe stuck in his mouth"[13] served as a horrible reminder of the killings. These violent acts and sights maintained a level of fear throughout the captivity. And although each day reduced the dangers, W.J. McLean recalled: "The war drums and the dance which they kept going most of the day and all night, with an occasional volley of rifle fire, kept us in a continuous state of nervousness and fear."[14]

There were added dangers for the female hostages. The women always had to stay in the company of others, never be alone. For safety, Kitty McLean remembered, "we carried a butcher knife in our belts to protect ourselves."[15] On one occasion, her sister Amelia stabbed an intruder's hand reaching into the tepee. Many Indian women, possibly because of their often abusive treatment and inferior status, provided empathy and support for their white sisters. No females were harmed, but several serious incidents occurred. On the day of the Frog Lake massacre, Métis prisoners John Pritchard and Pierre Blondon had purchased the wives of murdered John Delaney and John Gowanlock for $30 and several horses, thus preventing the women from becoming Indian wives – an outrageous affront to western frontier society. Another crisis involved Little Poplar threatening, with a revolver pointed at W.J. McLean's head, to seize young Amelia McLean for his seventh wife. A rifle placed against Little Poplar's chest by Blue Skybird ended this frightening confrontation.

During the ten weeks of captivity one macabre incident dramatically demonstrated the primitive belief of the Indians. One morning a poor wizened female, named Puskayak (She Wins), started ranting hysterically. Custom dictated that this aberrant behavior signified a witigo (wendigo), a dangerous cannibal who, for the safety of the tribe, had to be killed before sundown. However, finding an assassin proved difficult. When offered a double-edged dirk for the terrible task, W.J. McLean refused citing religious grounds. Those Indians approached likewise stated that this killing violated their religious beliefs. At last a Métis named Charlebois (Charles Ducharme) declared himself a nonbeliever of any god and accepted the gruesome assignment.

The woman was carried a short distance from the camp. Charlebois, decorated grotesquely in war paint and soot, spoke to the assembled: "My friends, you asked everybody to kill that woman and nobody would do it. After I strike her, don't say I struck the old woman and laugh at me."[16] He then clubbed and shot the demented woman. An Indian accomplice, using a sabre, quickly decapitated the poor victim.* A grisly scene followed: the Indian, clutching the severed head by the braids, "tried to throw the head over a clump of willows, but the braids caught in the branches and the head stayed there with its hideous face swinging three or four feet above the ground."[17] The Indians fled in terror. "It was," recalled Goulet, "the most horrible murder I ever heard of."[18] W.J. McLean echoed his words: "The scene was indescribably horrid."[19] Prisoners Quinn and Goulet cremated the woman's body.

Incidents such as this, so unexpected and violent, added to the mental strains afflicting many hostages. The future was so uncertain. Theresa Gowanlock recalled: "My mental anxiety, verging on derangement, was my worst trouble. I never knew what next was coming."[20] Elizabeth McLean remembered when her father was wading in a stream, several Indians loudly remarked that white skin would make good eating. Elizabeth did not know whether it was a joke intent on upsetting her or not, but remembered, "one never knew what was ahead."[21]

A lack of news concerning the rebellion brought further apprehension. On this point, Theresa Gowanlock told a news reporter: "We had heard nothing of the troops coming, nor had we heard anything of Riel's rebellion further than early March."[22] Likewise, W.J. McLean informed a reporter: "All this time the whole camp was ignorant of Riel's overthrow and Poundmaker's surrender."[23] What news they did receive remembered one hostage, "caused great consternation in camp."[24] One inaccurate report had 200 Métis from Edmonton coming to avenge the killing of the two priests. "Big Bear," remembered Reverend Quinney, "was frightened by this, for the Crees considered the half-breeds to be allies."[25] There was never any question that eventually the soldiers would come. What would happen then?

Becoming hostages entailed a sudden and dramatic change in daily routines. On the first evening in the Indian camp, as Factor McLean prepared his family of nine children for bed in tents pitched in the snow, he bitterly

*At the Indian trials in September 1885, Charlebois and Wawasehewin (Wawasehoween) received the death sentence for executing an elderly woman. In November 1885, this sentence was commuted to twenty years' imprisonment for Charlebois, ten years for Wawasehewin. A second Indian accomplice, Bright Eyes, received a ten-year prison sentence.

Imasees – Big Bear's Son, 1895

Imasees, Big Bear's son and a key instigator of the Frog Lake killings, escaped hanging by fleeing to the United States. When he returned to Canada ten years later legal authorities chose to overlook his crimes.

commented that the Indians "slept in our comfortable beds at Pitt."[26] The hostages were assigned to daily onerous camp chores, mainly attending to the firewood and water supply, cooking and cleaning, and guarding the horses. The Indians "wanted to work us to death,"[27] wrote Theresa Gowanlock in her account of two months in the Indian camp. Stanley Simpson described himself as being "a kind of slave."[28]

Although the pillaging had yielded the Indians an extensive accumulation of goods, the hostages received scrawny horses, shabby clothing, and inadequate food. There was no soap, but as one hostage ridiculed, its lack "was only felt by the whites."[29] Moreover, the captives' few remaining possessions with the were subject to the whims of the Indians. Wrote one prisoner, "When any Indian fancied an article of apparel, a horse, or anything belonging to the captives, he unhesitatingly asked for it."[30] As these requests were actual demands, the article was always surrendered.

The hostages watched helplessly as the improvident natives squandered their newly acquired wealth. Outwardly, the prisoners gave an appearance of contentment. Trader McLean, having lost most of his family's treasures, remarked, "In spite of this I had feign to content myself with the woeful lot."[31] * Likewise, his daughter Amelia remembered, "We never let those Indians know we were downhearted."[32]

The unsanitary conditions of the Indian camp disgusted the prisoners. They regarded the camp as filthy – infested with lice, swarming with flies, and overrun by lean, vicious dogs. The Indians were described as "very unclean and filthy,"[33] and the tepees as reeking "with filth and poisonous odors."[34] The absence of latrines bothered some prisoners. Naked boys, racing with bows and arrows after gophers, offended Theresa Gowanlock's sensitivity.

Many hostages loathed the Indian cooking and eating habits. One wrote: "The Indians would kill ten to fifteen cattle a day and then gorge themselves on food. They would eat eight or nine times, then follow the gorge with a dance."[35] Observing a whole rabbit – hair, eyes, and all – boiling in a stew pot was a revolting experience. Stanley Simpson bolted from the tepee upon learning the main ingredient of a stew he had just consumed was dog meat. Later, Simpson recalled the incident to a Toronto reporter with a twist of humor: "I was very hungry and the dish didn't look bad."[36] Besides, Indian custom regarded it an affront to refuse food placed before a person.

Accommodations usually were with Wood Cree families, or the "friendly Indians," which, to the captives, was "the best way to distinguish the Wood from the Plains Cree."[37] The large McLean family, though, found

*The government compensated the losses suffered by settlers. For the McLean family this amounted to $3,358. See Canada, *Sessional Papers*, *1887*, Vol. 13, No. 3, Claim 124, p. 524.

Wandering Spirit, 1885

As war chief of Big Bear's band, Wandering Spirit incited the killings at Frog Lake. He was hanged with seven other Indians at a public execution later that year.

themselves under Little Poplar, an influential Crow Indian who had arrived from the United States six months earlier. Besides being a "very active and turbulent agitator, Little Poplar proved to be an indifferent caterer."[38]

The hostages carefully assessed the disposition and attitudes of each Indian captor. War Chief Wandering Spirit always had a cloudy personality and always carried his Winchester. On several occasions, he had violently denounced the presence of whites in camp. Another Indian, Catfish, was just a nuisance, prone to annoying actions, such as feigning axe thrusts at passing prisoners. The hostages attempted to please their captors. André Nault, by masquerading as a hunchback clown, found that he delighted Little Poplar. Earlier friendships helped. William Cameron, at his capture, was comforted when a leading chief of the Wood Cree declared Cameron "a friend [who has] given us help when we needed it."[39] Cameron developed close ties with Meeminook (the first Indian killed by the soldiers) and with Lone Man, a prominent brave. Lone Man, uncle to murdered Indian Agent Thomas Quinn's Indian wife, promised to supply Cameron with a rifle when the soldiers arrived. Cameron, not wanting to kill his rescuers, claimed his aim was poor and instead offered to play the violin during the expected engagement. That Lone Man and war chief Wandering Spirit were bitter enemies held possible dangers for Cameron.

It helped to know the interrelated Indian families. Little Poplar, for example, was Big Bear's nephew and also related to Cut Arm, a leading Wood Cree chief friendly to the prisoners.[40] Also important was knowledge of Indian customs and codes of behavior. When an Indian called teenager Kitty McLean "little sister," she knew that her acceptance of this adoption meant he would "do anything for you."[41] William Cameron, certain that Indian custom deterred anyone from accosting him, clad himself in a blanket and walked about the camp at night. He found "a great deal of satisfaction in wandering around among the cutthroats and listening to their councils."[42]

The captives were enveloped by a sense of helplessness. When the Indians told William Cameron and Stanley Simpson that they had "the honor" of raising the rafters for a thirst dance, there was no choice but to agree. They despised this task, remembered Cameron, but made the best of it, "whooping as wildly as the redskins did."[43] Most often, however, the captives endured ineluctable tasks in bitter silence. Upon his capture Cameron had dutifully adjusted watches taken from the dead for the new owners, and observed in silent outrage the butchered head of a pet dog. Theresa Gowanlock watched helplessly as playful Indian children carelessly destroyed prized photographs and broke family keepsakes. Mrs. McLean could only seethe with anger while watching an Indian dance in her expensive dress, purchased for a Governor General's ball. Possibly the most outrageous insult involved Indian men dancing in the white vestments of the murdered priests. This was, in Father Legoff's words, "vraiment satanique."[44] Annoying situations had far less effect upon the children and adolescents. Amelia McLean, aged fourteen, simply tore her stolen hat off the head of an adult male Indian and threw it in the fire. The incident soon passed and her sister recalled, "we were all laughing at the whole ludicrous affair."[45]

Humor mollified the hardships of captivity. At Fort Pitt, a superstitious Indian had chopped an organ to pieces in search of a hidden devil. The retelling of the incident was always a source of amusement. The replacement of their beautiful beaded buckskins with an ill-matched assortment of ribbons, bells, dresses, jackets, made the Indians a sight to behold. Louis Goulet recalled watching the Indians leaving Fort Pitt: "There never was in all the world a circus parade as comical . . . it was hilarious but we didn't dare laugh. They took themselves very seriously."[46] Stanley Simpson's extra glass eye became a special source of amusement. An elderly one-eyed Indian dandy, called Dressy Man by the whites (because of his fancy clothes – stovepipe hat and swallowtail coat), experimented with the eye piece. When he complained that he still could not see, Simpson dryly explained that the glass eye had a blue iris, unlike the brown iris of Dressy Man's natural eye. Nevertheless, Dressy Man continued to use the eye piece, warwhooping and "proudly popping it in and out to the envy of others."[47]

William B. Cameron and Horse Child – son of Big Bear, 1885

Cameron had escaped the Frog Lake killings and spent two months as a prisoner in the Indian camp. This photo was taken in September 1885 at the time of Big Bear's trial, where Cameron testified for the Crown.

The captives received varying treatment. A farm instructor from Cold Lake, John Fitzpatrick, was well treated because he was an American.* Not so Robert Hodson. The Indians regarded Hodson "as some new variety of grub and . . . would like to have killed him out of mere idle curiosity to see him squirm."[48] Perhaps in revenge, Hodson later acted as the hangman at the public execution of eight Indians in Battleford.

Like the American John Fitzpatrick, the large McLean family usually enjoyed good relations with their captors. W.J. McLean told a Toronto reporter in July that in spite of his family's hardship they "were well treated with the greatest respect."[49] McLean, age forty-four, was called "Straight Tongue" because of his fair dealings with the Indians; Helen, his wife, "Medicine Woman" because of her medical help to the natives. Having been raised at a trading post, the children had an understanding of Indians and a knowledge of Cree. In addition, they astonished the Indians by speaking Saulteaux, a language unfamiliar to many of the Cree bands. At Fort Pitt, two of the teenaged McLean girls boldly entered the warrior camp to see their father. The Indians admired this brave act.

The captive children easily adjusted to the Indian camp. Asked by a reporter if the Indian children had been good to him, six-year-old John McLean exclaimed, "You bet they were!"[50] In a fascinating account of his captivity written eighty-three years later, Duncan McLean remembered life as an eight-year-old hostage:

> My personal memories of those days are, for the most part, of the good times. Everything wasn't bad, and I remember the camp fires at night, bacon and bannock, my Indian friends, and my family.[51]

Hostage Malcolm McDonald told a *Montreal Star* reporter that the children "appeared quite at home, running about from tepee to tepee in the camps and joking with the Indians."[52]

During the eight-week period between the Frog Lake Massacre on April 2 and the arrival of the Field Force on May 24, the Indian camp moved only in the Frog Lake - Fort Pitt area. The Indians broke camp with what the whites regarded as unbelievable delay and disorganization. Once under way, the captives enjoyed the freedom of movement. The Indians, remembered Elizabeth McLean, "did not seem in any hurry, sometimes staying in the same camp for two nights."[53] The improving spring weather made life more enjoyable. One Métis prisoner recalled:

*The Cree band apparently held the belief that American troops would come to help their cause – an idea that would make their insight into the campaign incredibly faulty. Yet, hostages recorded that the band expected twenty wagons of ammunition and 10,000 Americans coming to assist them. See McLean, "*The Last Hostage,*" p.5; Cameron., *Blood Red the Sun*, p. 72.; McLean, "*Tragic Events at Frog Lake,*" Whole No. 47, p.5; and Hughes, *The Frog Lake "Massacre,"* p.318.

> The spring weather turned warm and everyone relaxed. We had the supplies from Fort Pitt. We slaughtered Hudson's Bay cattle for fresh meat, played games in the daytime and danced at night.[54]

The hostages entertained themselves by conversing, singing, and reading the two books available – the Bible and *Robinson Crusoe*. A strong faith in God helped some devout prisoners withstand their captive ordeal. Family solidarity, too, countered adversities. Elizabeth McLean remembered her little six-year-old brother, shaking with fatigue, exclaiming to his older brother, "I'm not going to let those darn Indians see me crying."[55]

The Indians loved gambling and dancing. Every night they danced. Little Poplar, wearing a Stetson adorned with feathers and carrying a Bowie knife and two six-shooters, used a whip to encourage any sluggish participants. The energy expended by the Indians in dancing astonished the hostages. Theresa Gowanlock wrote: "I cannot conceive how human beings could march all day, as they did, and then dance the wild, frenetic dances that they kept up all night."[56] Stanley Simpson added a negative observation that while on the warpath the Indians "could tramp all day and dance all night, though while eating the bread of idleness they were unable to lift a hoe."[57] Their plunder had ended any need to hunt or work, and although the Indians squandered this new wealth, supplies lasted until the arrival of the soldiers.

Frequent council meetings, always held beneath the Hudson's Bay Company flag, served as social gatherings for the men and arena for Indian policy. Sometimes strong emotions erupted. Once Wandering Spirit, goaded by an old man questioning why the whites remained in camp, sprang to his feet with his rifle and was only restrained by other braves levelling guns at the war chief's head. It was a tense moment for William Cameron. At times, the hostages were required to read written information to the council. One newspaper article stated that 2,000 soldiers had arrived in Saskatchewan. Many Indians refuted this account as a lie. Yet, truth was required because literate Métis could confirm the information. Pointed questions, too, were extremely disconcerting. An uneasy Cameron remembered being asked whose side he favored – Riel or the police? The answers to leading questions always required tact and care.

The Indians were engrossed with the numbers, military strategy, and weaponry of the "soldiers." Yet, they often rejected the answers given as exaggerations. "Look at the few Red Coats at Fort Pitt. Is that plenty?" retorted Wandering Spirit. "We could finish them off like young ducks."[58] The band's knowledge of white numbers and military power came from first-hand observations of Canadian settlement. The three Provisional Districts of the North-West Territories had a white population of 15,000 scattered over 700,000 square kilometres. Most band members lacked the personal experience of the Blackfoot chiefs from southern Alberta, who were sent at government expense to visit Manitoba in 1884. In 1885, that province had 100,000 white settlers. Winnipeg alone, with a population of 20,000, almost equalled the entire Indian population in the North-West Territories.[59]

The hostages found that each passing day lessened their dangers. One prisoner wrote, "Our captors began to look with more friendly eyes upon us and our dangers seemed to grow less."[60] William Cameron and Stanley Simpson were even offered wives. Both men declined – Cameron with an excuse of poverty, "a dependable year-round defence."[61] Simpson lied that he had a wife which, by white man's rules, prohibited a second marriage. In a show of trust, the Indians provided Cameron and Simpson with guns and pitchforks for hunting and fishing excursions. The men had admirable outdoor skills. On one outing they astonished the Indians by returning with forty fish in less than one hour.

Cameron and Simpson immensely enjoyed the freedom of their hunting trips, but escape was out of the question. First, it would take days to reach the nearest safe settlement. Second, the Indians had declared that any escape imperilled the lives of those remaining hostages. Usually the hostages were not closely guarded. The Frog Lake captives could have easily left when the Indian warriors went to Fort Pitt, but after weighing the alternatives they chose to await the return of the war party. Likewise, Métis Louis Goulet returned across the ice-choked North Saskatchewan rather than escape. When Henry Quinn escaped briefly, the hostility of his fellow captives surpassed the anger of the Indians. Later when the troops approached, the hostages took special precautions to physically restrain Quinn.

In the middle of May, Poundmaker's Cree band called for a union of the two rebel Cree bands near Battleford. Poundmaker offered carts to facilitate the move and promised a great reception for which sixty cattle were being held. A Métis prisoner read the message from Poundmaker to the council. Not trusting his account, the Wood Cree asked McLean to confirm the reading. No longer did they implicitly trust the Plains Crees.

A major grievance against the Plains Crees was the killing of cattle. The Plains Crees chose to kill the animals from the 400 head after the fashion of the buffalo hunt, wildly exciting and dangerous as little care was given to the direction of bullets. This indiscriminate slaughter, with little concern about the ownership of the animals, led to bitter disputes and a feeling of "bad blood."[62] There was, in William Cameron's words, "no love lost between the two bands."[63] The hostages observed that the two Cree bands began "grouping themselves at opposite ends of the camp."[64] In addition, each night Wood Cree sentries now guarded those tents occupied by white captives. Obviously the safety of the hostages was becoming crucial.

The rigid discipline the Plains Cree once asserted over the camp was eroding. It was unusual to observe the Plains Cree War Chief Wandering Spirit acting as a peacemaker between two Indians involved in an angry dispute over the ownership of a horse.

The hostages viewed Poundmaker's invitation as a very dangerous proposal. Led by McLean, the white male captives immediately began to sabotage any plans for movement. Using the Indian dissension as a focal point they carefully probed the feelings of the Wood Cree Indians. They found Cut Arm, a prominent Wood Cree chief, very discontented with camp affairs. At the beginning of the rebellion, he had escorted the Reverend Quinney and his wife from Onion Lake to safety at Fort Pitt. Could the Wood Cree chief be counted on as a supporter? Stanley Simpson and William Cameron asked the Wood Cree why they allowed Wandering Spirit's men to kick them around as if they were dogs. They reminded the Wood Cree that they had not killed anyone. These persuasive arguments quickly gained support amongst the Wood Cree following. Still, Cameron recalled, "it was a perilous business for which we might be betrayed and pay with our lives."[65]

The arrival of four Saulteaux Indians from Riding Mountains in the Swan River district accelerated the intrigue. W.J. McLean knew the men and their language. "I sounded them out as to their sentiment," remembered McLean, "and found that they were loyal."[66] The Saulteaux became effective co-conspirators at the council meetings.

Each night the male white hostages held secret meetings to plan council strategy. This led to a secret gathering with all the leading Wood Cree men present. "I incited their anger," McLean wrote, "by telling them the Plains Cree were treating them like children."[67] He further belittled the Wood Crees for being coerced by a group they outnumbered three to one. McLean declared his opposition to joining Poundmaker's camp. The Wood Crees accepted his arguments, which mainly related to transport problems, and promised to delay any movement. In addition, the Wood Cree leaders agreed with McLean's suggestion to send scouts eastward to ascertain the military situation in the North-West.

McLean's strategy proved efficacious. At a disruptive meeting, the Indian council accepted the Wood Cree refusal to move camp until accurate information came from Batoche. A Métis captive and an Indian companion accepted this six-to-eight day assignment. At McLean's suggestion, they agreed to inspect Battleford en route. Within two days, the scouts returned. A shaken Indian informed the camp that "the earth trembled at Battleford with soldiers and horses."[68] This news disheartened the Indians. Was the government as powerful as the hostages had claimed? All plans for movement ended. Instead, in an effort to reconcile the two bands, the Plains Cree proposed a Thirst Dance.

Thirst Dance

To lessen tension between the Plains and Wood Cree factions of Big Bear's Indian camp, the band organized a Thirst Dance. In this ritualistic dance youths must pass a test of bravery to become a warrior. The unexpected arrival of the Field Force abruptly ended the festivities.

The dance, which usually continued unabated for three days, was one of the tribe's most important events. During the rites, young men endured torture and lacerations to qualify as warriors. A circular area, dominated by a high centre pole and surrounded by supporting poles covered with tents and branches, served as the site.

Within twenty-four hours electrifying news abruptly terminated the dance. Two Indian scouts arrived from Fort Pitt: to the west they had observed a large camp of soldiers. This news created panic and "the dance dissolved into a stampede."[69] Father Legoff recalled: "Had lightning struck the sacred tree it could not have caused greater consternation."[70] Chaos reigned. The warriors herded the prisoners into a group and placed the Indian women and children beside them to deter enemy fire. "Hardly were we seated," remembered teenaged Elizabeth McLean, "when we were told to break up camp, gather our few belongings and set off."[71] For the Indians, the premature ending of the dance "was interpreted as an omen of misfortune and loss."[72] Learning that during the dance the Hudson's Bay flag had been upside down, further upset the superstitious natives.

For the prisoners, the long-expected arrival of soldiers was an exhilarating moment. Was their captivity about to end? Cameron wrote: "We could have shouted, but the slightest sign to betray the delight we felt would have been our undoing."[73]

Even though help was near, a salient fact remained: they were still prisoners and subject to many dangers. That night Wandering Spirit, looking black and forbidding, warned the hostages that he planned to fight and if anyone left to join the soldiers, others "would pay with their lives."[74] Until the soldiers freed the hostages, only excited speculation was possible. "There was nothing possible for us," Cameron wrote, "but to wait."[75]

CHAPTER 10

Contact with the Indians

Photo on Previous Page :

Traders at Fort Pitt, 1884

CHAPTER 10
Contact with the Indians

"One of the boys scalped Meeminook. This scalp hung for a long time in a billiard hall which was on the corner of First Street East and Ninth Avenue."

– E.A. Hayes, Steele's Scouts

In the late afternoon of May 24 an advance party, led by J.K. Oswald of Steele's Scouts, reached the Frog Lake settlement. It lay in ruins with debris scattered in all directions. Strong odors attracted soldiers to a cellar or well. Trooper Hicks described the gruesome scene:

> Two men went down and handed up the parts to those above who then buried them. The men who went down to get the bodies wore gas masks consisting of a sponge saturated with army rum. They had the freedom of the camp that night.[1]

The hole contained four charred corpses, indistinguishable after fifty days of decomposition. Only beads identified the remains of the two priests. Years later, in a newspaper article, Trooper E.A. Hayes recalled: "It fell to us to remove the bodies. This we did and laid them in a row. Even now, fifty years hence, I can still see them with their hands and feet burned off."[2] The other bodies were those of John Delaney and John Gowanlock. Gowanlock had been horribly mutilated: both legs were severed near the thigh, and the arms above the elbows.

Canon McKay, while hunting mallards at a nearby pond, stumbled over a fifth decaying corpse, identified as that of young William Gilchrist. He had been shot in the back at close range. Nearby was the body of George Dill. After Surgeon Pennefather examined the corpses, Canon McKay conducted the burial service according to the rites of the Church of England. Members of Steele's Scouts buried the bodies in a nearby cemetery.

The main column of the Field Force arrived early the following morning. To the annoyance of Steele's burial detail, soldiers in the Winnipeg Light Infantry exhumed the bodies and Captain Frank Clarke administered the Roman Catholic funeral rites. Following the second interment, the troops unsuccessfully searched the surroundings for more bodies. Everywhere the

Sketch of Frog Lake, April 1885

Sketch of Frog Lake showing the buildings sacked by warriors in Big Bear's band the first week in April, 1885. The bodies of nine murdered men lay exposed until the arrival of the Field Force seven weeks later.

littering and vandalism evinced the rage of the Indians. In Gowanlock's house, the wallpaper was slashed to ribbons and the floors littered with books, papers, and letters. Surgeon Pennefather observed "not a single article of furniture or even cooking utensil was left."[3] When Pennefather saw large pike congregating in the nearby mill pond, he erroneously "thought it not improbable that the villains had ended their hellish work by throwing the bodies in the river."[4] But a further search by soldiers found no more victims.

The senseless waste at the tiny settlement elicited a sense of sadness, of futility; this beautiful and lonely spot once held meaning and a future for those now dead. Was all that remained of their efforts now only mutilated corpses and wanton ruin? Pennefather wrote:

> It was sad to see a place, which had evidently much pains bestowed upon it, rendered waste. A pretty garden, tastefully laid out, surrounded one of the cottages, and in front of the mission was a large, well-tilled field, ready for cropping.[5]

A second emotion aroused was hatred against the "savages." Scout Joseph Hicks bitterly expressed these sentiments:

> Up to this time the eastern troops expressed sympathy with the 'Poor Indians' and lots of us doubted whether some of the men, particularly the members of the 65th, would fight the Indians when we got at them. But what a change of attitude the scene at Frog Lake made. It was then the other extreme.[6]

First-hand observance of the havoc and murder increased the urgency to rescue the hostages with Big Bear. "It was a horrible sight," wrote the Reverend John McDougall to his wife, "and will do much to hurry us on the trail of the villains."[7]

Of utmost concern was the fate of Theresa Delaney and Theresa Gowanlock, wives of two of the murdered men, now helpless prisoners in the Indian camp – an abhorrent thought to most westerners. Many sensational stories had circulated "as to the atrocities perpetrated by the Indians on prisoners they had captured, especially on several females." [8] This gave most soldiers in the Field Force an exalted sense of duty to uphold the honor of these two unfortunate white females, even though no one personally knew the women. While advancing downstream, ill-founded rumors concerning the fate of the women reached the Field Force and the soldiers had become incensed. One officer wrote: "Had Big Bear and his band fallen into our hands while these reports were credited, I do not think man, woman, or child would have been spared." [9]

At noon, scouts brought news that Indians were at Fort Pitt, sixty kilometres to the southeast. Strange immediately organized a marching column from Steele's Scouts and the Winnipeg Light Infantry, while the 65th continued downstream by boats. The supply wagons were to follow the trail taken by the foot soldiers. By a forced march, foot soldiers reached Fort Pitt at 7:30 that evening.

Only smoking ruins gave evidence of Indians. One storehouse remained standing amid a field of broken furniture, books, merchandise, "strewn about as if scattered by a whirlwind." [10] The tainted air from nearby poplars led scouts to the badly decomposed body of Police Constable David Cowan, only eighteen years of age when killed by Indians on April 13. His body had been terribly mutilated, handcuffed, and his heart removed. Hostage Louis Goulet had witnessed several Indians eating the heart: "Take a look at this," Goulet was told, "an Indian can eat the heart of a whiteman, but a whiteman can't eat an Indian's." [11] Near Cowan's body, the uneaten portion of his heart was impaled on a stick. Nearby was Cowan's dead horse. The scouts immediately dug a grave and reverently buried the young man's body, "the rattle of musketry his only funeral requiem." [12]

The mutilated corpse had revolted the entire column. This barbaric act was, wrote one French Canadian soldier, "la guerre indienne . . . plus féroce et plus barbare." [13] Everyone wanted revenge. Canon George McKay recalled kneeling beside Cowan's body when a "burning righteous wrath" took possession of him. Turning to a companion he shouted, "You take the Bible and give me the gun." [14] The uncivilized abuse of the bodies at Frog Lake and Fort Pitt, Scout Hicks wrote, "did not allay the harsh feelings of the men toward the Noble Red Man." [15]

The following morning, May 26, fatigue parties cleaned out the ruins and constructed a stockade around what remained of the fort. The poor condition of the horses necessitated a short rest and access to open grazing. As supplies had not arrived from Edmonton, the shortage of food meant

Key Persons of the North-West Rebellion, Fort Pitt, 1884

From left to right: *Thomas Quinn, murdered at Frog Lake, was the Indian agent for Big Bear's band; Inspector Francis Dickens commanded the Fort Pitt Mounted Police detachment and made the controversial decision to abandon the post; James K. Simpson and Stanley Simpson (both hostages in the Indian camp) and Angus McKay, area fur trader.*

reducing the individual daily rations by one-fourth. Upon learning of food thefts, General Strange reacted harshly, declaring "anyone stealing is not worthy the name of man. He will therefore be considered a brute, and will be flogged."[16] This threat proved effective and no further food thefts occurred. Although scouts found an Indian cache of 100 bags of flour and fifty sides of bacon, Strange, fearing the supply might be poisoned, refused to allow its use. His decision further angered the *Manitoba Free Press* correspondent travelling with the column. "Strange," he wrote, "has entirely lost the confidence of those he commands and not one hour passes that deep mutterings of discontent are not heard."[17]

At Fort Pitt, General Strange, unaware that General Middleton was accepting Poundmaker's surrender at Battleford, expected that Big Bear and Poundmaker would unite their forces rather than allow themselves to be attacked separately. But where were the Indians? Based on his belief that the Indians "habitually follow their old trails," Strange ferried two scouting parties across the North Saskatchewan to examine three known Indian trails.[18] This reconnaissance, however, failed to detect any signs of Indian movements.

A misunderstanding in orders apparently followed as the troop under Police Superintendent A. Bowen Perry proceeded to Battleford, a 150-kilometre journey that took thirty-six hours. With Perry were seventeen Mounties, five scouts, and the missionaries, McDougall and McKay. Meanwhile at Fort Pitt, General Strange angrily awaited their return. He recorded:

> Unfortunately, Captain Perry took it upon himself to ride into Battleford, with his whole detachment, without sending me any information and I neither saw nor heard anything of him for nine days.[19]

Strange further suggested that Perry possibly sought some 'Kudos' from Middleton for opening communications.

The loss of the twenty-five man scouting detail, all mounted, caused unnecessary military difficulties at a critical moment in the campaign. First, with over one-half of the Montreal 65th serving at garrison stations along the route, the striking force that left Calgary now numbered 515 scouts and soldiers, along with about 160 teamsters.[20] Second, the loss of Perry's unit required the immediate training of an artillery unit for the "Macleod gun."

The Indians had cleverly attempted to conceal their movements, even to the point of removing "every particle of horse and cattle manure."[21] A letter found east of Fort Pitt, however, indicated that the band had remained north of the river. That afternoon, Steele's Scouts discovered the trail taken by Big Bear.

Ninety-two men under Steele began the pursuit. By midnight their circuitous route of fifty kilometres placed them in dense brush near the North Saskatchewan River. From this point campfires in Strange's camp, only five kilometres westward, could be seen. Steele, with three men, moved into a dark valley where they hoped to bivouac the scouts. Suddenly an Indian jumped up and ran. Scout Joseph Butlin fired. The Indian returned two shots, which passed between Steele and Butlin, before moving in the direction of Scout Tim McClelland, "who dropped him straight."[22] A wild shooting scene ensued. As Steele recounted, "we were in the midst of a yelling, whooping band":

> The hot flashes of the Winchesters of the Indians almost singed our faces, and several times we had to pause lest we shoot each other. This lasted a minute, when the Indians departed with headlong speed to the eastward, exchanging shots with my rear party as they passed by.[23]

Throughout the gunfire the shouts of Butlin and McClelland "could be heard a mile away."[24]

Fort Pitt, 1884

After Big Bear's warriors brutally murdered one Mountie, the Police detachment fled downriver to Battleford, leaving the residents no options but to surrender themselves to the Indians.

The Indian party contained twenty men.[25] After a cursory search in the dark underbrush for warriors, Steele ordered his men to lie on the ground and prepare for an expected attack. It started to rain. Two miserable, uneventful hours passed before the light of dawn allowed the men to reorganize.

The sudden skirmish resulted in one fatality, an Indian named Meeminook from Saddle Lake – a location approximately halfway between Edmonton and Fort Pitt. When Strange first viewed the body, the tall athletic bronzed body had upon his breast "the Queen's medal . . . an ornament about the size of an agriculture trophy for a prize pig."[26] On a second occasion, Strange observed the Indian naked; without his police tunic, without his medal, and without his scalp. The mutilation allegedly was the work of Montana teamsters who, "when opportunity offers, pay the redskin in his own coin."[27] One scout carried Meeminook's ear in a waistcoat pocket. When Angus McKay, brother of Canon George McKay with the Field Force, arrived at Fort Pitt with Middleton's force on June 2, he went with a companion to view the dead Indian. They found the naked body, dead for over a week, bloated to a huge size. A rope remained around Meeminook's head and it was obvious that a trooper "had galloped around the prairie with the rope attached to his saddle pommel, trailing the body in the grass in circles, the trails of which were still visible."[28]

At the end of the rebellion, Meeminook's scalp "embellished" a Calgary pool hall. According to Scout E.A. Hayes:

> One of the boys scalped Meeminook. This scalp hung for a long time in a billiard hall which was on the corner of First Street East and Ninth Avenue.[29]

The abuse of Meeminook's body matched the cruel defilement of the corpse of Police Constable Cowan.

In assessing the skirmish with the Indians, Second Lieutenant R.G. MacBeth, W.L.I., observed:

> there was great satisfaction when the routine of the long march was varied on the 27th of May by our coming into contact with the wily and light-footed foe.[30]

With the Indians at hand, all members of the Alberta Field Force readied themselves for further combat.

At daylight, May 27, scouts under Steele followed the main Indian trail. Their discovery of nearly two hundred campfires gave an approximate size of Big Bear's camp. Steele directed a small detail under Scout Whitford to move ahead. Within half an hour they returned, "riding for dear life,"[31] pursued by a large party of yelling warriors. Steele's men rushed forward, dismounted, and prepared for the onslaught. Steele recalled that "as soon

Mounted Police Drill, Fort Pitt, 1884

Inspector Francis Dickens (third row far right), son of the novelist Charles Dickens, is seen here with his detachment at drill practice.

as the savages caught sight of us they halted at a respectful distance and galloped away."[32] Whitford, who knew Cree, related his good fortune at hearing the Indians discussing his approach, thus preventing the ambush.

Shortly after this incident General Strange arrived. Once the wagons were corralled, and left for the teamsters to guard, the Field Force began an advance through difficult country. After moving about five kilometres, the men reached the base of a prominent elevation called Frenchman's Butte (now Frenchman Butte). About noon, an advance party of eight men began ascending a trail toward the summit. Suddenly, Indians appeared between them and the column following about 200 metres in the rear. Gunfire drove the Indians away.

This shooting forced the entire column to take cover. As the men intently watched the bald summit of Frenchman's Butte, Indians appeared. Trooper Hicks, in the advance party, recalled:

> They had gathered in considerable numbers, both mounted and on foot. They were yelling 'Astom Schmognus, Asum Pugumawa,' saying, "Come on white man and fight."[33]

The Indians circled the hill, Strange recalled in his autobiography, as an obvious signal to a hidden party, "displaying themselves in a way very unusual for Indians."[34] This was the first sighting of unfriendly Indians for the rank and file, and the setting accentuated their impressions. In his memoirs, Steele recalled the dramatic scene:

> a fine-looking band of Indians appeared on the summit of a large round butte, about 1500 yards distant. They were galloping in a circle to warn their camp, their excellent horsemanship and wild appearance making a remarkable picture as they were silhouetted against the blue sky.[35]

Strange ordered the firing of shrapnel shells to clear the ridge. The first shot fell low, but the second blast burst right over their heads, scattering the riders. Harry Strange directed the field piece. Gunner Jingo referred to his son as "phlegmatic Harry, . . . a fellow so infernally lazy that nothing will hustle him."[36] Apparently, once in action, Harry Strange was capable of precise shooting. In a letter to an old friend, General Strange acknowledged that in "35 years I never saw better."[37]

The Alberta Field Force divided into two groups and advanced on foot in the direction of the departing Indians. For many untested recruits, fears of a savage Indian ambush were uppermost. Private James McConnell wrote: "it was queer going through the bushes and every moment expecting a volley from the enemy."[38] The thick stands of small trees made progress difficult and hindered communications between the two groups, but eventually the men reunited and climbed the summit of the hill. Not an Indian was in sight.

For several hours the soldiers advanced in an eastward direction. The troops were joined by the 65th, alerted on the barges by the noise from the nine-pounder. That night a corral of wagons, called a kraal, served as a defence. Inside, the horses grazed while the men slept under the wagons. Because of the dense forest and total darkness, special security precautions were ordered. Everyone kept his rifle by his side, in preparation for an expected assault. In the event of an attack Strange warned his men to be careful as "night firing is not effective, except occasionally on friends."[39]

The warm night proved uneventful. Strange expressed surprise "that we were not molested that night."[40] A soldier in the Winnipeg Light Infantry echoed his general's view: "I have never been able to make out why the enemy . . . did not make short work of us in the darkness."[41] The Indians instead chose to remain in their camp. The advance sentries could see their fires glowing in the distant trees. On May 27, about fifty kilometres northeast of present-day Lloydminster, the Alberta Field Force had finally caught up with Big Bear's band.

CHAPTER 11

Frenchman's Butte

Photo on Previous Page :

Soldiers in the Winnipeg Light Infantry in Edmonton, May 1885

CHAPTER 11

Frenchman's Butte

"Montreal and Winnipeg should feel proud of their boys."

– Winnipeg Daily Times, *June 20, 1885*

At daybreak the Field Force arose without the customary bugle accompaniment and prepared for the day. The Winnipeg Light Infantry shared their meagre rations with the 65th who, in their haste to join the main party, had left their supplies and blankets on the boats. (Luckily for them the evening of the 27th had been very mild.) A dismounted van-guard of Steele's Scouts led the advance along a narrow three-kilometre trail. This route took them past the Indian Thirst-dance encampment where the number of campfires led scouts to inaccurately estimate an opposition of 700 braves.

The exact number of warriors in the Indian alliance was not known. All white estimates greatly exaggerated the Indian strength. The *Toronto Daily Mail,* for example, reported 800-900 warriors.[1] Those hostages in camp provided smaller numbers. William Bleasdell Cameron numbered warrior strength at 240 Wood Cree, 80 Plains Cree, and a handful of Chipewyan.[2] George Mann told a Montreal reporter that the camp held "20 tents of Chipewyans, 150 of Wood Crees and 75 of Plains Crees, which make between 300 and 350 braves."[3] Father Legoff wrote, "Big Bear never had more than 200 warriors."[4] Trader W.J. McLean, a prisoner for seventy days, stated their were "not more than 150 actual fighting men."[5] Having women and children to protect, seriously weakened the Indian fighting strength and mobility.

The possibility of being outnumbered meant little to the soldiers. In the thirty-eight days since leaving Calgary they had marched a long way for this chance to fight Indians. "The Crees under Big Bear have captured Pitt from the Police and we are going to take it back or lose our hair,"[6] wrote a young Mountie, Alexander Dyre, to his mother in Ontario. Moreover, the gruesome discovery of mutilated bodies three days earlier had hardened the inexperienced soldiers' resolve. Despite all their "gung-ho" enthusiasm, only General Strange and two subordinates had fought under battle conditions.

The trail led past a wooded descent, into a valley. To the north, a steep hill separated the advancing soldiers from Indians waiting in concealed rifle pits. The hill constituted a perfect natural fortification for the Cree defenders. The soldiers advanced from the southwest towards the river valley, some 500 paces wide, containing the sluggish Little Red Deer river which expanded into swamp and muskeg. This open area, in the words of scout Joseph Hicks, "looked like a nice green hay meadow but when you tried to go on, it disappeared and you were up to your neck with no bottom."[7] Above this protective moat of water and muskeg a steep escarpment, barren of trees, extended to the edge of the rifle pits. The summit of the hill was covered with timber, throughout which the five rows of carefully concealed rifle pits remained invisible. General Strange described the approach to the Indian lines in a letter to a friend:

> The enemies [*sic*] position formed a salient hill with a natural glacis perfectly clear of cover. The rifle pits were along the crest just at the edge of the thick bush behind. The front and flanks were protected by an impassable muskeg and creek.[8]

Soldier R.G. MacBeth considered the Indian position "to be impregnable."[9] Similarly, Private McConnell of the Winnipeg Light Infantry described the site "as better than any fort in the Northwest Territory."[10] But that morning, ignoring the Indians' strategic advantage, his force's sparse rations, the danger to the hostages in the Cree camp, the possibility of inferior numbers, and Middleton's earlier orders not to advance beyond Fort Pitt, "Gunner Jingo" chose to attack.

On the opposite hillside, streamers, of red and white calico drooped from tree branches in the silent and still air. These streamers were, in Strange's words, "so at variance with the usages of Indian war"[11] that he immediately distrusted their presence. They were, in fact, arranged to entice the troops to advance along the desired angle of fire for the rifle pits. Strange knew "the enemy wished to draw us into an ambuscade, and calculated that I would go blundering on with my Force."[12] Thomas Bland Strange, in spite of his rashness in advancing that morning, was observant enough to avoid this trap.

With a scout, the general rode out into the valley. All remained silent. At the stream, mud prevented further reconnaissance so Strange and his companion returned to the main body. Some members of Steele's Scouts reported hearing a horse neighing in the bush on the opposite hill. Chief guide and interpreter Alex Rowland told Strange that he was certain Indians were there. Strange answered, "We will find out."[13]

Big Bear and General Strange

Illustrations in the Canadian newspapers portrayed the Indian and Métis insurgents unfavourably. See Walter Hildebrandt "Official Images of 1885." Prairie Fire, *VI, No. 4, November, 1985, pp. 31-38.*

Strange's military expertise was artillery. It comes as no surprise, then, that his assault began with an artillery barrage of the concealed positions on the wooded knoll. His son, Lieutenant H. Bland Strange, brought the nine-pounder into position, and through the early morning mist discharged a shell into the hillside. Immediately, "fifty shots" [14] came back. "The shower of bullets sounded like a flock of snow birds as they flew over our head," [15] remembered one surprised trooper.

It is uncertain how many Indians opposed the Alberta Field Force. The Indian force, according to one account, totalled 120 warriors.[16] Some of these men guarded the Indian camp, located three kilometres to the north. Father Legoff claimed that only fifty men held the positions along the summit of the hill.[17] The Indian defenders, too, were poorly armed. Factor McLean doubted if there were more than sixty rifles in the whole Indian camp.[18] But for Private McConnell, the weaponry and the number of Indians on the opposite hillside at that moment was immaterial. He only recalled dodging bullets: "I tell you it was no fun having bullets whistling in such close proximity to our ears." [19] The time was 6:10 a.m. The Field Force returned the fire. It was the beginning of a shooting exchange that would last over three hours, until 9:40 that morning.

Although General Strange and his scouts referred to the skirmish site as "Stand Off Coulee,"[20] the conflict that morning of May 28 is generally called the Battle of Frenchman's Butte.* In fact, the prominent landmark, which rises fifty metres above the surrounding countryside, is located two kilometres south of where the forces engaged in battle. It was on the summit of Frenchman's Butte where the Indians had circled on horseback the previous day, until driven off by Harry Strange's shelling.

Excluding the teamsters, Strange's force consisted of four companies of Winnipeg Light Infantry numbering 180 men, possibly 100 police and scouts under Steele, and 103 members of the depleted Montreal 65th – in all about 400 men.[21] The Field Force lines extended for about one kilometre. Police and Steele's Scouts held the left front while the 65th under Lieutenant -Colonel Hughes, and two companies of the Winnipeg Light Infantry under Major Thibeaudeau, maintained the right. Two companies of the Winnipeg unit under Lieutenant-Colonel Osborne Smith remained in reserve. Major Hatton's Alberta Mounted Rifles covered the right flank where thick woods screened any Indian approach. The teamsters formed a zareba to the rear.

The troops faced a distinct disadvantage in terms of position and cover. There was little that they could do other than lie prone behind the improvised timber defences. When several soldiers advanced toward the stream, they sank in mud to their waists. Even had they crossed the swamp area, the open grassy incline in front of the Indian rifle pits would have made any attack a costly undertaking. It was a steep climb even without weapons. General Strange wisely ignored the clamouring of the soldiers in the 65th "to be led across the muskeg in a bayonet charge against the Indians."[22]

From their camouflaged rifle pits the Indians raked fire down on the soldiers. "The bullets were flying like hailstones all around,"[23] recalled McConnell. The soldiers returned fire from 400 metres at an enemy who, in MacBeth's words, remained "practically invisible, only the puffs of smoke from their rifles and the 'ping' or thug of bullets indicated their presence."[24] This was an unusual baptism of fire for the infantry: lying for hours and shooting at distant, perfectly protected targets. To their credit, the men maintained excellent discipline throughout the skirmish. "During the three hours they were under fire," observed a reporter from Winnipeg, "they smoked and chattered cheerfully as if they were engaged in a skirmishing drill on a field day."[25] Troop movements remained minimal. Scout Hicks recalled that this action "was noted for the loss of good ammunition rather than the destruction of the enemy."[26]

*All sources in 1885 refer to the hill as Frenchman's Butte. The Surveys and Mapping Branch, Department of Energy, Mines and Resources, in Provisional Map of Canada 73F/12, title the village and region as Frenchman Butte.

The Indians and male prisoners had spent the previous night digging the rifle pits. Early that morning, Little Poplar had incited and harangued the less militant Indians to prepare for the battle. "Will they," he taunted, "be knocked on the heads like rabbits? Does a few redcoats make them sick?"[27] Yet during the skirmish, Little Poplar, whom Father Legoff considered "the leader of the camp,"[28] patrolled the women's camp. Big Bear also remained with the women and children for most of the battle. He had arrived on horseback early in the conflict with the exaggerated announcement that twenty soldiers already had been killed. Throughout the distant shelling, the old chief continued to encourage the camp members. Two statements were to prejudice his trial in September. One was his remark that hostage complaints of hunger would be satisfied "by white flesh and plenty of it";[29] a second, that he wanted "his men to cut the head of the white people off the same as he cut a piece of tobacco off."[30]

At the battle site Wandering Spirit, the war chief, directed the defences. Until wounded in the wrist, another Plains Cree, Oskatask, taunted the soldiers after each cannon shell explosion by yelling "Tan at ee!"[31] (This was his version of "Stand at Ease," a drill procedure he had earlier observed in American forts in Montana.) Prisoner George Mann, who regarded most Indian combatants as cowardly, was impressed with the bravery and leadership of Cut Arm, the Wood Cree chief. "I have confidence in our young men," Cut Arm proclaimed. "They will never run away, but fight while there is a drop of red blood left, and we will destroy the white robbers, who have taken our country from us."[32] But other than one ineffective movement toward the teamsters, the Indians remained near their rifle pits. They did not even steal horses, observed one soldier, "at which they are much better than fighting."[33]

Although many Indians fought bravely, some warriors were unnerved by the attack. One prisoner related: "I never saw such cowardice in my life . . . many on the fighting line never fired a shot."[34] One Chipewyan warrior admitted being afraid. When he told a Cree companion that he was leaving to see if his family was safe the Cree joined him. "I found," the Chipewyan told his captors at Beaver River, "that he was as big a coward as I was."[35]

Against the advancing Field Force, Big Bear's Crees followed a military strategy that would only contain the soldiers, never win. Everyone knew that an army would come. Yet, the band failed to coordinate military action or even establish regular communication with the two other areas of insurgency. This was abysmal military planning. Allowing the government forces to advance virtually unharassed deprived the Indians of many advantages of mobility and terrain. Further, since the sacking of Fort Pitt six weeks earlier there had been no attempts to augment the diminishing ammunition. In effect, through inaction, lack of foresight, and satisfaction with present circumstances the Cree band seriously limited its future options.

On the Trail after Big Bear

On their march from Calgary to Saskatchewan the column had followed primitive trails without bridges, and encountered snow, rain, hail, and scorching heat.

At the battle site the Field Force, unable to dislodge the Indians by an assault, relied on the "Macleod gun." Throughout the battle the nine-pounder continually catapulted shells toward the Indian trenches, but because of the dense trees the shrapnel was ineffective. One shot did achieve startling accuracy. Aimed at an Indian who had hoisted a flag, the shell broke the staff in half. For this shot, all the troops gave the gun detachment three cheers. According to Father Legoff, the field piece wounded five Cree warriors and caused one fatality, an Indian named Kahweechetwaymot.[36] The warrior, who was responsible for two murders at Frog Lake, passed an agonizing night before dying in the morning.

In spite of its limited field success, the nine-pounder had a decided psychological impact. The explosions could be heard in the Indian camp, each reverberation a disquieting reminder of the presence of soldiers determined to kill Indians. "The cannon frightened the Indians very much,"[37] observed prisoner George Mann. Cameron recalled that one old woman had asked: "What had the poor Indians done that the white soldiers should come and kill them all with their big guns?"[38] Likewise, Mrs. Quinney related:

> An old woman asked, "What have the poor Indians done that the white men shoot them down?" "Grandmother," I replied, "have you forgotten so soon how they murdered the priests and the other people at Frog Lake and how they killed a policeman at Pitt. The cannons are demanding our release, and if you don't let us go they will come and take us, and then you will know what you will get."[39]

Throughout the shelling, riders constantly arrived in the women's camp, always bringing encouraging news of the fighting. "It is customary for Indians to boast of their prowess and bravery," wrote W.J. McLean, "[and] . . . during the fight some braves would find their way back to the women and children and tell them they had just killed a man."[40]

The sound of the gun brought hopes of freedom for the captives. The explosion of the shells, in Theresa Gowanlock's words, "sounded beautiful, it was sweet music to my ears."[41] Cameron remembered feeling intoxicated with cheerfulness at the nearness of the troops. "And what music in the ears of us captives," he wrote, "was the earth-rocking roar of that nine-pounder field gun."[42] Yet, for the time being, the hostages had to carefully suppress their true feelings.

Neither side made any headway in the battle. After three hours of inconclusive fighting Strange, citing the "great disadvantage"[43] of the troops, ordered Steele's Scouts to withdraw from the front, regroup, and on horseback flank the enemy's right. He hoped this movement would push the Indians toward the North Saskatchewan where Middleton's troop steamers were thought to be advancing.

Soldiers in the Winnipeg Light Infantry in Edmonton, May, 1885

In key situations, General Strange choose this battalion to impress the Indians as they had red tunics like the Mounted Police.

To cover Steele's maneuver, a heavy fusillade bombarded the enemy positions and the 65th pushed slightly northward. The scouts moved 2.5 kilometres without turning the Indian flank. Strange later concluded that some Cree defenders had perceived Steele's movement and conducted a parallel march. In any event, Major Steele failed to achieve his objectives. Then when two scouts finally succeeded in crossing the valley, a message arrived from Strange ordering the return of all the scouts.

Many factors contributed to the decision to withdraw from the battle site. After more than three hours of fighting it appeared unlikely that the Cree positions could be dislodged. The soldiers were hungry, the horse teams had been harnessed for eight hours, and only one day's rations remained. Most important, individual ammunition allotments were low and the nine-pounder had only twenty-two shells left. Led by Osborne Smith, subordinate officers advocated a cessation of hostilities.

Strange accepted the advice to retreat to more open ground. "I did not think," he wrote, "it advisable to sacrifice men for doubtful results."[44] With supplies and two companies of the Winnipeg Light Infantry expected to arrive by scow at any moment, there was the assurance that the next attack would take place under more favourable conditions.

Before the withdrawal, Strange asked about the condition of the casualties. He was astounded to hear one officer say that Private Joseph Lemay, 65th Battalion – who "would die anyway"[45] – remained badly wounded in an advance position. Moreover, when ordered to command a stretcher party to assist the wounded private, the officer replied to the incredulous Strange that he had "been shot at quite enough today, and I am damned if I go down there again."[46] Strange would never have left a fallen comrade on a battlefield. There was no question of his bravery. He ordered his son to open fire and with Doctor Paré, a stretcher party, and Father Prevost began a search for Lemay. *Gunner Jingo's Jubilee* relates:

> Father Prevost, Chaplain of the 65th, also followed me, crucifix in hand, to administer the last rites of his Church. We found the man well to the front, lying in an exposed position, and I must admit some impatience, which the good Priest did not seem to share, during the confession of sin, and suggested to the brave Padre the desirability of lumping the lot, which he did; and putting the dying man into the stretcher, under Dr. Paré's direction, the party moved up the hill, and I brought up the rear with the man's rifle.[47]

As the party ascended the hill the firing grew hotter, the rear man dropped his end of the stretcher, and "Gunner Jingo" took his place. With a sense of pride, Strange was the last man off the battlefield. Lemay owed his life to the "Buckskin Brigadier." And to everyone's amazement at Fort Pitt, Lemay "was around before the camp broke up."[48]

Factor W.J. McLean, who had offered one thousand dollars to anyone contacting the soldiers concerning his family's whereabouts, related that "he was thunderstruck"[49] by Strange's decision to withdraw. "The Indians were thoroughly scared," he told a newspaper reporter five weeks later. "I really believe they would have turned and fled, leaving us and everything behind."[50] The *Calgary Herald*, in an article titled "Struck-by-Thunder McLean," defended Strange's actions. Included was a letter by Strange which refuted the military second-guessing by the former hostage, now acting "more in the spirit of an enemy than a friend."[51]

Considering the three hours of firing, the number of casualties was remarkably slight. A young Mountie, Alexander Dyre, who survived that day (only to succumb to typhoid fever while on garrison duty in Battleford that fall), vividly described the danger:

> A bullet grazed so close to the hand I was holding my rifle with as almost to burn it, while others struck the ground between my long legs and whistled around my head like devils let loose. McRae was shot in the leg not two feet from me.[52]

During the skirmish, some men in the Field Force showed little heed to the dangers. Samuel Steele, for one, rode back and forth on his huge horse ordering others to seek cover; and while his gun crew crawled about on their knees, Harry Strange, who in his father's words was "the best shot at man in the force,"[53] stood upright to observe the trajectory of each shell with his field glasses. Three men were wounded in the Field Force: Private Joseph Lemay, 65th, shot through the lung; Private Joseph Marcotte, 65th, shoulder wound; and Police Constable J. McRae, shot through the leg.

Inaccurate information shocked Private Marcotte's family in Montreal. A news item in the *Toronto Globe*, June 1, 1885, reported his death:

> Joseph Marcotte, No. 3 Co. 65th, was a printer by trade and was working on the *Herald* when ordered to the Northwest with his battalion. He was unmarried and was looked upon as a steady young fellow. His father and mother were informed of their son's death in the fight by Bishop Fabre.[54]

In Montreal that same day, at a special church service (to bless a banner made by ladies for the 65th), Reverend Father Hanson declared that the unit "was now consecrated by fire and blood."[55] Research fails to reveal when Marcotte's anguished family learned that, far from dead, their son was recuperating in the fresh air of the great northwest.

The battle at the Little Red Deer River ended with the combatants moving in opposite directions. The Indians, unknown to the Field Force, had almost exhausted their supplies of ammunition. To effect a safe retreat, Strange ordered the firing of the field piece until the troops exited the ravine. As the force moved south, dismounted Steele's Scouts covered the rear. The Field Force retired ten kilometres westward to open ground, where at 4:45 p.m. the men corralled the wagons, turned the horses loose to graze, ate hardtack and drank tea. Later, members of the 65th went to retrieve supplies from their barges but found that the boats had drifted downstream to an island. The battalion's lack of tents, supplies, and rations required the Field Force return to Fort Pitt, another eight kilometres distance. The small fort also provided makeshift hospital facilities.

That evening the soldiers relived the battle. Wounded constable McRae had to be moved from the field under arrest as he had refused to quit firing until his fifty rounds were gone. Some men, like Sergeant McKay, "proudly exhibited caps shot through, as evidence of close-enough calls."[56] One soldier excitedly recalled having a bullet pass under his chin, covering his face with dirt. Private James Sullivan's scarlet tunic had three bullet holes – yet he was unharmed. The Winnipeg soldier's explanation was simple: his tunic, placed at the end of his rifle barrel and held above his concealed position, had attracted the enemy's attention and fire. And police constable R. Weldon proudly displayed a new hat, won from General Strange. Strange had approached Weldon and said, "You are said to be a good shot. You see that fellow on horseback close to the bush. Sight at 450 yards and if you hit his horse or himself I will give you a present."[57] Weldon shot the horse. It had been an exciting morning – a day to remember. D.R. Bremner, in a newspaper article twenty-five years later, wrote: "I do not forget the 28th of May when so many of us got our first baptism of fire."[58]

Strange generously praised his men. "Never in his military experience," he told them, "did he see a bolder attack made upon a stronger position."[59] With more battle experience they would correct mistakes in maneuvres – the green-coated Montreal men had bunched too closely when moving across open ground. The mistakes aside, Strange concluded, "it was remarkable for green men and horses to do such fine work. It reminded him of old times."[60] In his official report the General declared: "All troops did their duty to my entire satisfaction."[61]

In retrospect, Strange's actions that day showed no outstanding military ingenuity or tactical skill. Early that morning his force had contacted an enemy holding a decided geographical advantage. General Strange's first impulse was to attack, regardless of the possible consequences to the hostages. After opening the battle by firing artillery shells at concealed positions, the soldiers had remained prostrate for the next three hours while bullets whistled all around them, fired by an enemy that remained mainly invisible and perfectly protected. This was an unusual baptism of fire.

Middleton did not think highly of Strange's performance that day, remarking, "it was a pity General Strange had not waited for my arrival, when a more decisive blow might have been struck."[62] This assessment overlooked the inadequate information Strange had received of the Saskatchewan campaigns. One message that reached the Field Force incorrectly stated that Middleton was moving west from Battleford by steamer, ten days before the skirmish.[63] During the conflict Strange "hourly expected to see the smoke of the steamboat, with reinforcements."[64] A letter to his wife reaffirms this belief: "After my last fight with Big Bear I did not push him, expecting every hour General Middleton would come up behind him and I did not want to scare him away."[65]

The Indians also had demonstrated inadequate military skills. The defensive position proved well-chosen, but the battle tactics lacked movement and even surprise. Wounding three soldiers would not deter a force bent on attacking the band. Nothing had been done to harass the troops or to jeopardize their supply line. And fleeing from this enemy offered only a brief respite: within five days freshly equipped troops under Steele attacked the retreating band.

Even though the Alberta Field Force had not won a military decision in the battle fought near Frenchman's Butte, it had achieved a psychological victory over the Indians. In assessing the aftermath of the battle, all advantages rested with the government. The arrival of soldiers further fragmented the tenuous Plains and Wood Cree alliance, leaving the Indian camp disenchanted and demoralized. Everyone recognized the government's firepower. The warriors knew that their women and children encumbered their fighting force, slowing them down, while the soldiers "travelled without women and children."[66] The band, moreover, had knowledge of the American army's strategy of total warfare. One devastating tactic had soldiers ravage Indian villages regardless of the season. With this in mind the initial attack by the Field Force foreshadowed burdensome days and growing despair in the Cree camp.

Following the battle, the Chipewyan allies left the Indian camp. For three weeks this small band of twenty families had wanted to return to their settlement at Beaver River. To gain Cree approval they had already made gifts of carts and forty head of cattle. The Crees had accepted these tokens, in Father Laurent Legoff's words, "with the most solemn unequivocal and gracious promises"[67] – but always some excuse, delay, or false promise ensued. After the attack by the Field Force, the Chipewyans were determined to leave the Indian camp. When Cree Indians came to investigate the departure preparations, they faced a resolute row of rifles. A day later, aided by inclement weather, the Chipewyans left while the Crees slept.

They moved northwestward quickly with the warriors guarding the rear. Only after travelling thirty kilometres did the band stop to eat. "We had every reason to fear that the Cree would attack us," explained Father Legoff.[68]

Six white hostages and perhaps five Métis families gained their freedom in the confusing aftermath of the conflict. The Métis included the ten-member John Pritchard family. At Frog Lake, Pritchard had purchased the wives of murdered Gowanlock and Delaney. These two white women, William Cameron – another survivor from the Frog Lake massacre, and the Reverend Mr. and Mrs. Charles Quinney, taken at Fort Pitt, wandered for several days before contacting roving scouts.[69] Twenty-seven whites and several Métis families remained with the Indian band. Not until these hostages gained their freedom would the soldiers stop their relentless pursuit of the Cree Indian band.

While the dispirited Indian camp faced a dismal future, the soldiers were more determined than ever. They were also encouraged the next day, with the arrival of supplies and the news of the fall of Batoche. One soldier, now with three hours' battle experience, confidently predicted: "We expect to attack them again in a week or so, and then we will wipe them out entirely."[70]

CHAPTER 12

Skirmish at Loon Lake

Photo on Previous Page :

A Member of Steele's Police Scouts

CHAPTER 12

Skirmish at Loon Lake

"This was a battle of action. The Scouts' rifles got so hot they had to be dropped on the ground to cool."

– E. A. Hayes

On June 1, four days after the skirmish, a small cavalry detachment under Sam Steele returned to "Standoff Coulee." The extensive defensive preparations amazed the men. Scouts counted 300 rifle pits in one stretch three -fourths of a kilometre along the ridge. One trench was fifteen metres long and two metres deep. Barricaded logs, loop-holed for defence, provided perfect cover and made most of the pits shellproof. Several circular trenches had been cleverly covered by tepees. To the rear (north) of the rifle pits a deep ravine acted as a natural defence against any encircling movement by the troops. From their observations, the scouts concluded that any assault against the Indian positions would have resulted in a serious loss of life to the attacking force. In view of the laborious construction, one scout – who claimed "the Indians find farming much too hard for them"[1] – suggested an equal effort expended on agriculture would have yielded a respectable crop.

Seven trails led away from the battle area. These paths, designed to confuse and delay pursuit, eventually reunited into two trails indicating the direction of the Indians' northward retreat. Sixty-five abandoned wagons and carts revealed a hasty Indian departure. Keen observation noted the absence of rifle cartridges – a sign that ammunition was scarce, necessitating the reloading of empty cartridges.

The abandoned battlesite and Indian camp were littered with plunder. It was, in Major C.A. Boulton's words, "a heterogeneous collection of savage and civilized articles."[2] Mountie William Parker described the campground as being "covered with bales of prime furs, valued at between forty and fifty thousand dollars, as well as an enormous quantity of household furniture, ornaments, silverware, cook stoves, bedding."[3] Most of the valuables quickly disappeared. The teamsters, with vehicles in which to store the goods, were the main culprits. Many of the troops were "angry at not getting a haul."[4]

Steele's Police Scouts, 1885

Members of Steele's Police Scouts participated in the arduous eighty-five kilometre ride from Fort Pitt to Loon Lake. Of the seventy-five horses used by the troopers only twenty-six survived the return to the base camp.

Samuel Steele was determined to badger the Indians. At 2:00 a.m. on the morning of June 2 he loudly roused his cavalry troops and in the predawn light ordered them to get eight days' half-rations, all the available ammunition, and follow him. As the men groped for their supplies, Steele raced down the trail "as hard as his horse could lope."[5] Quickly the troopers followed. Steele wrote of his determined pursuit of the Indians:

> We could not wait for either the pack-animals or pack-saddles. The supply of ammunition was small, but there was no help for it, as no time was to be lost. . . . Strange informed me as I moved off that General Middleton had landed, and would be sure to send his mounted troops in support.[6]

Steele had sixty-two men at his command: twenty Mounties, twenty Steele's Scouts, and twenty-two Alberta Mounted Rifles. Everyone was eager for action as it was "generally believed that once he [Middleton] came all chance for other fights would be lost."[7]

The Indians had retreated through a lightly timbered region interspersed with sloughs, muskeg, and waterways. They burned what they could and discarded unwanted articles along the trail. At key places warriors felled trees to obstruct pursuit. "They did," wrote trooper Hicks, "the very things they could to make us trouble."[8]

The troopers found the trail extremely difficult. Mosquitoes and horseflies tormented their horses and forage was mainly tough slough grass. As a measure of the suffering, only twenty-six of the original seventy-five

Captain R.W. Rutherford's Painting of the Loon Lake Crossing

Following the skirmish at Loon Lake, the Indians moved north into inhospitable brush country while Steele's force returned south for supplies.

horses that began the pursuit, survived the ordeal. Scout Hicks recalled the problem of dying horses: "When a man lost his horse he started to walk back to where we started." [9]

About noon Steele's force contacted several Indian rear scouts and fired at them. Canon McKay dropped one Indian with a scalp wound, then fired a few shots over his head "to see if he could increase his speed." [10] McKay recalled:

> Of course, I could have killed the Indian but after all I was a clergyman and I did not plan on killing an Indian if I could frighten him into doing my bidding. [11]

The Indians soon returned the fire as the troops crossed a meadow. One man received a bullet wound, but, in Steele's words, "We pushed on gaily." [12] Perhaps the most startling campaigner was Canon McKay whose fierce "war whoops would make Sitting Bull turn green with envy." [13] The Indians evaded the charging troops and Steele pressed forward quickly, hoping to reach the main Indian camp before a warning arrived of his pursuit. Thomas "Jumbo" Fisk, the wounded scout, chose to continue northward with the force. To conceal their camp, they had no fires that evening. Supper was without tea and the men slept on the wet, cold ground.

Steele's force contacted the Indians near the southwestern corner of Loon Lake on the morning of June 3. Already that day they had spent over seven hours on the trail. Trooper R.L. Barber recalled:

> We rode until 12 o'clock midnight and camped between two sloughs, building a barricade with trees and our saddles. We took up Big Bear's trail at daylight, which was about two o'clock in the morning and came upon him about 10 o'clock. [14]

It had been a determined pursuit. In approximately thirty-one hours the scouts had ridden eighty-five kilometres over difficult terrain.

The Indian camp occupied both shores of a narrow water crossing referred to as Two Lakes, Loon Lake being unmapped at that time. A count of seventy-five campfires at the Indians' last stop meant that the scouts would be outnumbered. From a high ridge, the men could see Indians crossing the ford.

Steele had planned to have Canon McKay speak in Cree to demand the Indian surrender. However, gunfire from an Indian sentry served, in Steele's words, as "a signal for us to attack and we rushed to the front with Indian yells." [15] The men, on foot, charged the brow of a steep hill southwest of the ford. The retreating Indians, believing that Steele's party held only six men, were exhorted by a chief to retake the position. To their surprise, they moved into an ambush. At the hilltop Steele's men waited "to punish a few of them." [16] One Indian died three paces from Mountie Fielders, two others as they ran from the scouts. A lively exchange of gunfire followed from concealed positions in the brush. The soldiers also fired volleys at two distant tepees. A fourth Indian died from this long-range shooting.

The soldiers, numbered even or odd, next raced down the ridge. At the bottom, the odd numbered men charged to the left and up the opposite hill; the even numbered group forced their way to the right along the lake toward the camp and ford. Both assaults pushed the Indians back.[17]

The skirmish continued with long-range firing from hidden positions. Steele had Canon McKay make a second attempt to contact the Indians. "When I appeared in the open," McKay recalled in his autobiography, "they immediately opened fire, some of the bullets coming uncomfortably close. One cut my jersey sweater." [18] As there was no response to McKay's call for surrender, other than steady fire from one position, Steele decided to withdraw and await reinforcements.

Ironically, in the confusion of the battle, the Indians also had attempted to open negotiations with the help of Factor McLean. Waving a white cloth on a long pole, McLean vainly tried to get the attention of the troops. He recalled: "I called to them as loudly as I could, both in English and in French, but the only response we would get was a volley from their rifles." [19] McLean also had endeavoured, on his own, to contact the scouts. Unfortunately his messenger, François Mellieu, Saulteaux Indian, was shot in the elbow and forced back. To see the soldiers, and yet not be released, discouraged the hostages. W.J. Mclean recalled that he "returned to camp a truly sorry man." [20]

The attack at Loon Lake killed Cut Arm, the Wood Cree chief friendly to the hostages. The indiscriminate shooting had endangered the hostages on the south side of the ford. Teenager Kitty Mclean had a bullet pass

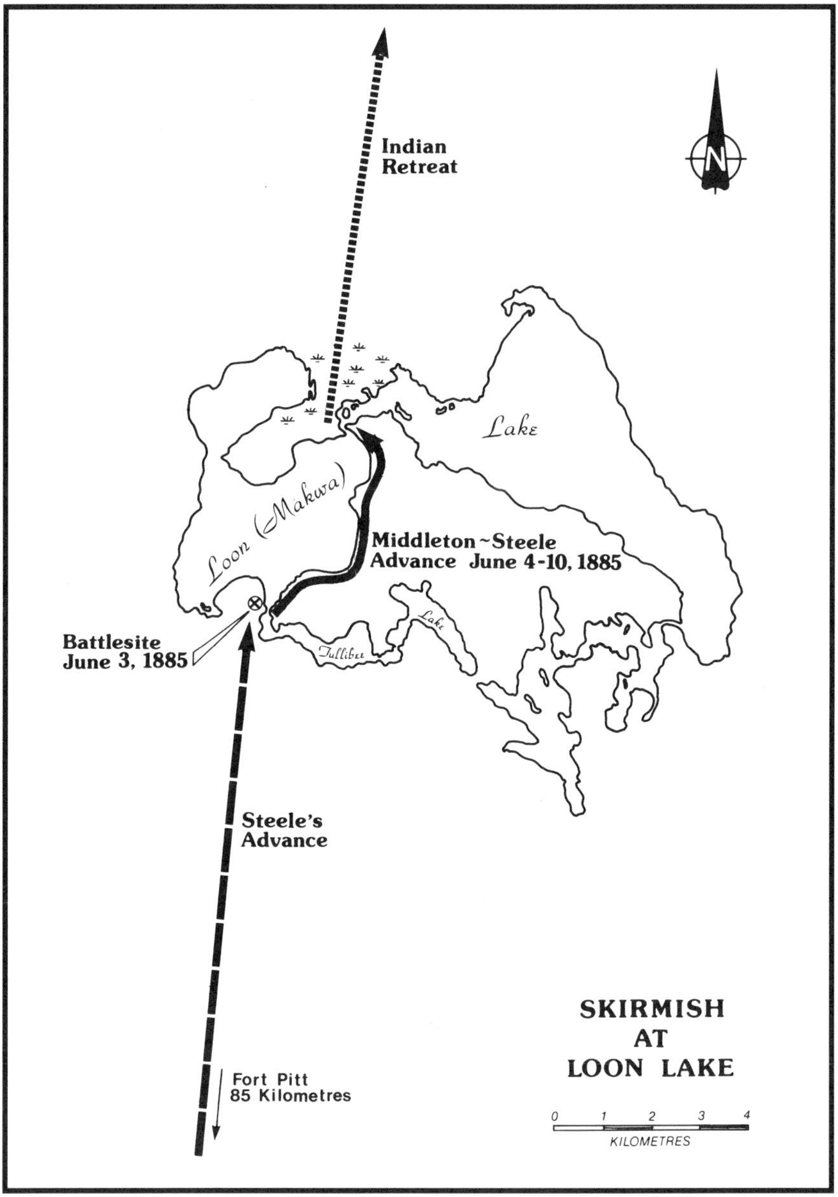
Indian
Retreat
N
Lake
Loon (Makwa)
Middleton~Steele
Advance June 4-10, 1885
Battlesite
June 3, 1885
Tullibee
Lake
Steele's
Advance
Fort Pitt
85 Kilometres
SKIRMISH
AT
LOON LAKE
0 1 2 3 4
KILOMETRES

between her head and that of a small Cree boy she was carrying across the ford. One soldier, fortunately, observed her blond hair and yelled at his comrades to withhold their fire.

Two troopers suffered wounds. The men recovered, but a bullet through Sergeant-Major William Fury's right lung ended his police career. "Long and meritorious service" made Fury eligible for the maximum pension of sixty cents daily for the term of his natural life.[21] Everyone identified the weapon which shot Fury as a Sharpe's rifle, the only such weapon in the poorly-equipped Indian force. "We know the whistle of it well," wrote Strange to his wife. "He was pegging at Harry and myself."[22] The other wounded trooper, Scout Billy West of Edmonton, received a bullet in his thigh.

In contrast to the battle near Frenchman's Butte one week earlier, the skirmish at Loon Lake had involved quick movements and close-range action. Trooper Hayes recalled: "This was a battle of action. The Scouts' rifles got so hot that they had to be dropped on the ground to cool."[23] Hicks remembered: "I had Indians run by me within ten feet and we were all busy attending to them."[24] One Mountie with his back to a tree, later found a bullet lodged in the centre of the tree. Another combatant believed that "a good time was had by all."[25]

The conflict lasted for about three hours. An attack across the ford (today called Steele Narrows) would have been too dangerous and only one day's rations and fifteen rounds of ammunition per soldier remained. Both the men and the horses were played out. "The worst of the situation," Steele remarked, "was that there was no sign of the promised support which should have been with me earlier in the day."[26]

The scouting force, therefore, prepared to retreat. Before leaving, Steele's men seized six Indian ponies and set fire to the tepees on the south side of the ford. A barrage of bullets directed at the unseen enemy followed, hopefully to cover the withdrawal.

After the cessation of gunfire the Indians headed northeastward around Upper Loon Lake, while Steele's men retreated to Fort Pitt. Early in the morning of June 6, Middleton's large advancing force contacted Steele's camp, and on the General's orders the scouts became part of Middleton's column.

The soldiers were proud of their military victory at Loon Lake. Steele's bold assault had killed five Indians.[27] The attack, moreover, proved that disciplined soldiers, with superior firepower, could easily pursue and harass the Indian camp. The Indians, according to three hostage accounts, were completely surprised by the fierce attack – even though they were aware that scouts were following their trail.[28] Most of all, the attack completely demoralized the Indians. They saw no possibility of

Skirmish at Loon Lake

The Illustrated War News *version of Steele's fight with the Indians. In the final skirmish of the campaign, five Indians died while two soldiers suffered wounds.*

a military victory. An escape into the inhospitable northern wilderness was the only alternative. One crippled female, Sitting at the Door, unable to maintain the pace, chose to hang herself on a tree limb.

Within days of the Loon Lake skirmish, the tenuous alliance between the Plains and Wood Cree terminated. The split was a simple matter. The larger body of Wood Cree delayed the morning departure until the Plains Cree had left, then headed in another direction.

No longer did Big Bear's band constitute a threat to the region. For the next month, all Indian energies were concentrated upon avoiding patrols and merely surviving in the harsh environment.

CHAPTER 13

After Big Bear

Photo on Previous Page :

General Middleton on Horseback

CHAPTER 13
After Big Bear

"All quiet on the northern front."

– *Staff Sergeant Walter Stewart*

Seven days after the capture of Louis Riel near Batoche, General Middleton moved his column westward from Prince Albert to Battleford. Near this settlement, on May 26, the general haughtily accepted the surrender of Poundmaker's band. This left Big Bear's following as the only rebel force.

On May 27, Inspector Perry's wayward scouting party arrived in Battleford with the news of Strange's arrival at Fort Pitt. Middleton immediately ordered a steamboat with men and supplies to reinforce the Field Force, upriver at least 160 kilometres. While en route, the task force encountered a courier travelling down river by canoe. He carried a report from General Strange of the engagement near Frenchman's Butte. After disembarking, a mounted corps continued to Fort Pitt, and the steamboat returned to Battleford for further orders.

Middleton, however, already knew of Strange's skirmish with Big Bear. Near midnight, May 29, a mounted scout had brought news of the fighting. Immediately the Battleford military base went into an uproar. A flurry of activity centred around Middleton's tent and "word flew around the camp that Middleton was going to take 'his boys' to crush Big Bear." [1] Sergeants moved throughout the large compound ordering the assigned units to leave tents standing and prepare to depart in marching order at sunrise.

A considerable force – 225 mounted men, 25 artillery personnel, 150 infantry troops, plus the necessary supplies – moved upstream May 30, either on horseback or aboard three steamboats. For the mounted column it was a difficult ride. Trooper James H. Johnston wrote from Fort Pitt:

> We arrived here this morning after the hardest time I have put in since leaving home. We rode here in a steady rain in two nights and one day. I got about one hour's sleep on the trip and snatched a little in the saddle. [2]

By June 3, Middleton's force had assembled near the charred ruins of Fort Pitt. While the main body established a base camp, the General rode with a small escort about twenty kilometres to Strange's camp near Frenchman's Butte.

Here at last was the opportunity for Middleton to remove Strange from command of the Field Force. Since early May, communications between Middleton and Minister of Militia Adolphe Caron had questioned the effectiveness of Strange's leadership.* Two concerns were foremost: first was Strange's arbitrary dealings with the Indians; second, his generous promotions had upset the whole militia ranking system.[3] However, once the Field Force had left Calgary, it was impractical to change command. Caron could only congratulate Strange's rapid advance and suggest, "would like you in dealing with Indians to do so through Indian agent."[4] Throughout May an exchange of cryptic telegrams passed between Caron and Middleton. Only a week before the meeting of the two unit commanders, Caron had telegraphed Middleton: "Strange I hear is making Majors of Police Officers, who in consequence take command instead of our men. I shall be glad when you relieve him."[5]

Acrimony marked the evening meeting between Strange and Middleton. Strange resented Middleton's arrogance, stating in a letter that his superior was "so puffed up over Riel's surrender . . . that he thinks there is but one Middleton."[6] During their conversation, the two men disagreed about Strange's deployment of troops. Gunner Jingo wrote of this exchange:

> He said I was wrong to have left my troops to protect my communications; . . . This is too brazen effronterey [*sic*]. He has had a telegram behind him all the way, he has not marched 100 miles to my 600, he has no enemy in the country he passed through until he reached the breeds. I had vast reserves of Indians only just on the balance between war and peace. It was only my promptitude in overawing them with troops that kept quiet some 2300 half breeds and Indians between McLeod [*sic*] and Edmonton.[7]

Middleton further expressed annoyance that Steele was trailing the Indians. He coldly rejected Strange's request that 300 mounted men reinforce Steele, exclaiming, "Not a man! Not a man! Who is this Major Steele? It should not have been done!"[8] Strange, in defence of his police scout's actions, countered: "Good God Man, what did we go for but to fight Indians!"[9] As one concession, however, Strange received permission to move his wagons and infantry toward Onion Lake, located about twenty kilometres to the northwest. More important, though, was that the meeting ended with General Strange remaining in command of the Alberta Field Force.

*In D.P. Morton and R.H. Roy, eds., *Telegrams of the North-West Campaign, 1885*, p. 238. Some examples include: May 4 – Middleton to Caron: "Afraid Strange will cause trouble – have always been afraid of this"; May 5 – Caron to Middleton: "Can you suggest any means of getting Strange to some other command than his present one?"; May 6 – Middleton to Caron: "Can't suggest means of getting Strange to some other command at present." Dewdney, also, was involved in the controversy regarding Strange. A letter (GAIA, Dewdney Papers, 1413) from Middleton to the Lieutenant Governor, May 3, states: "I am sorry to hear that Strange has not been acting with discretion. The fact is I have always been afraid of his proceeding. He is and always was rather odd and I was astonished at his being employed."

Middleton declared his intention to station at Fort Pitt until definite information came from Steele. Before returning to that base, he inspected the May 28th battle site. He acknowledged the natural glacis as a superb defensive position, but regarded the numerous rifle pits as "not well placed, a good many of them being too far back on the plateau." [10] The General concluded, unfairly in light of the inadequate communications, that "it was a pity General Strange had not waited for my arrival, when a more decisive blow might have been struck." [11]

At 2 a.m. the night of June 4, a courier brought the news of Steele's skirmish at Loon Lake. At once, Middleton organized a strong force to follow the line of Steele's advance. Lieutenant Colonel Bowen van Straubenzie was placed in charge of Fort Pitt, while Strange was free to rejoin his troops at Onion Lake.

The men in the Field Force enjoyed their mission. Two months of marching together in the wilderness had created an esprit des corps. The men viewed themselves as "the western column," independent and successful.[12] A common dislike for the pompous General Middleton further cemented their sense of unity and purpose.

All the men resented the treatment accorded two Field Force scouts by the Commander-in-Chief of the Canadian militia. On May 21, one day after leaving Victoria, Strange had sent the two men ahead by canoe to contact Battleford. The scouts, hiding by day and travelling by night, slipped past the Indian encampment at Fort Pitt and successfully reached their destination. But General Middleton, who had just arrived in Battleford by steamer, belittled their efforts. He even refused Scout George Borradaille's request to replace a lost pistol, claiming that "it was not necessary, as he himself would go through the country with a stick." [13] Upon his return to the Alberta column on May 29, a note pinned to Borradaille's hat – "I was not at Fish Creek – I was not at Batoche" [14] – clearly demonstrated to the Field Force that Middleton did not respect their contribution to the campaign. In a poem, one soldier described Middleton as "a man we all hate" – words undoubtedly expressing the general feeling of the Field Force.[15] As for walking through the country with a stick, a sarcastic Thomas Bland Strange noted that "when he did come, he arrived with steamers, carrying a Battalion of Infantry, Gatling guns, and Cavalry." [16]

Under Strange, the Field Force returned to Frog Lake and then moved north toward the Beaver River. Middleton's force, at the same time, continued northeastward following the Indians' retreat. How long they would be gone, no one knew: "We might be back in a week or we might be away a month," [17] wrote one soldier. The country was a rugged wilderness – Loon Lake was not even on the maps.

The Steamer *Northwest*, 1885

The steamer Northwest *arriving at Battleford with General Middleton and troops on May 24, 1885. After accepting Poundmaker's surrender, Middleton relied on the* Northwest *and two other steamers to help move 400 soldiers and supplies upstream to Frog Lake Landing.*

Although Middleton had doubted Strange's comments concerning the difficult terrain, he soon admitted that the trail "was terrible, owing to the numerous muskegs."[18] To help the advance, Dominion Land Survey Scouts preceded the main body. They cleared the trail and brushed swampy areas. The surveyors, too, did not forget personal interests and whenever an abandoned Indian camp came in sight, "there was a great rush for loot and trophies."[19] "We all looked for trophies," remembered Survey Scout A.O. Wheeler. "Maddock found a battle-axe and I a buffalo powder horn and case of razors."[20] One camp yielded a large quantity of hidden furs. At another location, a mound of dirt was thought to cover the corpse of a hostage so Middleton directed the exhumation of the body. It was that of Man-Who-Talks-Like-Another (Kahweechetwaymot),[21] who was badly wounded in the skirmish near Frenchman's Butte. His decomposing body was a hideous sight. A soldier commented on the discovery: "He is a disgusting object, but we think of the Frog Lake settlers and feel rather glad – you see he is a good Indian now."[22]

After only sixteen kilometres of difficult marching, Middleton decided to continue with mounted men only. The infantry, "heaping curses on the General's head,"[23] reluctantly departed southward for Fort Pitt. The General ordered the second gatling gun to be brought up, as he said, "more to console the mounted force from the loss of infantry than from any advantage I expected to derive from it."[24] In spite of its vaunted firepower, Middleton recognized the gun as ineffective in bush country. Also, to expedite the march, all tents, except one for Middleton, were left behind.

A record of the mundane daily routine of the mounted men exists. Assistant Surgeon Haultain recalled:

> The orders would invariably be: Reveille at 4 a.m.; start at 5:30. After getting up and giving the horses oats, we would have breakfast and tea, hard tack and corned beef . . . strap up our waterproof and blankets behind the saddle, and oats and hard tack and tinned beef in front. After the command 'Saddleup' from the captains of the different corps . . . would come to 'attention', and line up two deep, then 'prepare to mount' and 'mount' and we were off for seven hours without a halt if the trail was good, mostly walking, with a canter now and then.[25]

Hordes of mosquitoes and horseflies (called "Bulldogs") plagued the advancing column. They were, in the words of one soldier, "inescapable, though we kept swishing them off our horses and ourselves, with branches plucked from the trees."[26] Middleton described the insects as "fearfully troublesome."[27] Each night, pickets were stationed and smudges lit to protect the tethered horses. The harassed animals would place their noses right in the smoke to avoid the hordes of insects. The men slept in a circle around large fires of spruce boughs. Saddles or oat sacks served as pillows and all feet pointed toward the warmth of the fire.

Survey Scouts Clearing the Trail to Loon Lake

An advance contingent of Survey Scouts prepared General Middleton's advance from Frog Lake Landing to Loon Lake by clearing the trail and brushing swampy areas.

A party conveying three wounded men from Steele's detachment to Fort Pitt, brought information that Steele's camp was only ten kilometres north. Before joining Steele, Middleton prepared the next phase of his campaign strategy. Scouts were sent to direct Colonel William Otter to advance his Battleford force northeast to Turtle Lake, for Police Commissioner A.G. Irvine to move a police troop from Prince Albert to Green Lake, and for Lieutenant Colonel Arthur Williams to transfer the Ontario Midlanders to Frog Lake Landing. In effect, there would be four columns and one base camp cutting off any Indian escape south. "It would," wrote Middleton, "be difficult for Big Bear to get away."[28]

With Steele's men joining their ranks, Middleton's force continued northward to Loon Lake. They discovered the battle site completely deserted. After crossing the ford, the men found three mounds with Indian dead and the crippled woman hanging from a tree, a victim of suicide. Scouts estimated that the retreating Indians were forty-eight hours ahead. However, the turbulent current between Upper and Lower Loon Lakes (today called Makwa Lake) prevented the wagons and gatling guns from further advancement. Middleton stationed twenty-five Mounties to guard the weapons and supplies. The remainder of the men swam their horses and rafted their saddlery across the fifty metre "Second Ford" while the General watched "with great interest."[29]

Beyond the crossing, a large muskeg area delayed further pursuit. Yet, as Steele pointed out, "delicate women and children had been able to traverse it a few days previously."[30] Middleton, too, believed further pursuit was possible. The rotund general rode forward, as he said, "to judge for myself . . ., but soon sank to my saddle girths and was extricated with great difficulty."[31] Quite likely the Indians and hostages had crossed before the ice was completely thawed; otherwise, as the Indians told hostage W.J. McLean, the muskeg "was impassable even to them."[32]

Two scouts succeeded on June 8 in crossing the muskeg area, which extended northward for several kilometres. Their difficulties, however, convinced Middleton to return the column to Fort Pitt. A commander of a scout unit agreed with this decision, stating: "We suffered here greatly from mosquitoes and flies and were glad when the order was issued to retrace our steps."[33] Besides, the men were tired of Middleton's indecision. We are, wrote one, "too sick of the vacillation of our commander to do much but swear mildly at ourselves for expecting anything else. Last night, mind you, the orders were to cross and pursue."[34]

Everyone recognized the futility of this mission. The Indians had not even been sighted. The most exciting moment had occurred when a cartridge belt fell into an evening campfire, causing a series of explosions that jarred the entire force from sleep. "It was some time," recalled A.O. Wheeler, "before order was restored."[35]

First Ford, Loon Lake

Troopers in Middleton's column are seen crossing the First Ford. One week earlier Steele's Scouts had indiscriminately fired at Indians crossing this waterway, nearly killing several hostages.

Perhaps, the men rationalized, the only good from this wilderness trek was an improvement in their diet. Nets strung across the stream outlets from the lake had yielded an astonishing number of fish. Still, as the men noted, only Middleton had marmalade and jam.

One soldier left this record of Middleton's return to Fort Pitt in the early evening of June 11: "We gave him three hearty cheers. Then the band struck up 'See the Conquering Hero Come'!"[36] The tune was ill-chosen. Middleton had spent eight days on the trail of the Indians. Little had been accomplished.

General Middleton's orders of June 7 at last gave the troops under Colonel William Otter and Police Commissioner A.G. Irvine a release from their monotonous garrison duties. Both columns welcomed the opportunity to move northward after the evasive Indians. They hoped to rectify the negative image of their units because of earlier actions in the campaign.

The 245 men in the Queen's Own Rifles had remained in Battleford since their inept attack on Poundmaker's band four weeks earlier. This forced inactivity, everyone agreed, was Middleton's retribution for their unauthorized assault on the Indians. "Otter was," in the words of one diarist, "being punished for his drive on Cut Knife Hill."[37] The arrival of Middleton's force on May 24 only increased the frustration of the Queen's Own. The general's troops, particularly an Ontario unit called the Midlanders, flaunted their success at Batoche. R.W. Rutherford, "B" Battery Canadian

Second Ford, Loon Lake

Warming weather caused a muskeg area just beyond this point to stop the soldier's advance, even though Indians with their prisoners had crossed this barrier only a few days before.

Artillery (who painted a series of watercolors of the campaign) wrote of the arriving column: "The whole force seems to be imbued with nothing but the sense of their own importance and valour after the Fish Creek and Batoche fights. We are nobody at all."[38] This resentment was heightened several days later when Middleton elected to take only his own troops westward to Fort Pitt. As the Midlanders broke camp on May 30, the Queen's Own remained in their tents, deliberately ignoring the customary three cheers given departing troops.

General Middleton's directive ordered the Battleford troops ninety kilometres north, past Jackfish Lake to Turtle Lake. Here was the long-awaited "second chance" for the Queen's Own. One diary entry announced the prevailing mood. The officer wrote: "We are very glad to escape the monotony of Battleford."[39] Confidently, a companion declared, "If Big Bear is around the men will punish him."[40]

The 385-man column, composed of the Queen's Own augmented by 140 men from four other companies, left Battleford on June 9. At Turtle Lake, an abandoned Hudson's Bay post functioned as headquarters for the column. From this point patrols searched the nearby area. They found some discarded supplies, but captured only one Indian. A second native was discovered serenely resting in a shallow grave until, as Lieutenant Cassels noted with disgust, "some unprincipled medical student made off in triumph with the skull of the poor occupant."[41] On June 16, Otter visited

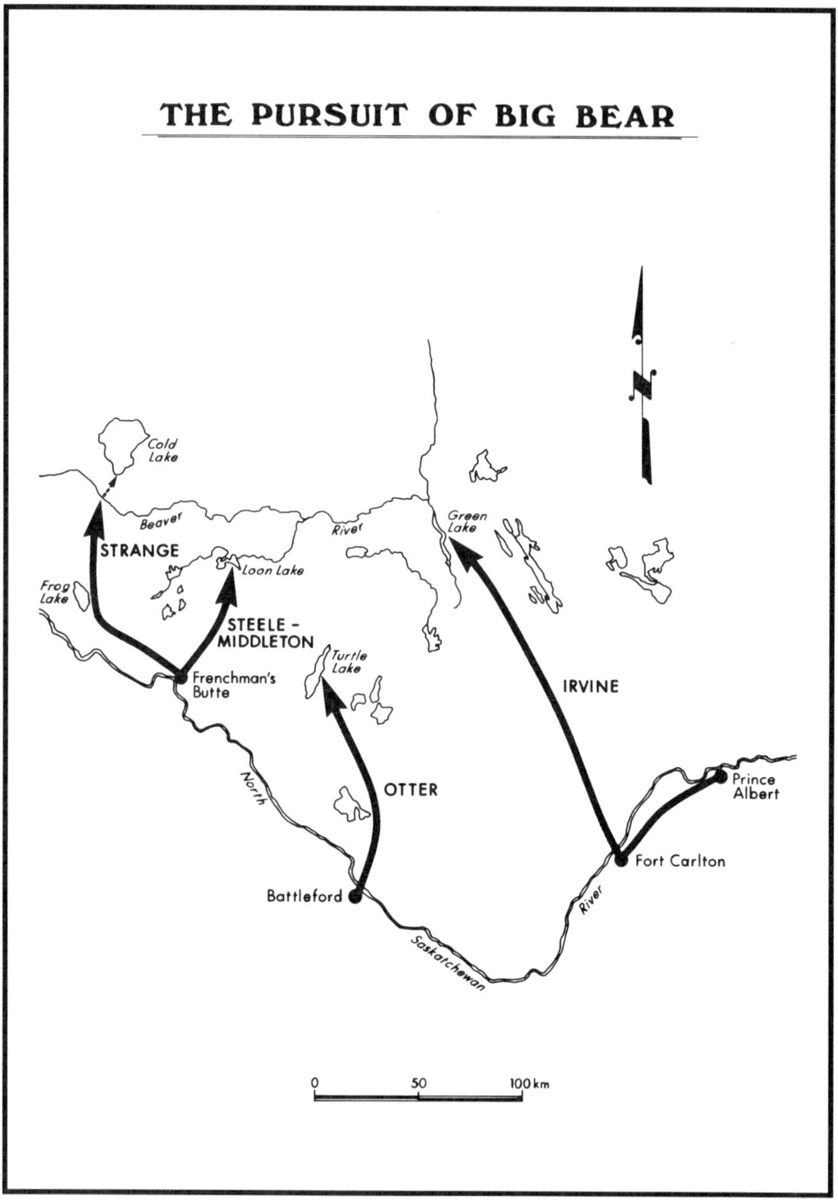
THE PURSUIT OF BIG BEAR
Cold Lake
Beaver
River
Green Lake
STRANGE
Loon Lake
Frog Lake
STEELE - MIDDLETON
Turtle Lake
Frenchman's Butte
IRVINE
North
OTTER
Prince Albert
Fort Carlton
Battleford
River
Saskatchewan
0
50
100 km

the Yellow Sky band of 150 Saulteaux Indians near Cedar Lake and found them to be friendly. Another movement reached an Indian camp at Birch Lake, approximately thirty-five kilometres east of Turtle Lake. The soldiers seized forty-three cattle and four horses, the property of settlers, from the Indians. Colonel Otter agreed to allow the band to move to Jackfish Lake, except for five men implicated in the thefts. Although the Indians professed to have no information of Big Bear, Otter "strongly suspected they knew something of his movements."[42]

Mounted scouting parties, helped by the five Indian prisoners, continued to probe the country to the northeast. Several couriers contacted Irvine's column on the Green Lake - Carlton Trail, but the whereabouts of the Indians remained a mystery. Big Bear's band had, by now, broken into small groups, making capture difficult. Little Poplar's trail was discovered heading south, but being about five days old there was no point in pursuit. Big Bear, known to be almost alone, remained at large. The scouts concluded that the old chief had used Little Poplar's trail to mask his movements.

For the men in Otter's force, the anticipated excitement of fighting Indians quickly faded. Instead, mundane routines regulated daily life in the camp. The hot daytime temperatures added to the disillusionment. While on inspection, June 18, twenty men fainted because of the heat. After the burning sun of the day, one soldier wrote to his father in Toronto that astonishingly "the nights are generally bitterly cold . . . [and] often ice formed on the water when you woke up."[43] The fierce prairie thunderstorms, described as "extraordinary celestial phenomena,"[44] were awe -inspiring sights for men living in canvas tents. Twice, violent hailstorms caught the soldiers in the open, once while swimming. An eastern soldier wrote that the hailstones were "of inconceivable size."[45]

Fortunately, the lake, twenty-five kilometres in length and surrounded by woods and white, sandy shores, had superb fishing and excellent swimming. Still this provided little entertainment in this so-called adventure. Each day brought increasing boredom. One soldier complained in his dairy: "Harry and I attempt to take a stroll this evening but are ignominiously driven back to camp by mosquitoes."[46] What had begun as a spirited assignment was now, in the words of one officer, "a goose chase with less satisfaction than before starting out."[47]

Everyone wanted to leave this wilderness. One soldier wrote on June 24: "We are pretty weary of marching about and our mission seems fruitless . . . we expect orders to march home. The sooner the better."[48] On June 28, the good news arrived. Wasting no time, by the evening of July 1, Otter's column was back in Battleford.

Colonel Irvine, Commissioner of the North-West Mounted Police, had marched a contingent of ninety-three Mounties northward from Regina to Fort Carlton in late March. The column arrived only hours after the

General Middleton on Horseback

General Middleton detailed a mounted column to follow the line of Steele's advance to Loon Lake. Within eight days the men were back at Fort Pitt, without even sighting the Indians.

Duck Lake skirmish. In the ten-week period following that engagement, Middleton's field strategy had stationed Irvine's force in Prince Albert. The reputation of the Mounties had been tarnished by the inactivity of Irvine's men, Inspector Francis Dickens' abandonment of Fort Pitt, and Inspector William Morris' lackluster leadership at Battleford. A derogatory term – "gophers" – became a widely-applied slur for the North-West Mounted Police.

Irvine's force consisted of 136 men, 127 horses, and nineteen wagons. As a mounted force, the police were the most far-ranging column in the search for Big Bear. From Prince Albert the contingent moved south-west to Fort Carlton where a steamer provided transport across the North Saskatchewan, opening the way north. Their assigned destination was Green Lake, a distance of 160 kilometres.

Early in the rebellion, Indians had sacked the Hudson's Bay post at the south end of this lake. Indian intimidation of a twenty-man repair crew from Prince Albert resulted in a hurried southward departure by the men. Would there be further difficulties at Green Lake? No one in Irvine's column was certain.

They reached Green Lake on June 14, after five days of travelling. Once the base camp was established, Irvine directed scouts at the north end of Green Lake to travel westward to Loon Lake, a difficult trip of over 100 kilometres, to find "news" of Big Bear. Other mounted patrols scoured the nearby countryside. Several caches of food were discovered but, as one Mountie observed, "nothing was seen of any hostile Indians nor anything learned to lead belief in their being in the vicinity."[49]

As with the other columns, the monotonous routine and discomforts quickly soured the military assignment. Having only four tents for the entire force meant that most of the men slept under wagons or tarpaulins. The mosquitoes and horseflies were troublesome and a food shortage became acute. By June 18, only enough food remained for a scanty breakfast. Later that day teams arrived with supplies, oats, and a steer which was immediately butchered. Within two days these supplies were consumed and the rations reduced to tea and hardtack. At Pelican Lake, the men demonstrated their anger, following a trying trip through dust, intense heat, and a hailstorm. In what police parlance called "a buck," an appointed delegation approached Colonel Irvine with an ultimatum: unless the food improved there would be no further patrols.[50] In response, Irvine ordered the slaughter of an ox.

Recognizing the disillusionment with the Green Lake assignment, Colonel Irvine sought to boost the morale of his force. At general parade on June 23, he reminded the men that the police force had surmounted all previous difficulties; therefore, until the surrender of the Indians they must endure further hardship and food shortages.

Artillery Mess on Big Bear's Trail

After two months, most of the initial excitement of the campaign had been replaced by the mundane routines of tending camp.

Another week was wasted before the news arrived of Big Bear's capture. The men quickly departed southward, reaching Fort Carlton two days later. After arresting a group of Indians near the trading post, the Mounties rode the seventy kilometres to Prince Albert.

Irvine's column arrived at their home base, escorting "sixteen evil-looking savages of Little Poplar's cutthroats."[51] As the police force moved slowly down the street in the driving rain, a Mountie stationed at Prince Albert recorded his thoughts on the futility of the Green Lake expedition:

> The men certainly looked haggard and worn. Their long blue cloaks were muddy and torn, their slouch hats out of shape, their spurs red with rust, and their boots indescribable . . . thin, bronzed, and with beards of scrubby growth, they were a grim, hard lot to gaze on . . . each man armed to the teeth.[52]

Three weeks earlier, companies under Otter and Irvine had rejoiced at the opportunity for action. In spite of arduous efforts, however, their assignment had become little more than a series of fruitless patrols, based around dull camp routines. For the soldiers and police, rather than rectifying earlier negative military criticism, each day had brought increasing disenchantment.

Middleton's third directive moved the Ontario Midland Battalion to Frog Lake Landing, as a support base for the Field Force. The "Midlanders," under Lieutenant Colonel Arthur Williams, with eight companies totalling 426 men, comprised the largest contingent in the rebellion. For those soldiers anticipating action, the encampment at Frog Lake Landing from June 7 to 21 proved disappointing. At no time were Indians contacted.

On one assignment, the Midland Battalion marched to the scene of the Frog Lake killings. The sight of the graves and the destruction made the men, in the words of one officer, "almost bloodthirsty for the time being."[53] The massacre and waste, wrote a second observer, served "as a warning against trusting an Indian unless the scoundrel is dead."[54]

The Midlanders prepared for battle on only one occasion. Spurred by a distant sighting of metal flashing and puffs of smoke, the troops quickly advanced in skirmishing order towards the area of fighting only to find a dozen soldiers destroying an Indian cache of flour by shovelling the material high into the air. Their maneuver across difficult terrain had been a waste of time on a hot June day. Moreover, for the contingent whose charge had overwhelmed the rebel positions at Batoche this exercise, "was perhaps the hardest, of the campaign."[55]

During the Midland Battalion's two-week sojourn at Frog Lake Landing, tedious garrison duties governed camp life. Of interest, though, because it predates a famous quotation associated with warfare, is a diary entry in which a soldier wrote: "All quiet on the Northern Front."[56]

CHAPTER 14

Strange to the Beaver River

Photo on Previous Page :

Soldiers of the Field Force in camp at Cold Lake

CHAPTER 14
Strange to the Beaver River

"In the wilderness toward the Beaver River the mosquito is king."

– Manitoba Daily Free Press

Middleton's return to Fort Pitt on June 11, following the inconsequential Loon Lake maneuver, again brought the general into telegraphic contact with Ottawa. Again, communication resumed regarding the question of Strange's command. Three telegrams, all dated June 12, illustrate the intrigue involved:

> To Hon. A.P. Caron
>
> Just arrived here after a fifty mile ride – got a despatch from Strange who is on the Beaver River . . . must start off tomorrow with the Cavalry to join – you can't trust him.
>
> Fred Middleton

> To Major-General Middleton
>
> Glad you are going to meet Strange – I agree with you about him. Can you relieve him of his command? Think it should be done as soon as possible.
>
> A.P. Caron

> To Maj. General Strange
>
> Glad to hear from you. I congratulate you and your command on work you have done. You must requisition for what you require.
>
> A.P. Caron [1]

Geographical factors, however, effectively foiled the removal of Strange from command of the Field Force. While Middleton was following Steele's trail to Loon Lake, Strange had rejoined the Field Force and moved his troops northward to the isolated Beaver River Mission, 110 kilometres northwest of Fort Pitt. Middleton, therefore, could only inform the Minister of Militia on May 15 that "it is impossible to relieve Strange at once . . . will do so as soon as possibly see opportunity."[2] Events proved otherwise, however, and Thomas Bland Strange maintained his command of the Field Force until the end of the campaign.

Strange led a tattered column to the Beaver River. At this point in the campaign, the men had already walked a great distance. The Mounties from Fort Macleod had hauled the field piece 900 kilometres. The column had followed primitive trails without bridges, and encountered snow, rain, hail, and scorching heat. On the open prairie, wrote one Mountie, "there is always wind."[3] It had been an arduous journey, one from which a newspaper correspondent saw the men suffering "far more hardship . . . than from the sharp ordeal of actual fighting."[4]

By now the men, Strange wrote, "were dead beat from marching in the rain and awful mud."[5] Lieutenant-Colonel Hughes, commander of the 65th, informed Strange that his soldiers could march no further, and that they wanted to return home. In response, Strange rode before the dejected battalion and addressed the men in French, citing an "ancien chanson":

> Malbrook s'en va-t-en querre - a!
> Ne sait quand reviendra![6]

His speech rekindled the spirit of the haggard soldiers. With cheers they marched off singing folksongs of Quebec.

Strange enjoyed good relations with his French-speaking soldiers. One member of the 65th, R.H. Metcalfe, wrote: "The general was much liked and used to address the Battalion in the French language which suited the boys, as possibly not more than ten per cent were English-speaking."[7] In turn, Strange spoke highly of the Montreal unit. A letter to his wife stated: "They have dragged our cannon through swamps and bushes, their boots are worn out. They are footsore and weary – but there was no flinch in them in the fight of which they bore the brunt."[8] Another letter to his spouse asked her to tell Lieutenant G. Amyot, commander of the Quebec troops stationed in southern Alberta, that Strange was "very proud and fond of [Amyot's] compatriot soldiers."[9]

Some Ontario newspapers, unquestionably fueled by Colonel Ouimet's enigmatic behavior, had assailed the resolve of French-Canadian soldiers in western Canada. A newspaper correspondent travelling with the Field Force countered all allegations of disloyalty. He wrote:

> The conduct of the 65th in the face of the enemy's fire, as well as in the long, tedious marches completely refutes the accusations brought against its officers and men. None speak higher of the 65th than do the Winnipeg contingent, scores of whom tell me that no braver men ever wore the Queen's uniform.[10]

"The Alligators," the 65th Battalion

A sketch of "the Alligators," as the 65th Battalion called themselves, struggling with the gun carriage while advancing to the Beaver River Mission. The Field Force received little recognition for their long difficult march.

Le Manitoba similarly praised the "bonne conduite" of the 65th.[11] And the *Calgary Herald* reported that Police Major Perry and Colonel Smith of the Winnipeg Light Infantry "both emphatically declare that they want no better soldiers than the 65th."[12]

The 65th showed a liveliness which Strange called "their cheerful alacrity."[13] The *Toronto Mail* correspondent, on the march to Beaver River, observed moroseness overcoming the Winnipeg men, "out of which they were only aroused by an outburst of song from a company of the 65th."[14] Soldier MacBeth, marching with the Winnipeg unit, remembered "how the Frenchmen of the 65th, almost shoeless and half-clad though they were, more than once helped out the horses of Perry's gun."[15] In their struggle through the water and mud, the 65th attached the sobriquet "The Alligators" to themselves.

The Field Force, left with only thirty-five horsemen from Perry's returned troop, followed a route from Fort Pitt to Beaver River that passed Frog Lake on June 5. At this charred settlement, the soldiers found the bodies of two victims of the massacre two months earlier. In a search for other victims, the men exhumed three graves covered with doors – only to discover Indian bodies. Their scouring of the area uncovered food caches which augmented the scanty rations of the column.

Moving northward, the advancing column followed a cart trail through country described "to lovers of nature, the prettiest in the world." [16] Twenty Alberta Mounted Rifles led the advance, followed by six companies of foot soldiers from the Winnipeg Light Infantry, fifteen Mounties manning the gun carriage, and in the rear, three companies of the Montreal regiment.

The heavy bush along the narrow trail was ideal for an Indian ambush. "The suspense of our boys when on the march was always great," wrote one soldier. "We never knew when to expect an attack. The ambush was always looked for." [17] At every stop came a never-ending picket and guard duty. And although the June darkness lasted but a few hours, the lonely nighttime sentry duty, a soldier recalled, "brought nerves to the utmost tension . . . not forgetting . . . the subtle character of our foes, the wary redskin, the knowledge that he often imitates animals so as to scout in close." [18]

The countryside abounded with wild animals. Observing wolves was a fascinating event as related in this account:

> Our pickets and sentries were also troubled with wolves and coyotes at night who prowled constantly close to our camp yelping and howling, but not molesting anyone. Orders were issued not to fire at them except in self-defence. The wolves were quite large and seemed ferocious coming closer at dusk and waiting around in a circle and snarling like mad dogs. [19]

Wolves waiting in a circle and snarling like mad dogs . . . this was certainly an indelible memory of the march through the wilderness of Saskatchewan! It would be a spellbinding story to relate – if the column ever saw civilization again!

The muskeg slowed the advancing column. At places the soft trail required leading the horses. Otherwise, as one rider recalled: "several times I thought my horse and self would disappear bodily, so far down did he sink." [20] The men hated the slime and stinking odor of the muskeg. After each step "the hole immediately filled with a black liquid, the foul-smelling juice of decaying vegetation and leaves." [21] Some soldiers cut holes in the toes of their boots "so the water would escape after each step in the swamp or the crossing of streams." [22] In muddy sections the heavy gun carriage attracted everyone's attention. As the wagon sank, sometimes to the axles, the drivers cracked whips and cursed the six heavy horses onward. The great snorting beasts responded by charging ahead, splattering the cheering bystanders. One bog was impassable for the struggling horses and their drivers, whose arms "were weary from whipping." [23] Soldiers had to dismantle the field piece and drag the parts through the muddy stench.

Innumerable insects inhabited the wet wilderness. In the swamps, sandflies "as they rose resembled a cloud." [24] Mosquitoes appeared everywhere and were, in the words of Strange, "almost unbearable." [25] One travelling

Burning Smudges in the Camps

Hordes of mosquitoes and horseflies (called "Bulldogs") plagued the four columns searching for Big Bear's band. Each night smudges were lit in the camps to protect the tethered horses.

correspondent acknowledged: "In the wilderness toward the Beaver River the mosquito is king."[26] The soldiers insisted that the insects deliberately followed the column.

In more comfortable surroundings, while at a reunion of veterans in Victoria in 1942, R.D. Bremner, Winnipeg Light Infantry, commented on the march fifty-seven years earlier. "I can't get away from it," Bremner recalled. "We lived through hell in the weeks we pursued Big Bear."[27] He remembered his trousers had one leg left, and that was shrunk to the knee. Many members of the 65th now were barefoot, while others had "muddy bloodstained rags tied round their feet."[28] In his memoirs J.O.M. Williams remembers the column now being plagued by body lice. "We were in agony," he recalled, "with no time or means to clean them off."[29]

For most of the distance to the Beaver River the troops marched "route step," meaning somewhat informally, with four men abreast. The general mood was cheerful according to one reporter:

> Some would have their pipes out; others were cracking jokes, and others singing popular ditties. Sometimes there was one broad grin from the head to the tail of the column. One company would sing 'John Brown's Body,' and the next company 'Red, White and Blue,' and the next 'Rule Brittania.'[30]

One unit received the sobriquet "the Salvation Army company" for repeatedly singing songs popularized by the recently-arrived (1882) church in Canada. The Field Force even had its own song, composed by one soldier to mock the wearing apparel of his marching comrades. It began: "If you want us to advance, you must give us all new pants."[31]

The Field Force at the Chippewyan Mission

For two weeks the Field Force remained stationed at the Chippewyan Mission, Beaver River. The tattered soldiers welcomed the needed rest.

An advance party reached Beaver River on June 7 just in time to secure the Hudson's Bay storehouse, about to be looted by the same Chipewyan band that had been in Big Bear's camp. The scouts relayed a message back to the main column – some twenty kilometres southward – to rush reinforcements forward. The men, anticipating action, hurried in Indian file through an almost continuous muskeg swamp in dead silence. As this was the only night march of the campaign, it was recalled as "the silent march."

When the Indians threatened to resist the troop arrival, their priest, Father Legoff, intervened and went to meet General Strange. The Field Force commander had the priest and the chaplain of the 65th return with an ultimatum demanding the Indian surrender within twenty-four hours; otherwise Strange "would burn every house on the Reserve, except the Chapel, the Priest's house, and the Hudson's Bay store." [32]

"We didn't need any lengthy speeches to induce those brave people to surrender . . . it was their only reasonable choice," [33] wrote Legoff. Within the prescribed time, the Indians arrived – thirty-three men, their families, and a pack of yellow mangy dogs carrying the Indians' belongings. Surgeon Pennefather, always hostile to the Indians, described the party "as a whole, very dirty and repulsive looking." [34] Lieutenant Brooks, Winnipeg Light Infantry, witnessed the surrender:

> A more pitiful-looking lot of human beings it would be hard to imagine. Men, women and children were literally in rags, in many cases not having enough clothing to cover their nakedness. They were more than half famished, and many among them were suffering from loathsome running sores. [35]

The party was not, concluded a Toronto reporter, "the noble red man, of whom Fenimore Cooper wrote . . . but a group of badly dressed, small-sized, swarthy men." [36]

The soldiers gave the Indians some bannock and the entrails of a bullock. Without hesitating, the famished prisoners cut the unwashed entrails into strips "with their teeth, and devoured it."[37] Watching the scene, one observer contended that "you could not help but feel sorry for the poor fellows [who] . . . were not a bad lot but seemed to have been dragged in by threats."[38] Sam Steele, though not present at the surrender, disagreed, maintaining Chipewyan claims of being coerced into rebellion were "sheer nonsense, mere romance."[39] Surgeon Pennefather, likewise, suggested "the proverbial lying of an Indian prevents any credence being attached to what they say, especially when their personal safety is concerned."[40]

After the Indians surrendered their weapons, they were placed in a prison camp for several days. At a court of inquiry, the Indians told Strange that their understanding was that the North-West would be sold to the Americans and only those who joined the outbreak "would receive any portion of the purchase money."[41] Strange decided to detain eight Indians as guilty of plundering, even though he noted that their chief witness, Father Legoff, "with true pastoral love of his flock, would gladly have exonerated them."[42] Legoff did, though, persuade Strange to hire twenty men as scouts and messengers.

The tattered appearance of the forty-five-year-old priest told of his five-week ordeal. A soldier in the Winnipeg Light Infantry observed:

> A tall, thin, spare man, I mistook him for an Indian when I first saw him. His face was tanned the color of leather, his clerical garb was frayed and worn, his shoes would have puzzled a cobbler to mend, and altogether he looked more like one of his flock than their shepherd.[43]

On the fateful day when his two colleagues had met their horrible deaths, Laurent Legoff, OMI, had been delayed from attending the Frog Lake services by his Chipewyan (Legoff refers to them as Montagnais) Indians. Several days later, delegates from Big Bear – "five mad dogs" in Legoff's words[44] – arrived at Beaver River to intimidate the small band. They enticed several Chipewyan warriors to participate in the Fort Pitt looting. Ten days later, another war party of Cree coerced Legoff's Montagnais to travel south on April 26 to join Big Bear's camp. For the native of France, who had served this band for most of his nineteen years in western Canada, it was an unhappy moment. "Nothing could be sadder to watch," he wrote.[45] There was no alternative other than to accompany his converts into the very Cree camp responsible for the brutal deaths of his fellow priests.

Everyone acknowledged Father Legoff's valuable services during the rebellion. One soldier observed "there was no more enthusiastic priest in the North-West."[46] A reporter from the *Toronto Mail* called Legoff an "intrepid and brave man."[47] Even gruff General Middleton conceded that Legoff was "a very worthy, good man."[48]

On the Warpath after Big Bear.

Swimming Horses, Beaver River

Waterways along the march often impeded movement. On their march north, troops swim horses across the Beaver River.

Of interest, late in life Laurent Legoff experienced a second period of captivity – but in circumstances far removed from an Indian camp in the wilderness. Almost thirty years later, while in Belgium to publish his Chipewyan dictionary, the hostilities of World War I led to his imprisonment in a monastery. Ever determined, Legoff immediately escaped to Switzerland, and from that country returned to the Cold Lake area.[49]

Following the surrender of the Chipewyan Indians, many soldiers and teamsters in the Field Force began confiscating Indian valuables for their own personal profit.[50] Former hostage William B. Cameron, had gained employment as a scout. He candidly relates his actions at Beaver River:

> with two other scouts I made rounds of the reservation. Revolvers at full cock in our hands, we galloped up to each cabin in turn. We found no Indians, but we did discover and appropriate some prime beaver and bear skins.[51]

The rationalization that "the Chipewyans were rebels and the confiscation therefore justified"[52] excused the plundering. Quickly, the seizure of goods became an undisciplined affair as troops and teamsters competed to obtain valuables. One party even brought a bloodhound from Fort Pitt to search for cached goods.

The soldiers and teamsters showed little respect for the property of the Indians or the church. One teamster returned to Alberta with eight hundred pounds (365 kilograms) of stolen goods in his wagon. The Field Force appropriated the band's herd of forty cattle. Scout Hayes recalled a cook carrying a rifle and a butcher knife, boldly announcing that he was going to get some firewood. That evening, Hayes recalled, "we had fresh veal."[53] One old man had $3,000 in furs stolen, and Legoff's church ornaments and personal goods disappeared. The priest declared in a letter to his superior: "As for the soldiers, they sacked the houses of all the poor Indians and destroyed everything they found in them."[54] The unchecked vandalism spared few windows. One of the nicest houses in the community became a latrine, which Legoff said was done "out of pure spite, for that house was a good mile from the Camp."[55] Father Laurent Legoff regarded the malicious destruction as "revolting," especially in light of the fact that as the soldiers looted, his Montagnais now "risked their lives in the army's service."[56] For his own losses, Father Legoff later presented the government a bill for $673 for twenty items destroyed or lost during the rebellion.[57]

From June 8 to June 24, General Strange remained stationed at the Beaver River settlement. Father Legoff's home and church served as his head-quarters. The Beaver Mission settlement was tiny – a few log cabins, some plowed land surrounded by rude fences, a few shaggy ponies, the herd of cattle, and numerous gaunt, vicious dogs. During the two-week encampment, the only contact with the rebels came when a lone Indian fired at sentries.

For the most part, this period provided a needed rest. Strange conceded in a letter to a friend that "things are drawing to a close."[58] Other than the daily camp routines, several mounted parties patrolled eastward and construction began on a scow and four boats. Swimming and bathing in the muddy river were popular recreational activities. Strange considered the health of his troops to be excellent. The weary horses were released to graze in nearby pastures. Many of the animals suffered from a hoof disease which Strange believed had been contracted from swamp water.

A tattered appearance characterized the Field Force. Reverend McKay recalled: "My clothing was threadbare . . . my trousers were in shreds up to my knees and I wore out my shirt and had to rely on my jersey sweater."[59] When newspaper correspondent Angus Kennedy arrived at the camp, he was astonished to find some members of the 65th doing sentry-go in bare feet – yet they "were cheery as larks and singing the old folk-songs their forefathers had sung in the France of the seventeenth century."[60] Kennedy found General Strange unceremoniously darning socks.

The lack of some supplies angered the soldiers at the Beaver River camp. Wrote one newspaper correspondent:

> There is no sugar in camp, no beans, no potatoes, no cheese, no coffee, no barley, very little hard tack, no oats for the horses, no soap to wash with, no chewing tobacco.[61]

The troops knew that abundant supplies had been forwarded to western Canada; yet, as the soldiers claimed, perhaps one-tenth of the supplies reached the front line camps.

George Ham, *Toronto Globe* reporter, however, contended that the idyllic pristine wilderness compensated for the spartan camp life. In his description of a church parade near the banks of the eastward-flowing river, Ham determined that beautiful natural setting far surpassed the gilded edifices adorning prominent Toronto churches. There was, too, a congruity between man and nature at Beaver River. Even the dirty canvas -covered wagons and the tough, motley congregation listening to the Reverend John McDougall harmonized with the surroundings. And the solemn group disbursed orderly and quietly, unlike the hurly-burly of so-called cultured Toronto assemblies.[62]

Notwithstanding the beauty and serenity of the land, few men in the Field Force remained thrilled with this adventure. This wilderness was mosquitoes, poor food, and an evasive enemy. The soldiers had not sighted Big Bear's band in weeks. Two months had passed since they departed from Calgary. They wanted an end to their isolation. Wrote one observer:

> Of what is transpiring in the rest of the world we are ignorant. We have heard that the Gladstone ministry is defeated; it has been rumored about camp that England and Russia are at war, but of what the real facts of the case may be we know nothing.[63]

The enthusiasm for the campaign diminished each day. It was likely there would be no further battles. The conclusion of the campaign was only a matter of time. The men wanted to go home.

Not all the Field Force remained stationed at the Beaver River Mission. After the column left Fort Pitt for the Beaver River, Middleton had ordered the Field Force to halt. "Fortunately," wrote Strange, "I did not get his letter to halt until I reached the Beaver River, had built boats, and sent 100 men over."[64] These soldiers, members of the Winnipeg Light Infantry, were detailed to Cold Lake.

This march, though only twenty-five kilometres' distance, took two days. The men broke a trail through heavy woods, water, and fallen timber. The weather was hot and the insects troublesome. Additional overcoats, supplied in lieu of tents, added to the misery of the plodding column. Twenty Chipewyan Indians, prisoners only a few days earlier, guided pack horses laden with the rations and utensils. The animals suffered immensely. More than once they "broke away from their drivers and plunged into whatever water might be near, glad to cool themselves."[65] At the sight of the lake, both animals and men raced to submerge in the cool water, making a remarkable and hilarious spectacle.

For the next five days the soldiers camped along a sandy beach on the south shore of the large, cold, clear lake. Written accounts described the physical setting as beautiful, with a thick forest of large pine trees extending to the camp. To the north, the lake appeared as "a gigantic and marvellous mirror."[66] Each day was sunny and warm, the nights clear and mild. The men passed an enjoyable time fishing and swimming. One enthused writer even declared that he knew of "no more desirable place on earth to settle in."[67]

A second patrol from the Beaver River base moved eastward. Six volunteers under Captain Charles Constantine, Winnipeg Light Infantry, headed on June 14 for the point where the Chipewyans had left Big Bear's camp. This route, described "as a sterile and worthless and rough a piece of country as to be found in the North-West,"[68] took five days. The horses suffered from insect bites. Blood oozed down their nostrils. Travelling reporter George Ham wrote of the journey: "How the Chipewyan women and children struggled through a march in this region is a mystery, unless one believes, like the Irishman's hanging, they are used to it."[69]

Late in the morning of June 14, one week after Strange had established his base camp, Middleton's cavalry force, accompanied by Steele's Scouts, arrived at the Beaver River. The scouts were happy to rejoin the western

Camp at Cold Lake

In mid-June Strange detailed a 100-man detachment to Cold Lake. Hardly had the men established the base when news arrived that all the hostages were safe.

column and received a great welcome. Middleton had wanted to send Van Straubenzie, his infantry brigadier, to Beaver River, but Strange outranked that officer.

Earlier trailbreaking by the Field Force facilitated Middleton's advance. One area was corduroyed for almost one kilometre and another swampy area was brushed for eight kilometres. The column proceeded northward at an easy pace and with lax discipline. The flight of a duck from a nearby marsh resulted in a wild scramble for eggs. On other occasions, whole groups of men sought sheltered spots for a "pipe parade." With care, one valuable match would light half a dozen pipes. For this journey the men sported gauze veils and linen gauntlets, a gift from a Toronto women's organization. Nevertheless, Middleton remembered "being torn to pieces by mosquitoes and flies." [70]

At the Beaver River base, General Middleton met with his subordinate officers. Following this meeting Middleton sent a messenger to telegram the Minister of Militia that both General Strange and Osborne Smith, Winnipeg Light Infantry, aspired for the command of the troops left in the North-West. Both men were, in Middleton's opinion, unsuitable for this posting. Adolphe Caron agreed. In a return telegram, the Minister of Militia answered, "You are right – Strange and Smith would never do." [71] Middleton also conducted a "pow-wow" with the Chipewyan band. Three Indians agreed to canoe downstream with Canon McKay, hoping to find information about the hostages.

Two days after his arrival, Middleton took a small mounted party to Cold Lake. Several writers questioned his motives, suggesting that this trip served only to satisfy the general's love for fishing.[72] In any event, no sooner had Middleton reached Cold Lake than Indian scouts arrived with a message that all the hostages were safe.

Unrestrained cheers from the soldiers greeted this news. At 3 a.m. on June 19, Middleton's party left Cold Lake for Frog Lake Landing. At Beaver River Middleton ordered Strange's troops to remain in camp. Everyone was discouraged. One soldier wrote: "Fred returned last night with two fish . . . Middleton damn fool anyhow."[73] Strange could only complain, "I am sick of this waiting business . . . enough now of this wretched war of which I am heartly [*sic*] sick."[74] On June 24, orders finally directed the troops stationed at Beaver River and Cold Lake to move to Frog Lake Landing. An observer described their arrival: "June 27 . . . the 92nd came in, and a very tough looking crowd they are. One man had a pair of drawers on for pants."[75]

From Frog Lake Landing, a waiting steamer transported the Field force to Fort Pitt.

Chapter 15

Freedom for the Hostages

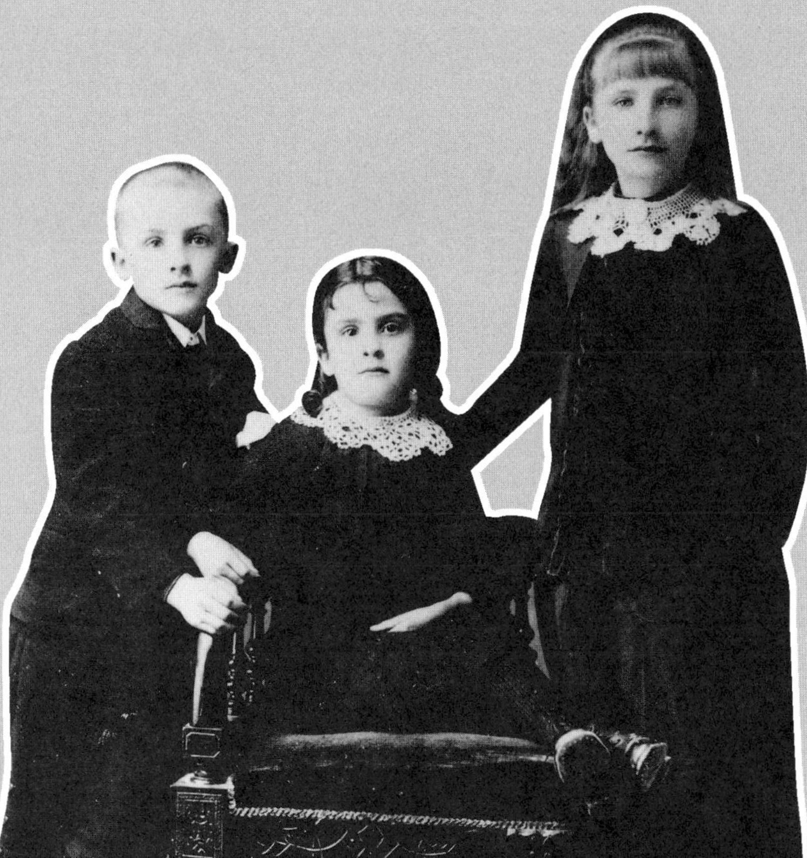

Photo on Previous Page :

George, Lottie and Blanche Mann – 1887

CHAPTER 15
Freedom for the Hostages

"I hardly know how we got through it, but we did."

– *George Mann*

The disarray and confusion following the skirmish north of Frenchman's Butte allowed six white hostages and most of the Métis families to gain their freedom. Still captive in the Wood-Plains Cree camp were twenty-two whites, several Métis men, and one Métis family. For these hostages, another three weeks of captivity remained.*

With the arrival of the Field Force had come the long-awaited hope of rescue, and although the soldiers remained out of view, each reverberation of the cannon confirmed the presence of help. Those hostages left with the Indian band were terribly disappointed, and faced Indian reprisals. When George Mann asked the Indians to release his family he was threatened with death if he "did not go on again."[1]

After Indian scouts returned from the battle site with discarded weapons and announced that the soldiers had withdrawn, it appeared that the skirmish had favored the Indians. Factor McLean regarded this news as "somewhat ominous, for we did not understand what it meant [and] had to suppress our feelings carefully."[2]

The Indian euphoria was short-lived. In fact, the band was terribly frightened. Everyone recognized the superior firepower of the enemy "Redcoats." Their arrival and attack were indications of determined soldiers bent on pursuing and killing Indians. The warriors could not match the soldiers in weaponry, and having to protect women and children was a decided disadvantage. The soldiers would only reorganize and strike again. Under the adverse circumstances the Cree camp chose to take refuge in the inhospitable wilderness. "Notwithstanding their vaunted bravery," observed one hostage, "they were all badly scared."[3]

---

*The hostages who went with the Wood Crees to the Beaver River included: W.J. McLean, his wife Helen, and their four daughters and five sons; George Mann, his wife and their three children; Malcolm McDonald; Stanley Simpson; John Fitzpatrick; Métis François Mellieu, his wife and their four children; Robert Hodgson; John Perry (Poirer?).

Two days of heavy rainfall masked the Indian withdrawal. All cumbersome vehicles and unnecessary supplies were abandoned in what quickly became a rout. A prisoner recorded:

> Well, a hasty retreat was made, and we rushed off pell-mell, each one struggling to get away, regardless of the wants of the sick or aged, and leaving broken carts and played-out animals by the wayside.[4]

The Indians deliberately took an exhausting route across swollen streams and treacherous muskeg "to make it harder for any troops that might follow."[5] At key places they felled trees to impede any mounted pursuit. Under the escalating pressure, McLean observed his captors "gradually daily getting more frightened."[6] A Métis hostage, Louis Goulet, agreed. "Each day, more and more, we could feel the beginning of the end," wrote Goulet. "The Indians had a woebegone look about them and the number of desertions increased every day."[7]

Several nights after the military engagement of May 28, at a camp near Horse Lakes an accidental discharge of a rifle, mistaken as an attack by the soldiers, clearly revealed the Indians' fears. A frenetic scene followed as women and children fled into the bush while the warriors indiscriminately "kept up a fusillade into the surrounding bushes, for ten minutes."[8] After this episode, many Indian women and children hid near the camp each night.

The northward flight quickly became an exhausting mental and physical ordeal for the entire Indian camp. The hostages faced added burdens. The McLean family had an old ox to carry their tent, but no bedding or provisions. Mr. McLean carried an eighteen-month-old child on his back. The older children helped their younger siblings cross swamps and swollen streams. Around each evening campfire, family members watched steam rise from their drenched clothing – a reminder of the exhausting day. Farm Instructor George Mann had an ox to carry his blankets, food, and three young children. He and his wife walked beside the slow beast, whipping it through swamps and muskeg. It was, he wrote later, "a rough time. I hardly know how we got through it, but we did."[9]

The Indians no longer bothered to conceal their trail. To prevent written messages, though, they unsuccessfully attempted to confiscate all the pencils in the whites' possession. The hostages, for their part, deliberately discarded useless personal articles, tied strings to branches, and left messages written on pages torn from *Robinson Crusoe*. Members of Steele's Scouts easily detected this evidence when they advanced along the trail several days later.

For the first time during the captivity, there was a scarcity of food. In 1968 Duncan McLean, only eight at the time, recalled how the Indians had discarded their supplies and then found it necessary to exist on dog meat.[10] Factor W.J. McLean estimated that the Indians must have eaten "three hundred or more dogs."[11] Unhappily, this number included the McLean family's pet Irish retriever. Prisoner Goulet observed, "As our supplies visibly shrank, the Indians became more and more discouraged."[12]

The deteriorating conditions increased the tensions between the two bands. One morning an old warrior, Big Hunter, stalked through the camp boldly denouncing the harsh treatment accorded the hostages and deriding the Plains Cree warriors for being "as cowardly as the loons who dived beneath the water at the least sign of danger."[13] In a reference to the Frog Lake massacre, he ridiculed the Plains Cree as "brave then, but when the troops came you run away like dogs."[14] His vitriolic words, noted George Mann, incensed the Plains Cree, "but as he was warmly supported by the Wood Crees, they had to grin and bear it."[15] No longer did the Plains Cree warriors unquestionably dominate the Indian alliance.

The Indian respite from the Field Force was brief. Six days after the battle near Frenchman's Butte, had come the attack by Steele's Scouts at the Loon Lake ford. After this skirmish the combatants moved in opposite directions: the Indians northeastward around the lake, while Steele, mainly because of a lack of provisions, back to Fort Pitt. His fierce attack again demonstrated the tenacity and firepower of the soldiers. Five Indians had died. The band was shaken and angry. Some warriors threatened to kill "a prisoner for every Indian killed."[16]

The Indians forced the white male hostages to dig a common grave for the dead. Years later, Elizabeth McLean recalled watching the Indians moving slowly up a ridge to the burial site. The funeral party appeared as a "tragic picture against the sunset."[17] A rainbow coloured sky mirrored on a lake still as glass, while hundreds of loons flew overhead. The scene was wonderfully peaceful – yet Elizabeth recalled that she and her sisters were filled with foreboding. Their father was attending the funeral services, but the other white men remained out of sight. Louis Mongrain, now leader of the Wood Crees after the death of Cut Knife in Steele's attack, had advised the white men to conceal themselves "because he feared a spirit of revenge."[18] Malcolm McDonald, a former police interpreter, found safety under a pile of furs when the wife of one victim stalked the camp with a knife.

The funeral was, in W.J. McLean's words, "a truly pitiable one . . . as characteristic of the Indians [and] loud in the lamentations for the dead."[19] Afterwards, Louis Mongrain helped placate the Indians: first, by comforting the father of one dead Indian and, second, by stopping a party of Indians approaching the McLean family.

Threats aside, the Indians realized the value of having unharmed hostages when the soldiers appeared for a third time. Factor McLean recognized this fact. He wrote: "The only reason the Indians kept us was to protect themselves in case they were cornered."[20] Another hostage observed:

Mann Children, 1887

George, Lottie and Blanche Mann two years after the rebellion. For the young Mann children captivity was an exciting adventure.

> Each of the prisoners had . . . a guard, a friendly one, and when any danger from the Plains Cree was anticipated, these faithfully occupied the tents of the captives, and if any harm was threatened were prepared to defend their own particular ward with their lives.[21]

Louis Mongrain even provided W.J. McLean with a rifle and unexpectedly Wandering Spirit began serving as a protective guard.

Once beyond the eastern edge of the lake, a swift-flowing river delayed movement. Since only three canoes were available for the transport of hundreds of people, the Indians constructed rafts made from cartwheels covered tightly with hides. The young braves effected the river crossing in a unique manner: each man drove his horse into the water, and holding the mane with one hand while swimming with the other, pulled a raft across using a rope held by his teeth. Using this time-consuming method, everyone safely reached the opposite bank. Once beyond a small hill the Indians reached an extensive area of muskeg which they chose to cross.

This route was extremely hazardous. "In places," Kitty McLean recalled, "we broke ice with our feet while overhead the sun beat scorchingly down on our uncovered heads."[22] Older members of the family, sometimes up to their armpits in water, carried the young. As they struggled through the mire, attention focused on an ox, bleating loudly with only its head and packsack above the quicksand. "We were," wrote Elizabeth McLean, "horrified to see him gradually disappear."[23] Only after four hours of strenuous struggle did everyone safely reach solid ground.

The exhausting route through the muskeg had brought tensions to a breaking point. Kitty McLean, in an address fifty years later, recalled drawing her knife and making stabbing gestures at Indians who were jeering her exhausted sister. The Indians, impressed by Kitty's boldness, responded by giving food and tea to her family.[24]

The following morning, the Crees separated into their respective bands. The parting was a simple matter: the Wood Crees delayed the morning march, stopping to smoke as Indians often did while on the move. Once the Plains Crees were out of sight to the east, the Wood Crees headed north as fast as possible. To hinder pursuit, the band members branched into small parties. The groups later reassembled at a prearranged location. By nightfall the Wood and Plains Cree bands were far apart.

Everyone in the Wood Cree camp was totally exhausted but there was a sense of relief at "being rid of the Plains Indians."[25] Understandably, the unexpected arrival of two prominent Plains Cree warriors on the following day caused apprehension. Elizabeth McLean recalled how the appearance of Wandering Spirit brought "a solemn stillness throughout the camp."[26] No one wanted to be associated with the war chief responsible for the Frog Lake murders. Ironically, compassion for the fierce warrior – whose hair had turned grey in weeks – came first from the McLean family.

McLean Children, 1895

A family picture of the McLean children, taken in 1895 – ten years after their seventy-day captivity in Big Bear's camp. From left to right: *top row – Helen, Duncan, Kitty, Bill; centre row – Freda, John, Eliza, Angus, Amelia; bottom row – Murray, Lillian, Lawrence.*

The second unwelcomed arrival was Dressy Man, one of the three men involved in the murderer of the Witigo. At the end of the rebellion, Wandering Spirit was hanged for murdering the Indian agent at Frog Lake while Dressy Man received a twenty-year sentence in Stoney Mountain Penitentiary.[27]

Two days after leaving the main party, the Wood Crees reached the swollen Beaver River. It had been a difficult journey with everyone "often up to their armpits in mud and water." [28] The shortage of food was acute. W.J. McLean pleaded with his captors for the release of all the hostages before they became too weak to travel. The Indians, who in his daughter's observation appeared "in a quandary," [29] rejected this request, stating that if the soldiers "came after them, they would have no one to intercede for them." [30] The Indians, though, did provide the captives with moccasins and a share of a moose.

At the Beaver River, the Indians constructed crude boats from raw hides lashed to willow frames. An entire day was needed to cross the flooded waterway. After camping for the night, the Indians moved to an open area about ten kilometres to the northeast. Here rabbits were numerous, but the Indians were so fearful of gunfire attracting soldiers that they set snares to trap the animals. McLean's family of eleven received two or three rabbits daily, hardly an adequate diet.

The mental and physical anguish of the fugitive band was now at a critical point. Under these desperate circumstances W.J. McLean, again supported by the Riding Mountain (Saulteaux) Indians, arranged a council meeting. After three days of discussion the Indians sent for McLean. The council greeted McLean kindly and with respect. Chief KeWin, as spokesman, asked how the release of McLean would help the Indians. Other questions related to the conflict: Was the master of the soldiers his friend? Had the government sent this man to kill Indians? Could McLean write to the Queen to prevent the soldiers from shooting?[31]

McLean's responses convinced the Indians that he could serve as a peacemaker. He reinforced the salient fact that as long as hostages remained in the Indian camp "the soldiers would follow them, should they travel to the sea."[32] Moreover, the soldiers were certain to defeat the Indians. Only through the release of unharmed hostages would the band receive sympathetic treatment from the government.

McLean agreed to act as a peacemaker for the Wood Crees. While he and Stanley Simpson wrote nine letters requesting leniency for individual chiefs, the other hostages quickly prepared for departure. Wandering Spirit sent criers through the camp announcing the release of the hostages and asking for gifts. The supplies provided were meagre – two pounds of bacon, eight pounds of flour, and mocassins. George Mann traded a blanket for five pounds of flour. The acquisition of three horses, though, provided helpful transportation for the children.

The company of twenty-eight left within the hour, lest the Indians change their minds. The date was June 18 and it was estimated that the 230-kilometre walk to Fort Pitt would take eight days. With them they carried a peace pipe and tobacco from the Indians as a gift for General Middleton.

Two Indians escorted the group to the Beaver River where two canoes were used to help the ex-hostages cross the river at about ten o'clock that evening. Three rabbits, shot during the walk to the river, provided a sparse supper. The following morning, the Indians left and an experienced Métis guide led the party southward. He found an easy route and the party moved along quickly, "fearing the Indians might change their mind."[33] The girls were cautioned against singing, in case hostile Indians were nearby. Stanley Simpson and a companion left the party to hunt. They shot nine rabbits which were eaten that day. That evening W.J. McLean recalled being "very tired but buoyed in spirit by our feeling of freedom."[34] Five rabbits, snared during the night, provided a meagre breakfast for the twenty-eight travellers. That day much of their route crossed a burned-out area where Simpson managed to kill only three rabbits and one partridge.

The extended daylight of June 20th enabled the party to walk until late in the evening, reaching the north end of Loon Lake. W.J. McLean described their feelings: "We certainly felt tired, also dejected at the prospect of

Queen's Own Rifles Bugle Band

A band at Fort Pitt greeted the arrival of the eleven-member McLean family, safely home after seventy days in the Indian camp. Upon their return the family was astounded to discover a large military base at the site of their former home.

nothing to eat for supper or breakfast."[35] Quickly their fortune changed: while the tents were being erected, Stanley Simpson went to the lake where he encountered and shot an ox. This was wonderful news. Elizabeth McLean described her feelings: "one can only imagine the excitement that this news caused for twenty-eight starving people."[36] The following day, everyone waited in camp while Stanley Simpson and a companion, using information provided earlier by an elderly Indian woman, left by canoe to locate a cache of food. In the evening, the men returned with a supply of flour, bacon and biscuits – enough food to keep the company until it reached Fort Pitt.

The following morning spirits soared as the ex-hostages continued southward. They crossed the water outlet of the lake using a bridge built by the soldiers. A copy of a Winnipeg newspaper, dated May 16, provided them for the first time with the news of Middleton's victory at Batoche. Someone found a letter tacked to a tree warning Big Bear not to harm the hostages. Two other letters discovered, written by a relative, made the McLean family "wild with joy and excitement."[37] Also found was the body of an Indian warrior killed in the battle at the ford, and the body of the Indian woman who had committed suicide. After several weeks of decomposition her body "was not a cheerful sight."[38]

At breakfast the following day a rumbling sound frightened the former hostages. Was it the croaking of frogs? Or a party of Plains Cree? Everyone watched intently. W.J. McLean described the moment:

> suddenly we saw the heads of two horses showing over the hilltop overlooking our camp, and immediately a man showed himself, and asked in English which was the best way to get down to our camp with his team. Just imagine, if possible, the sudden transition of our feelings. We hailed him in an ecstasy of delight, though we did not know who he was. However, we knew that he was not one of our dreaded Indians.[39]

The teamster brought news that a scout had observed their camp early that morning and ridden back to tell W.J. McLean's brother-in-law to bring supplies. Within half an hour the relative, Sam Bedson, arrived to a tearful and joyous reunion. With Bedson were supplies of bon-bons, cakes, and clothing for the entire company.

At last the sufferings, hardships, and dangers of the captivity had ended. No one was more relieved than Mrs. Helen McLean. For the last two months the expectant mother had protected and cared for her nine children. Her words reflected the anguish she had endured: "It's all like a horrible dream to me and I can scarcely realize that our troubles are ended. It has been terrible. Thank God, thank God, it's all over at last."[40] Teamsters transported the weary travellers to Fort Pitt. When they entered the sleeping camp at 4 a.m. on June 24, the McLeans could not believe their eyes. All around the ruins of their home were hundreds of tents.

Surrender of Big Bear

Big Bear, in chains, with his captors at Prince Albert shortly after his surrender to the Mounted Police in July, 1885. For one month the old chief had easily evaded four columns of troops searching for his band.

Despite the hardships, the former hostages were remarkably well. The women and children, observed one soldier, "though ragged, did not look much the worse for their terrible experience with the Indians."[41]

The steamer *Marquis* provided temporary living quarters for the former hostages. General Middleton and his staff came with greetings. Factor McLean presented the general with the peace pipe sent by the Indians. Middleton, in turn, expressed pleasure over the safe return of everyone. McLean proudly recalled Middleton's statement:

> He made manifest his satisfaction with the course of my actions with, and influence over the Indians during my captivity, and said the country owed me a very great debt, for in this matter alone I had saved many hundred thousand dollars and probably some valuable lives to the country.[42]

Only eleven days earlier, Middleton had sent a telegram to the Minister of Militia which stated that McLean "deserved hanging."[43] But the general's true feelings aside, all that mattered was that everyone was both unharmed and safe. That evening, from the river bank, a band played before the *Marquis*. Although the music re-established a sense of "civilization," thoughts, too, must have wandered, recalling the two months in the camp of Big Bear.

Middleton, on June 26, considered the rebellion effectively ended. A count of campfires informed scouts that the Plains Cree had fragmented into many small groups. Big Bear was known to be with only one councillor and two boys. In this light, General Middleton surveyed the situation:

> I received news that Big Bear's band had broken up, so with Batoche captured, Riel and Poundmaker prisoners, Big Bear powerless and a fugitive, and all the prisoners released, I considered my work nearly done, and began to make arrangements for breaking up the force.[44]

The "capture" of Big Bear on July 2 concluded the campaign. The old chief arrived at Fort Carlton with Horse Child, his twelve-year-old son. Since the skirmish near Frenchman's Butte, the old chief had walked hundreds of kilometres and easily avoided the four columns of over 1200 troops. But the final weeks had been a trying ordeal. Horse Child later recounted that some members of Big Bear's starving group nearly fainted when the smell of frying meat drifted over from a nearby camp of soldiers.

Ironically, it was Sergeant William Smart, the man left in charge of the ferry at the burned-out fort, who arrested the most wanted Plains Indian in the North West. In the words of a cynical Thomas Bland Strange, Smart was "about the only man on the Force who had never gone after him."[45]

CHAPTER 16

Heading Home

Photo on Previous Page *:*

Winnipeg Victory Arch

CHAPTER 16

Heading Home

"If I had $1000 I would not be any better off in this place."

– *C. Rannie*

With their arrival at Fort Pitt on the morning of June 27, the Field Force joined the largest concentration of troops assembled during the rebellion. The addition of the Field Force to the four scouting troops, four infantry companies, and two artillery units in camp made Fort Pitt, for that final week in June 1885, the largest populated centre in the entire North-West Territories.[1]

The camp, located on a small hill almost a kilometre north of the North Saskatchewan river, formed a rough square extending about one kilometre on each side. Shelters made of tree boughs served as reading rooms and a mess. Along with the rows of tents housing 2,100 soldiers and teamsters, Fort Pitt was a remarkable sight in the thickly wooded wilderness. Barges and steamers along the broad North Saskatchewan River added to the picturesque setting. To complete the scene, there was a small prison compound where Métis prisoners moved about, though hindered by an 18-kilogram (40-pound) ball attached to one leg.

The soldiers were bored with life at this remote military base. Nothing of any military consequence had occurred for weeks. Time, in the words of Chaplain Daniel Gordon, "hung heavily."[2] He wrote:

> Day followed day and week followed week, but we remained a month at Pitt expecting that each day would be our last there. There is some meaning in a soldier's life when he has fighting to do, but our experience at Fort Pitt led us to conclude that it must be a wearisome kind of life in barracks.[3]

A deckhand aboard the *Marquis* agreed: "There is nothing for the troops to do but kick about the grub."[4] Apparently there was justification for the complaints about the food. One soldier wrote:

> we were tired, unspeakably tired, of our unchanging bill of fare, canned beef, pork, beans and hardtack, relieved only now and then by fresh beef and vegetables. Our only beverage was tea.[5]

When mild cases of scurvy developed, possibly the result of tampered lime-water casks, some soldiers staged a hunger strike. This protest ended quickly after Doctor Ryerson gave the fifty men on sick parade an emetic, after which he "heard no more complaints."[6]

The fickle June weather increased the growing dissatisfaction in camp. One letter relates: "Today it was very hot, tonight it is cold enough for snow and will freeze before morning."[7] Fierce thunderstorms and violent wind gusts assailed their camp. The soldiers, protected only by canvas tents, were awed by both the splendor and destruction of the prairie storms. Signs on tents – "Imperial Hotel: on the European Plan," "5th Avenue Hotel," "Hotel du Cochin Noir" – ridiculed the living accommodations.

Sporting events helped "kill time." Contests in track and field, rifle target competitions and baseball games were popular. The post held stag dances with music emanating from an assembly of bugles, drums, homemade instruments, and cooking utensils. For those men interested in hunting, the countryside abounded with wildlife. Rabbits and ducks were especially plentiful. The gophers fascinated the eastern troops. In a letter to his brother in Montreal, one soldier wrote of returning from an excursion to find his tent "a menagerie," with no fewer than fifteen gophers racing about with strings attached to their necks.[8] Anyone able to endure the mosquitoes found the nearby lakes teeming with fish. One soldier recalled catching nine large pike in twenty minutes. Fishing near Fort Pitt, however, was another matter. A reporter from the *Montreal Star* complained that the excessive number of anglers made it impossible to approach the river bank.[9]

The spartan camp life gave everyday items extra value. Private Robert Monro recalled that "soap – white, pink, or yellow – scented or unscented, became the most treasured possession the boys possessed."[10] The cooks engaged in a lively business selling pies for twenty-five cents. With its increasing scarcity, tobacco became a commodity for which "any amount [of money] was freely offered."[11] One soldier confessed to exhuming an Indian grave, knowing that tobacco would be buried with the brave.[12] For many men, though, money had little use. C. Rannie informed his brother in Ontario that he had only spent three of the ten dollars in his possession. "If I had $1000," Rannie concluded, "I would not be any better off in this place."[13]

The arrival of mail brought a "general stampede for the letters."[14] For the North-West campaign the government had waved restrictions regarding the shape, transparency, or variety of perfume on the so-called "pink letters." Second, only a two-cent stamp was needed for all letters forwarded to those on active service – a saving of one cent. Parcels brought welcome gifts – honey, clothing, paper, envelopes and condensed milk. Those letters researched provide information on the soldiers' families and communities, give political observations, and express pride in serving Canada.

Many letters include prayers for safety and express relief that the soldier's name "was not on the casualty list."[15] Extracted from the letters of one mother is a list of concerns:

> Who are your companions? . . . Do you have a comfortable bed to sleep on? . . . And are you much exposed to the cold? . . . I hope you took plenty of warm socks with you. . . . I hope you have religious services; I am happy you decline anything stronger than ginger ale. . . . We don't think you were at all wise in bathing in the Saskatchewan or swimming so early for it was too cold.[16]

One letter was addressed to a soldier at "Qu'Appelle, North West Territories, or elsewhere."[17] And Miss Violette Wood in Birtle, Manitoba received an unusual letter. Her soldier correspondent, having no paper, wrote a message on a piece of birch bark, added a two-cent stamp, and sent his communication eastward by river steamer.[18]

Not all the news from home was good. Some married men found that while they were serving Canada, their families were experiencing financial hardship. In the Senate, a member rose to call attention to this problem.[19] The letters also reveal concerns over future employment. One drummer boy in the Winnipeg 90th reflected that his paper route replacement was making more money selling war editions of the *Winnipeg Sun* than he was earning on duty in Saskatchewan. In camp, the poorly-paid soldiers resented the idle teamsters, who were receiving six to ten dollars daily.

The general dissatisfaction increased tensions. Friction between the various military units nearly resulted in several large-scale brawls. Everyone criticized General Middleton's inability to end the campaign. One scout wrote: "Everyone got terribly tired of camp and lived in the daily expectation of receiving orders for home, but the long-deferred orders never came till we had despaired of ever getting them."[20] And it didn't matter how they were to return, downriver or overland. The commander of the 10th Grenadiers wrote: "I care little which way we go so long as we set out soon."[21]

Not surprisingly, the long-awaited announcement that they were returning home elicited, in scout H.P. Rusden's words, "exuberant rejoicing."[22] He recalled: "The whole camp was in a state of ecstasy at the prospect of leaving the most dismal hole in creation and getting back into some sort of civilization. The main thing looked forward to, I think, was getting a good square feed."[23] In a flurry of activity, they disassembled the camp. The bowers were torched and the baggage readied. The steamers *Marquis* and *Northwest* prepared to transport the infantry battalions downriver. Since the capture of Batoche, the river steamers had served as important transport vessels. The dimensions and stateliness of the steamers surprised the soldiers. The *Marquis,* on which Middleton travelled, was 65 metres (202 feet) long

Steamer *Northcote* Towing a Barge

Steamers were leased to the Canadian government for $250 a day. Their final service involved transporting several thousand soldiers down the Saskatchewan River to Lake Winnipeg.

and had a 1.1 metre (4 foot) draught. It had up-to-date machinery and amenities such as a piano, mirrors, and carpets. And at $250 per day, they provided their owners with substantial revenue. This transportation of troops, however, was the last service of importance for the prairie steam-wheelers. With the completion of the transcontinental rail line, seasonal river transport became obsolete.

The steamer *Baroness* had moved upstream to collect those members of the Field Force serving in garrisons. While awaiting the return of the *Baroness,* General Middleton used the occasion of Canada's eighteenth Dominion Day to celebrate with a great parade of his forces.

The 6:30 a.m. parade contained a tough assembly of soldiers. Joseph Crowe from Ontario's Midland Battalion, described his regiment's appearance:

> We had long discarded our regulation headgear and all the officers and men had fashioned caps made from the bags that held the oats. Our boots were in a bad state of repair, with no hope of replacing them. Our faces and beards were tanned and bleached by the sun, and our hair reflected our amateur barber's skill.[24]

"We were," he admitted, "a hard looking lot."[25] At this moment, though, appearances mattered little to the men. Middleton's review happily signalled the end of the campaign and the beginning of the return home.

After the parade, the cavalry units departed overland. The previous day, Hatton and Steele's Scouts had started the long ride back to Calgary by way of Edmonton. The scouts hurried to the Saddle Lake Indian Reserve to stop any pillaging by teamsters, and managed to prevent one act of looting.

The following afternoon, the *Baroness* returned from Edmonton. A waiting throng of enthusiastic comrades invaded the vessel as it docked. It was a happy time, a joyous affair for the 65th finally reunited, in the words of Sergeant Charles Daoust, "apres 72 jours de separation."[26]

In the early morning of July 3, the force embarked downriver. The whistles of the steamers, the bands, and the reciprocating cheers from the men made the departure a boisterous affair. "This was the beginning of the end of the campaign," wrote one newspaper correspondent, "and the delight of the soldiers knew no bounds."[27]

Those men remaining at Fort Pitt "were astounded to see what an extensive scale the provisioning had been carried on."[28] One observer recorded:

> The east bank of the river was simply lined with tons of oats and piles of boxes of hard tack and corned meats. There was as much still going to waste and ruin as would feed a regiment for a year.[29]

The mountain of supplies attested to the determination of the Canadian government to suppress this uprising. One requisition alone from England had consisted of 10,000 Martini Henry rifles and two and one-half million rounds of ammunition – thousands of bullets for each opposing rebel.

With the eastward departure of the flotilla, the units of the Alberta Field Force headed their separate ways. As mentioned, Steele and Hatton's mounted men were moving westward toward Edmonton. General Strange, the 65th of Montreal, and fifty members of the Winnipeg Light Infantry boarded the crowded steamers for the long journey to Winnipeg. Another 200 members of the Winnipeg unit remained at Fort Pitt to supervise the prearranged surrender of the remaining members of Big Bear's band.

Tragedy struck the flotilla soon after departure. On the morning of July 4, Lieutenant Colonel Arthur Williams of the Midland battalion died of typhoid fever. His death stunned the soldiers. More than anyone else, Williams epitomized the vigor and independence of the young nation. His battalion's assault on the Batoche rifle pits had refuted the established belief that only British officers could lead the Canadian militia. As one soldier wrote: "We have the men, as the campaign proved – for our own country and our own defence . . . we have the officers, too. Is it not quite time that this appointing British officers should be done away with?"[30]

Moments before Williams' death, Sergeant Prima Valiquette of the 65th, on board the *Baroness*, had died in agonizing pain from appendicitis. This was the fourth death involving men assigned to the Field Force. All deaths

Fort Pitt, N.W.T.

A Church Parade at Fort Pitt. In June, 1885 this military camp was the most populated settlement west of Winnipeg.

were of a non-military nature. Near the end of April, A. Blais of the 9th Quebec battalion had died in Winnipeg of tonsillitis. A second member of the Quebec company, Private Marois, had died of pneumonia on May 3, and was interred in Calgary. A teamster was another fatality. Following a thunderstorm about thirty kilometres south of Edmonton, Alexander MacKenzie, a former Mountie of the 1874 march, was struck by lightning. The *Edmonton Bulletin* dramatically described his death:

> He said to the cook, "This is worth a dollar," and raised his cup to his lips for a second drink . . . when there came a blinding flash of lightning and crash of thunder which almost stunned the men standing around. The air was filled with blue fire and the smell of electricity. . . . MacKenzie was lying on his back near the fire quite dead with electric flames coming out his mouth and nose.[31]

That no deaths occurred during combat was remarkable. In three engagements, lasting a total of five hours, hundreds of shots had been directed at the column. Six men had been wounded, while in turn seven Indians had been killed.*

The 65th, shocked by Valiquette's tragic death, impatiently endured their boat's slow progress to Battleford. Upon reaching the settlement, the surprising sight of Joseph Lemay, wounded five weeks earlier at Frenchman's Butte, aroused "une veritable ovation"[32] from the excited contingent. Shortly thereafter, this elation was subdued by the funeral of Sergeant Valiquette. After the rites, conducted by the company's chaplain Père Prevost, each soldier, Sergeant Daoust recalled, "retourne au bateau en silence."[33]

At Battleford three units, the Quebec Battery, Ottawa Foot Guards, and Queen's Own Rifles, joined the crowded flotilla for the journey to Winnipeg. The 65th and the Winnipeg Light Infantry found themselves "packed like herrings in a box."[34] Although the steamer *Northwest* held over 600 men one soldier declared, we "consider ourselves fortunate in not having been sent across the prairie."[35]

At the moment of departure, strong winds delayed travel. Once under way the next day, a snowstorm struck. The *Northwest* smashed into a bank, throwing one soldier into the river. All navigation stopped for one hour. The soldiers reacted in astonishment. This was July! Two days earlier the maximum temperature had been 34° celsius. This western territory was truly incredible. Was nature conspiring to prevent their return home? One soldier observed of Saskatchewan: "It is impossible to avoid swearing in this country. The nature of the climate requires exercise in this form."[36]

---

*In comparison, the two columns in Saskatchewan suffered far greater losses. The main force under General Middleton had twenty-six battle fatalities and eighty-eight men wounded. Colonel Otter's skirmish at Cut Knife Hill had resulted in eight battle deaths and fourteen soldiers wounded.

On the morning of July 8 the boats reached Prince Albert. During the two-hour stop, most of the soldiers visited Big Bear. The poor Indian had arrived, in the words of a Mountie, "in a pitiable condition of filth and hunger."[37] The police proceeded to give him a good scrubbing in a tub at the barracks, though this was anything but enjoyable for him. The sixty-year -old Indian, described by the *Illustrated War News* as a "cruel and remorseless savage,"[38] received degrading treatment. The soldiers called on Big Bear en masse. One wrote:

> Big Bear was the focus of attraction. . . . He was brought out to exercise, and seemed rather afraid at the unexpected amount of interest he was causing, as he shuffled along in his leg-irons, through a long lane of eager, sun-burnt faces.[39]

Their long-sought adversary was, in the words of one viewer, "a pathetic sight."[40]

Shortly after noon the town's 1500 residents gave the soldiers an enthusiastic sendoff. The mayor spoke to the men, lauding their courage and accomplishments. Following his speech, each soldier received a cigar – a gift from the town. Then with several bands playing "The Girl I Left Behind Me" and lastly "Auld Lang Syne", the boats departed. It was a nostalgic occasion: the troops were leaving the great North-West Territories. Their destination was Winnipeg – some 1500 kilometres to the southeast.

A swift run brought the boats through a series of rapids to The Forks, the confluence of the two Saskatchewan rivers. At this location a sheer prominent butte, 120 metres high, impressed the men "as a second Quebec or Gibraltar."[41] A steamer with canvas-covered hospital barges from Saskatoon awaited their arrival. Once the wounded men from the battles of Fish Creek and Batoche were moved aboard, the flotilla pressed eastward. At a speed of between twenty and twenty-five kilometres per hour, it would take the 1500 men ten days to reach Winnipeg.[42]

The presence of many sandbars meant limiting travel to daylight. Even so, frequent delays occurred when the boats ran aground. The men viewed the progress of the steamers as a contest to relieve the boredom, and enjoyed waving good-naturedly each time they passed a stranded vessel. The scenery was described as "grand in the extreme, unmarred by the hand of civilization, nature is here seen in all its wild beauty and simplicity."[43]

The journey down Saskatchewan River covered at least 1000 kilometres. Some soldiers enjoyed this segment of their return home. For Montrealer Charles Daoust, "le paysage devient de plus en plus pittoresque."[44] R.S. Monro, of the 90th Winnipeg Rifles, happily remembered that the "excursion down the Saskatchewan was one which I never have forgotten."[45] Lieutenant Preston enjoyed an appreciation of history during short stop at Fort à la Corne and Cumberland House. For two soldiers there was a remarkable reunion: An officers' party, enlivened by a punch containing five gallons of rum, developed into a convivial gathering. During the evening, two officers, with the same surname, discovered that they were long-lost twin brothers. In celebration, the brothers "climbed the table and sang a rousing duet, which was received with great applause."[46]

Many men, though, found the river journey a time-consuming affair, aggravated by innumerable sandbars and the onerous tasks of wood cutting and loading. Newspaper correspondent Angus Kennedy recalled: "The mosquitoes ate us up by night and the sandbars held us up by day."[47] One sandbar delayed Kennedy's boat for eight hours. When grounded, poles and pulleys were used to nudge the vessels loose. A second method, when possible, was to attach a cable to a large tree and use a steam winch to free the craft. The delays annoyed the soldiers. The question on everyone's mind, wrote one adventurer, was – "When will we get to Winnipeg?"[48]

The Pas served as a point to reunite the flotilla. The first arrivals found this trading and mission settlement to be a dismal swamp, inhabited by a few Indians and a large number of vicious dogs described as great wolves. The dogs commanded the narrow pathways. "When you met one on the trail," wrote R.G. MacBeth, W.L.I., "it was wisdom to step aside and give him the right-of-way."[49] Needless to say, the safe arrival of all the boats was good news. Only fifty kilometres remained before the Saskatchewan River entered Cedar Lake.

The river now diverged into many channels bordered by unattractive marshy flats abounding with wildlife. Travel became slower and directions were harder to discern. Near the mouth of the river all the watercraft assembled at a small native settlement. The Indians were amazed to see soldiers. At once, the military band assembled and began playing loudly. As expected, the Indians scattered. All along the Saskatchewan, whenever Indians were encountered and time availed, band members had delighted in achieving this response.

After the 120-kilometre crossing of Cedar Lake, the flotilla reached Grand Rapids. This settlement of one hundred inhabitants was located at the point where the Saskatchewan River empties into Lake Winnipeg. The sight of the whitewashed Hudson's Bay Company building aroused excitement. At last the river run was over. However, the spectacular rapids, six kilometres in length, necessitated the transshipment of all supplies. A dilapidated five-kilometre horse tramway was used to convey the baggage to waiting steamers and barges on Lake Winnipeg. To the amazement of the men, here in the wilderness, telephone communication connected the store-houses at each end of the tramway. And yet, as the Hudson's Bay factor told one soldier, it had not been until June 7 that he had learned of the rebellion.

As compensation for the extra work required, many soldiers enjoyed their spare time shooting the rapids. Another popular recreation was fishing. The river and nearby waters teemed with fish. Part of a lengthy poem claimed:

Welcome Arch in Winnipeg

The troops who marched under the Welcome Arch were no longer in the "dry" North-West Territories and they soon crowded local taverns, which remained open all night by the mayor's special proclamation.

> A fragment of your shirt-tail for a bait,
> They're on the jump before it strikes the water.[50]

Even acknowledging the exaggeration associated with the pastime, this poetic account does appear incredible.

On July 13, the flotilla departed on its 500-kilometre journey to Winnipeg. Cramped conditions ruined any prospects of a pleasant voyage. One diary relates: "We were so crowded that we had to sleep in sitting or standing postures."[51] The immense size of Lake Winnipeg caused further problems. One turbulent eight-hour storm tossed seasick men around in their barge until "they had then no desire to live."[52]

On July 15, eleven days after leaving Fort Pitt, the flotilla reached Selkirk. As a welcome, the town's ladies had arranged a luncheon in a beautiful park. Many soldiers, however, had other interests. Unlike the North-West Territories, Manitoba was "wet" and the drinking establishments of the small town quickly filled with soldiers. One observer wrote:

> There are only a few buildings here, but four of them are saloons, and the stuff they sell must be the worst kind of firewater as we had not been more than 15 minutes ashore when there were several rows on among the men.[53]

Later that day, a special train transported the soldiers to Winnipeg.

The returning soldiers presented a ragged spectacle for the enthusiastic citizens of Manitoba's capital, but their unkempt appearance was of little importance. What mattered was that the troops had returned, in particular the two Winnipeg units – the 90th "Little Black Devils" and fifty members of the Winnipeg Light Infantry.

The men were welcomed at a great reception. It appeared that every one of the city's twenty thousand inhabitants was on hand. All along Main Street were arches and banners. A Triumphal Arch of Victory, built at a cost of $500 to City Council, demonstrated the welcome greetings. The men marched down Main Street, in the words of a local newspaper, to "a continual ovation."[54] "The people," wrote a member of the Black Devils, "were wild with joy."[55] Such enthusiasm erased "all the hardships and dangers of the campaign,"[56] remembered MacBeth, of the Winnipeg Light Infantry. It was, he realized, also exactly three months to the day since his unit had departed for Calgary.

After the prescribed official reception at City Hall, the men were released to celebrate. An obliging mayor, by proclamation, declared that the taverns could remain open all night. Furthermore, the police were instructed not to interfere with the anticipated revelry. Joining the 1500 soldiers from the Saskatchewan River expedition were another 1000 men who had arrived by rail from western stations. The young men were free to "let off steam." Behind them were the rigors and dangers of war. Ahead lay the future. Lieut.-Colonel George Denison recalled:

> I never saw such a scene as Winnipeg displayed that night. The streets were crowded with men of various regiments, all mingled together in the highest good humour, a great many good-naturedly drunk and singing and shouting.[57]

Regarding the spirited celebrations, officer J.A. Forin commented: "the boys are doing the town."[58] Surveyor A.O. Wheeler agreed: "the boys painting the town red."[59] In less diplomatic language, L. Miller, Queen's Own Rifles, described his unit "as nearly all drunk."[60]

A diary entry on July 16 – "le matin, la pluie commence à tomber"[61] – indicated what was in store for Winnipeg. "It rained as only it can in Winnipeg,"[62] recorded a soldier from the Maritimes. That day twenty-four millimetres of rain fell on tent camps already muddy from a storm two days earlier.[63] Undeterred, the men sought refuge in vacant buildings and the doorways of shops. Rain was not going to stop the revelry.

After several days, the celebrating waned. On July 18, officer Forin's diary noted: "about time we got out of Winnipeg."[64] Already eastern regiments were boarding trains for the journey home, leaving Winnipeg to revert to a quieter life style.

The 65th Regiment travelled directly to Montreal by rail. Since their trip westward, workmen had completed "the gaps" north of Lake Superior. No doubt the soldiers contrasted the return journey with their rigorous experience four months earlier. Who could forget tramping through deep snow and huddling for warmth in open boxcars?

On the morning of July 20, the seven-car train arrived in Montreal. This was, reported a correspondent, "a gala day in this great city, where everything was made subordinate to extending an enthusiastic welcome to the gallant 65th Regiment on its return from the North-West."[65] The main avenues leading from the Canadian Pacific depot were decorated profusely with streamers, banners, and flags. Tens of thousands of the city's 200,000 inhabitants greeted the train's arrival with wild enthusiasm. A reporter wrote: "It was a demonstration that your correspondent has never seen equalled."[66] At the sight of the brave men, reported the *Montreal Star,* the "female enthusiasm was indescribable."[67] The warm response from his hometown residents was, for soldier Daoust, "impossible à decrire."[68]

From the station, the unit marched to a great "patriotic welcome" at City Hall. All along their route enthusiasm soared. One soldier remembered: "le passage était littéralement bloqué, l'enthousiasme ne se ralentissait pas et les bravos étaient ininterrompus."[69] Following the official welcome by the mayor, to which Colonel Ouimet responded, the regiment proceeded to Notre Dame where the "Te Deum" was chanted. Then the men were released for family reunions. For the family of Joseph Marcotte, the soldier incorrectly reported killed near Frenchman's Butte, this must have been an emotional moment.

After almost four months' service, the men were civilians again. This was a day that they had been happily anticipating – but with the long-awaited moment came an emptiness. Sergeant Charles Daoust succinctly recorded: "Le campagne était finie."[70]

In southern Alberta, the 232 men of the 9th Voltigeurs of Quebec City had served garrison duty at Gleichen, Fort Macleod, and Calgary. A few soldiers had seen limited active duty escorting teamsters to Edmonton. Since the general inactivity had disappointed all in the battalion, authorities arranged a trip to the Rockies. The Voltigeurs were reunited in Calgary and a special train of seven cars moved the men and officials westward on July 8. Major James Walker of Calgary outlined special landmarks. The soldiers visited the abandoned mining town of Silver City and viewed spectacular Castle Mountain. "Voila! le citadel. C'est Québec!" a *Herald* reporter heard the men exclaiming.[71]

The train passed westward through tunnels, across timbered bridges, and near cascading waterfalls. One diary recorded the scenery as being "des plus beux à voir."[72] The trip terminated at Donald, British Columbia, the first crossing of the Columbia. This community provided dinner, and speaker Chief Justice Matthew Bigbie declared that interprovincial relations between British Columbia and Quebec were "rendered closer by the visit of the 9th to Donald."[73] Colonel Amyot responded on behalf of his unit.

Donald had mushroomed into a "boom town" of some 1200 men as railway construction continued. Also attracted to the locale were about thirty women described as "de mauvaises réputations."[74] Their conduct – in smoking, card playing, drinking and street brawls – shocked young medical student Arthur Potvin. Never had he observed such outrageous behavior.

On the return journey the train stopped at Canmore for a view of "les Trois Soeurs," a striking mountain landmark. On Thursday morning, July 9, the unit was back in Calgary. The men remained two hours for final farewells, the purchase of mementoes, and a civic lunch provided at the Grand Central Hotel. The small town gave the blue-coated men a rousing send-off. The *Herald* reported:

> when the train bearing the 9th battalion finally left for Winnipeg and Quebec, most of the town was on the platform to see them off, and the train steamed off amid the mingled cheers of Calgary and Quebec, the beating of drums and the tooting of trumpets.[75]

In Winnipeg the men paraded to the grave of Achille Blais, a member of their unit who had died April 20. Blais represented the frailty of life. Here he rested "loin de sa patrie, loin de sa famille en deuil."[76]

On July 17 the battalion reached Port Arthur where, at noon, they embarked on the Canadian Pacific steamship *Alberta*. Two battalions from Ontario occupied the front section of the vessel while the Quebec unit arranged

Winnipeg Victory Arch

A horse-drawn streetcar represented civilisation for those soldiers returning to Winnipeg after two months in an almost empty wilderness. To the soldiers of Canada the North-West Rebellion was a great adventure. In contrast, for many of the Métis and Indians, the conflict signified the end of a way of life.

quarters in the rear. One correspondent recorded the fraternization between the 600 soldiers on the crowded craft as "a pleasant feature"[77] of the journey. While crossing Lake Superior, the Voltigeurs delighted the 1100 passengers with Indian war dances:

> It was an inspiring sight to witness the officers of the gallant 9th squat themselves in a circle on the poop deck, and after gravely passing the pipe of peace around, rise one after the other to relate wonderful feats they had performed in the way of horse-stealing and lifting scalps. Then it was grand to see the entire group rise to their feet and move around in exact imitation of the peculiar step of the so-called dance of Indian braves.[78]

During these performances, members of the 9th "made themselves perfectly agreeable to the ladies."[79] These vivid interpretations of Indian ritual implied that the soldiers had performed daring deeds in the wild west. Who on board would suspect that the 9th Voltigeurs of Quebec City had not fired one shot in the rebellion?

Beautiful weather made the two-day voyage across Lake Superior a pleasant experience. At Sault Sainte Marie a problem arose when American authorities refused transit of the canal for the transport of Canadian troops. This meant a march of twenty kilometres across Canadian soil to Lake Huron. An exchange of telegrams between Sault Sainte Marie, Ottawa, and Washington resolved the problem after several hours, allowing the steamship to proceed, provided that the soldiers remained out of sight.

At Owen Sound, two "arcs de triomphe" greeted the arrival of the vessel. Young girls gave the soldiers flowers and refreshments, and ladies provided a lunch. The local Salvation Army band played music and their singers gave a rousing performance. A sign carried by one female warned of the need for salvation. It read: "Ready When Jesus Comes."[80]

After minor transportation delays, the Voltigeurs continued their homeward journey by train. Throughout Ontario flags, signs, and banners greeted the Quebec soldiers. The welcome reached its climax in Toronto where fifty thousand people lined Yonge Street to observe the Queen's Own Rifles, Royal Grenadiers, and 9th Voltigeurs on parade. Along the route the French Canadians eagerly responded to onlookers' calls for a French song. At the end of the parade the soldiers quenched their thirst with free beer. Later that day the clergy provided lemonade and a hot supper, while Mrs. Thompson, wife of one minister, played patriotic music on a piano. At the rail station, every soldier received a cigar, thanks to the generosity of a local merchant. One recruit wrote of the hospitality:

> Dans cette ville essentiellement anglaise et protestante, on nous rendait hommage à nous français et catholiques. Nos voisins savent reconnaitre nous dévouement à la cause sacrée de la patrie, notre amour du devoir.[81]

The warm reception in Ontario formed a lasting impression upon the Voltigeurs.[82] On July 20, in Ottawa, the 9th paraded on the lawn before the Parliament Buildings and served as a guard of honor for the prorogation of the session. Upon their return to Quebec City, speeches, parades, banquets and excursions continued for four days.

Members of the Field Force from Alberta – teamsters, scouts, Mounties, and the cowboy contingent – returned home overland from Fort Pitt. On Saturday, July 18, the mounted units of the Field Force approached Calgary. At midday, Mayor George Murdoch rode to Nose Creek. As the sun broke through the clouds, there came the distant reflection of "a hundred rifle barrels coming along the Red Deer Trail."[83] Murdoch raced back to inform the town that "the boys were coming in at last and would be here in the course of an hour."[84]

At 2 o'clock the column reached George Hamilton's ferry. Steele's Scouts led the advance, followed by Hatton's Alberta Rifles, then James Oswald's Calgary Scouts. The *Herald* described "the boys" as looking well in their Montana broadcloth, though some of their coats were torn and the horses appeared thin. Their cowboy hats – "blazoned with glorious words"[85] – informed onlookers of their adventure.

For days Calgary had been preparing a welcome. Two arches carried messages of welcome and victory. Under one arch of evergreens, Mayor Murdoch read a welcome, to which Steele responded. The spectators then gave "three cheers and a tiger for the boys,"[86] after which the troopers disengaged and joined the happy celebrations. At the rink, Mr. Millward's band gave a concert. Later at Boynton Hall, one hundred and fifty guests attended a banquet. This gathering was, in the *Calgary Herald's* opinion, "the most brilliant affair ever arranged for in Calgary."[87] If gauged by the number of arrests for the illegal sale of alcohol, the reception and dance that night indeed became a boisterous affair.

On July 27, nine days after the Field Force arrived in Calgary, Police Inspector A. Bowen Perry's small detachment of sixteen Mounted Policemen returned to Fort Macleod. Welcomed by a piper, playing the inappropriate "Marching Through Georgia," the entire town enthusiastically greeted "the gallant little detachment of C Troop from the perils and hardships of the campaign in the North."[88] The local druggist recalled that "the men were quite overcome with the warmth of the reception."[89] They had been gone since April 17 (over three months) when Perry and his men had left with the field piece to join General Strange's second column.

After leaving Fort Pitt on June 29, the Fort Macleod troop rode to Swift Current, Calgary, and then home – thus completing a gigantic loop of the North-West Territories. Inspector Perry's log book estimated that his travels covered 1308 miles or over 2100 kilometres.[90] It was an incredible ride – one matched by few military columns in history.

The last members of the Alberta Field Force to reach home were two hundred men from the Winnipeg Light Infantry, stationed at Fort Pitt to effect the surrender of Big Bear's band. These proceedings had been structured to intimidate the defeated Indians. The Cree band sat in an open field surrounded by armed Winnipeg men, dressed in their faded scarlet tunics. Osborne Smith and Indian Agent J.M. Rae dictated the terms of surrender. First, the natives were forced to deliver all weapons; second, those Indians accused of crimes were named and escorted to a stern wheeler for transport to Battleford. Finally, the assembly was told that because the Queen had a forgiving heart, they could return to their reserves – "but they would not be trusted with arms again until they had shown that they desired for the future to live in peace with their white neighbours."[91]

On July 25, Osborne Smith received orders to leave Fort Pitt. In the past weeks "malarial fever" had wasted most of the men. Rather than follow the Saskatchewan River route taken by their comrades three weeks earlier, the soldiers immediately headed southward for the rail line. On August 13, these last members of the Alberta Field Force arrived in Winnipeg. A festive gathering and cordial welcome greeted them.

CHAPTER 17

Epilogue

Photo on Previous Page :

York and Simcoe Battalion, marching to Humboldt

CHAPTER 17

Epilogue

"My great adventure."

– *Robert Monro*

The North-West campaign concluded after 100 days with Canada firmly in control of its vast western prairies. Over 5,000 combat soldiers, almost entirely Canadian in nationality, had marched against the rebels. Their presence proudly demonstrated that Canada could overcome complicated logistics, and field a potent force thousands of kilometres from its largest centres of population. In response to this military crisis, the government, though on the verge of bankruptcy, exigently raised five million dollars. The campaign, too, proved that a transcontinental rail system justified its enormous costs.

The military outcome of the campaign was never in doubt. True, there had been initial limited rebel successes, an alarming possibility that the area of conflict would spread, and potential dangers to certain settlements. The government, however, had vastly superior numbers and resources, telegraph and railway communication, and, unlike the insurgent forces, a coordinated plan of action. The insurgents were, to cite an analogy used in the *New York Times,* like a pygmy attacking a giant.[1]

Even on the Canadian prairies the whites held an advantage in population, a fact ignored in the few studies of the rebellion. Of the 48,362 inhabitants of the North-West Territories, 20,170 Indians and 4,848 Métis made up slightly more than one-half the population.[2] With the inclusion of Manitoba, the white population dominated the western plains. A census for that province in July, 1886 listed a population of 108,640, with the white element numbering over 95,000.[3] Winnipeg's population of 20,238 alone exceeded the entire Indian population in the North-West Territories. The city provided more than one thousand soldiers to fight the insurgents, more men than the entire rebel force. In total, on the western plains, whites numerically exceeded the Indian-Métis combined population by a significant 80,047 people.

The Alberta Field Force was helpful in containing and suppressing the North-West Rebellion. The force accomplished its directives quite admirably: the majority of the Indian and Métis in the District of Alberta remained loyal, and once Strange had worked out the necessary logistics, the column marched across a vast region to confront rebel Indians. Through its visual presence, the force served Canada far better than it had at the rather undistinguished skirmishes near Frenchman's Butte and at Loon Lake. Above all, the force demonstrated fortitude and purpose of mission. Nothing could suppress the ardor and enthusiasm of the inexperienced recruits. Few military columns in history have surpassed the distances marched by the Alberta Field Force that spring in 1885. Few military columns ever travelled through such an empty wilderness.

In the final analysis, the formation of the Alberta Field Force had minimal effect upon the suppression of the rebellion. Quite simply, Riel's disorganized, ill-equipped and uncoordinated rebel resistance was certain to face defeat. Canada was not going to allow a handful of prairie rebels to jeopardize the grand vision of a nation from sea to sea.

In Thomas Bland Strange, the Field Force had a capable commander. No doubt his personal whims caused concern, but he was a tireless campaigner and competent organizer who produced the desired results. Under Strange, a career soldier, the Alberta Field Force accomplished all its assigned tasks. Gunner Jingo, in his book, outlined the effectiveness of his command:

> My long line of communication . . . was never seriously interrupted, I never lost a supply train, and in the end, Big Bear's band was dispersed, the white captives set at liberty, and Big Bear himself and his subchiefs, surrendered. And this was accomplished with a minimum of casualties to my Force.[4]

Thomas Bland Strange, rightly, could pride himself on his achievements.

Strange had never intended to lead a military column northward to Frog Lake. His decision to organize a rudimentary home guard was related to concerns for his family's safety and his ranching investments. It was General Middleton's campaign strategy, directing three troop units to Calgary, that engendered the Field Force. It fell to Thomas Bland Strange – bilingual, having organized the area defences, and with professional military skills – to command these troops.

At the conclusion of the rebellion, General Strange returned to his ranch. One reference likened Gunner Jingo to "a modern Cincinnatus, [who] beat his sword into a ploughshare and resumed the cultivation of the arts of peace."[5] For the valuable services rendered, the source acknowledged "the Dominion owes him a deep debt of gratitude."[6] Strange agreed. He had done much for Canada, and the country should reward his achievements.

This was not to happen. Up to the point when he left Canada in the Spring of 1888, Strange experienced unending disappointments. Most immediate was the forfeiture of his $200 monthly military pension, based upon the regulation that he had returned to active service. Quite rightly, Strange belaboured this loss of revenue and until the pension was restored one year later, this matter was a persistent grievance.*

Disillusionment followed in the aftermath of the rebellion. Strange felt betrayed that the commanders of his Quebec contingents, Amyot and Ouimet, bolted the Conservative party during the furor over Riel's fate, that Big Bear was released after only six months' imprisonment, and that Middleton's official report minimized the contribution of the Field Force in the defeat of the insurgents. In response to these events Strange commented that "the campaign was more than futile."[7]

Further, Strange's personal aspirations for public office met with failure. First, there was the Government's rejection of Strange for the office of North-West Mounted Police Commissioner. Prime Minister Macdonald, in a confidential letter, suggested that the best way to deal with Strange was to indicate that the succession had already been determined. Macdonald added:

> Strange is too old altogether and too much of a mere gunner to have control of the Police force, besides his crazy fear of the Indians which almost amounts to semi-insanity.[8]

Second, in the aftermath of rebellion, the Federal government created four constituencies in the troubled region. At the urging of friends, Thomas Strange decided to stand for Parliament in the Federal election in late February 1887. But which party should he represent? After rejecting the political leadership of both established parties of that day, Gunner Jingo characteristically chose to campaign as an independent.

Strange, as expected, supported measures which promoted regional economic growth and immigration. He bitterly opposed the prohibition legislation in the North-West Territories, maintaining that any visitor to Calgary could easily observe the failure of this ill-advised legislation. The town was, in Strange's words, "the most drunken place I ever saw."[9]

Citing a lack of money, Strange withdrew from the campaign about the first week in February. The *Herald* considered this decision unfortunate:

> we believe a large number of electors will regret it. General Strange is a man of large and liberal views on public questions, his character is irreproachable, and had he entered the field as a straight party candidate he would have been a tower of strength.[10]

*Nowhere in his writings, however, does Strange document his economic gains from military service. The Sessional Papers 1886, Vol. XIX, No. 13, p. 535 record that Strange's pay and allowances totalled $2,752, a considerable sum by 1885 living standards.

The victorious candidate in Strange's constituency was D.W. Davis. Strange ridiculed the electorate's decision: "It seems incredible. He is the worst robber and scoundrel in the N.W. – and that is a big country to choose from."[11] That Davis was a former American soldier, only fueled Strange's resentment. Strange loathed Americans.

By now Strange was completely discouraged with his ranching interests. Economic reverses, adverse weather conditions, ongoing problems with the nearby Indians, and a severe injury from a horse kick thwarted his optimism. A letter, written by his wife in February 1887, related: "Tom is getting so disheartened and out of spirits he talks seriously and often of leaving the country."[12]

In late 1887, Strange decided to end his ranching career. He was bitter: "I have given the best years of my life to the service of Canada and I only want to get out of it and never see it more."[13] In a letter to an old friend in Quebec, Strange expressed the timeless lament of older generations. "Our poor Canada," he declared, "has sadly deteriorated since you and I were young."[14]

Strange retired to England. In 1894, at age sixty-three, he wrote his autobiography, *Gunner Jingo's Jubilee.* For another thirty-one years he lived in retirement in a London suburb. One military comrade in Canada continued to correspond with the old gunner. Strange's letters were, he recalled, "strong and fearless like himself."[15] On July 9, 1925 Strange died.

Half a world away in Alberta the evening paper failed to report his death; the morning paper, on July 10, carried a short note, page seven, "General Strange Dies." The article briefly outlined Strange's career and incorrectly referred to his nickname as "Gunner Jinga."

Gunner Jinga! How quickly people forget! On this very day, exactly forty years before, Thomas Bland Strange and his Montreal soldiers had been aboard the *Baroness* on the broad North Saskatchewan River en route to Winnipeg. Three months earlier, they had left Calgary to begin a remarkable adventure. Now it was all over.

For the most part, Thomas Bland Strange remains a forgotten figure. Once, almost everyone in western Canada knew Gunner Jingo. A volume of Canadian biography in 1888 contained eight full pages on General Strange, describing him as a "conspicuous figure on the Canadian scene."[16] Today, few history texts recognize his contribution to Alberta's history. The Collins Dictionary of Canadian History does not even include his name.[17]

There remain two geographical features which bear the name of the man who led the Field Force northward that spring in 1885. West of Gleichen, an uninhabited locality bears the name Strangmuir. And forty-five kilometres northwest of the town of Jasper, isolated Mount Strange thrusts 2,870 metres skyward.

In the spring of 1885 it seemed inconceivable that within months Canada's spirit of solidarity would be quickly shattered. It was, on November 16, 1885, with the hanging of Louis Riel. Because of his execution, Canada was divided, largely on the basis of language. The joint accomplishment of the 65th Battalion from Montreal, the 9th Voltigeurs from Quebec, and the Winnipeg Light Infantry was forgotten. Protestant Ontario endorsed Macdonald's action. Roman Catholic Quebec condemned it.

Although Canadians in the North West probably would not have admitted the fact, Riel's uprising had in several ways immediately benefited them. Enormous military expenditures had stimulated a depressed economy. After years of procrastination and delay, the conflict brought quick action on many aggravating issues. By June 1885, the residents of St. Albert received their long-awaited land titles, and the following year all three Provisional Districts finally obtained Federal representation. The uprising alerted authorities to the need for improved communications. During the rebellion telegraphic lines were constructed from Edmonton south to Calgary, and between Medicine Hat and Fort Macleod. The violence also indicated a need for greater regional protection resulting in an increase in the North-West Mounted Police presence to over 1,000 men. Calgary received a contingent of one hundred Mounties, making the police a large segment of the local population. Many residents of this ranching frontier, however, must have viewed the new recruits with wonder. Even the Police Report of 1885 admitted: "A large population are unable to ride, and are unaccustomed to horses." [18]

Ottawa rewarded those Indians who had remained neutral during the conflict. For some natives this included a two-week train excursion to eastern Canada in 1886. Receptive audiences in Toronto, Montreal, Quebec City, and Ottawa along with the eastern press flocked to observe the picturesque Indians from the plains as they were introduced to the "wonders of civilization." It proved to be a triumphant, though fatiguing, tour.

Was the purpose of this trip, like the visit of four southern Alberta chiefs to Winnipeg in 1884, to demonstrate the formidable power of white society? This plan may have succeeded, although some Blood Indians declared that they were most impressed by the monkeys in the Toronto zoo.

In western Canada officials distributed gifts to loyal Indians. The Stoneys at Morley received forty sheep; Pakan saw Victoria renamed in his honor and for his "great loyalty throughout" received $100, two cows, one gun, and two oxen; Woodpecker, in Samson's band, for being "generally good," received two oxen; and Blue Quill, "Who kept his men quiet," also received two oxen.[19]

Authorities dealt forcefully with those Indians responsible for depredations and violence. These Indians, mainly from the bands of Big Bear and Poundmaker, lost their annuity payments for three years, had their horses

Indian Chiefs in Ottawa, 1886

The Canadian Government awarded loyal Indians with a trip to Eastern Canada. Blood, Blackfoot, and Peigan chiefs are photographed with Mayor McDougall of Ottawa (front left) *Father A. Lacombe* (front right). From left to right: *North Axe, Peigan tribe; Three Bulls & Crowfoot, Blackfoot tribe; Red Crow & One Spot, Blood tribe.*

and firearms confiscated, and now required permission to leave the reserve. The victors helped themselves to Indian possessions. Bands of soldiers and armed civilians scoured the country in search of loot. "Whatever of value they found," wrote one former prisoner in Poundmaker's camp, "was appropriated as spoils of war."[20]

The destitute Indians suffered enormously. One soldier remembered watching "a family of Indians picking up the crumbs we left behind – a miserable lot of people shivering with the cold."[21] For the suffering Indians, disarmed and with forty-four of their leading men in prison, it was futile to resist the government.

Big Bear and Poundmaker received three-year sentences in Stoney Mountain Penitentiary. At his trial in September 1885, Big Bear faced a court which followed baffling procedures and was conducted in a language that had to be translated. The charge of treason-felony was a concept alien to his culture and difficult to translate. In effect, it was explained that Big Bear had attempted to seize the Queen's crown. The Cree language contained no word for crown. An observer recalled that Big Bear turned to him and said:

> These people all lie, they are saying that I tried to steal the Great Mother's hat, how could I do that? She lives very far across the Great Water, and how could I go there to steal her hat? I don't want her hat and I didn't even know she had one.[22]

The witness concluded, "I believe the old man thought to his last day that at least part of the punishment he got was for stealing the Queen's hat."[23]

Even though much of the evidence was inconclusive and several witnesses spoke favorably on Big Bear's behalf, the court contended that the duty of a loyal Indian was "not to be found in the rebel camp, but where law and order prevailed."[24] An association with a rebel band, his established record of contumacy, and the government's intention to weaken the Cree leadership precluded any possibility of innocence. Until the situation in Saskatchewan stabilized it was better to remove the old chief from the region.

Imasees, Big Bear's son and a key instigator in the Frog Lake killings, escaped a certain hanging by fleeing to Montana Territory. When he returned to Canada ten years later, legal authorities chose to forget his crimes. Little Poplar, described by the *Saskatchewan Herald* as "the greatest scoundrel of them all,"[25] also fled to the United States. He was murdered in August of the following year. Court trials found Wandering Spirit and seven other Indians guilty of murder. In Battleford, on a bitterly cold day in late November 1885, a force of 350 police and military personnel stood guard at the public executions. The scaffold, constructed seven metres above the ground, provided an unobstructed view for several hundred Indians assembled to view the deaths. C. Whitehead, one of the Mounties, recalled the aftermath of the executions:

> The bodies were duly placed in the boxes and we escorted them to the trench that had been excavated in the frozen ground with some difficulty. To our dismay, we found they would not fit in the grave, and we had no tools or dynamite to blast the hole bigger, so it was necessary to put them in sideways.[26]

The stark burial was a tragic ending to the prairie Indian resistance against the white intruders.

For fifteen years the Plains Indians had suffered terrible hardships – smallpox, whisky traders, the disappearance of the buffalo, and starvation. Many Indians, furthermore, failed to comprehend the magnitude of the impending white influx. One young pioneer girl, travelling with her family from Fort Ellice, had recorded in her diary in 1879: "As we passed the Indians they all came out and laughed at us."[27] Yet, within six years, economic circumstances had relegated the Indians to the confines of reservations. The vast Canadian prairies were open for the settler.

In 1885, the Indian population in the North-West Territories numbered 20,170, or forty-two percent of the total population. By the end of World War I, the former area comprising the North-West Territories, now the provinces of Alberta and Saskatchewan, held 18,644 Indians, even fewer than in 1885.[28] In the same time period, the white population in Alberta

York and Simcoe Battalion, Marching to Humboldt

Not all units engaged in battle. For many eastern men the chief impression of the campaign "was the immensity of the great central Canadian plain." These troops are seen marching en route to the Touchwood Hills and Humboldt.

and Saskatchewan had mushroomed to 1,145,000 people – an incredible increase of 4900 percent since 1885. It was one of the greatest land settlements in world history. The indigenous peoples of the region became a tiny minority – less than two percent of the population – in a land which older Indians recalled as being theirs alone.

In contrast to the unhappy plight of the prairie natives and many Métis, the soldiers who marched that spring in 1885 enjoyed a great adventure in an exciting new land. Time quickly effaced the hardship and boredom of the campaign. Making tea from water "alive with tadpoles, centipedes, and leeches, and many kinds of water bugs"[29] became only a memory – something to recall of the march. Captain Hamlyn Todd wrote of the "happy days, yet they ever linger with me."[30] Eustache Fiennes, fifty years later, was quoted as saying, "I found the campaign terribly exciting."[31] For G.H. Needler, the chief impression that spring "was of the immensity of the great central Canadian plain."[32] Alex Laidlaw echoed Needler's impression in one word – "immense."[33] Henry James Grassett, in a letter to Toronto, wrote: "You can form no idea of the vastness of this land of solitude, which has so fitly been called the Great Lone Land."[34]

No soldier who marched across the plains ever forgot the magnitude of the natural elements. There had been beautiful sunsets, the magnificent aurora borealis, and violent thunderstorms. While in Calgary soldiers from Montreal had marvelled at a strong warm wind "appellent Chinouck."[35] In the June evenings, the men had read or played poker late into the evening. The clear air and rolling, often treeless landscape had enabled viewers to see great distances. During their short three-month campaign, the weather had held incredible contrasts: some troops moving north from Calgary suffered snow blindness in April; two months later, soldiers fell from sunstroke. But aside from the ubiquitous mosquitoes, as one soldier observed, "The North West had been a splendid country for soldiering and one in which the sick had become well and the weaklings had become strong."[36]

No one ever forgot the excitement of leaving for the western plains. At Union Station in Toronto 10,000 well-wishers had gathered to witness the departure of one contingent. A newspaper recorded:

> Never in the history of Toronto has there been such intense excitement as shown this morning. They left the drill shed following the band playing "The Girl I Left Behind Me." Along Kent Street the wildest excitement prevailed, the cheering being continuous.[37]

Immense throngs of people, too, had welcomed the boys home. Rifleman Forin, in the Queen's Own Rifles, remembered Toronto as "quite bewildering, thousands upon thousands met us and one continuous deafening cheer went up along the whole line of march . . . something I will never forget."[38] George Denison wrote of the welcome: "There must have been from 100,000 to 125,000 out to see us. What struck me was the extraordinary enthusiasm of the people."[39] Especially rewarding for the young men in the campaign had been the attention shown by young women. Charles Daoust, aged twenty and travelling west with the 65th Battalion, forever recalled being greeted on the train, late at night in Brandon, by "jolies jeunes filles."[40] J.A.V. Preston described his return to Toronto in these words: "I never realized how many pretty girls there were in the City and how very interesting and human they could be."[41] Back in London, nineteen-year-old Laurie Hyttenrach thrilled as girls in white dresses placed bouquets in the rifle muzzles of the soldiers. In 1885, Canada enthusiastically honored its volunteer army serving in the great North-West.

One hundred years later, a government ignorant of historicity disregarded the men of 1885. In 1985 Canada commemorated the North-West Rebellion with a postage stamp entitled 'Gabriel Dumont Batoche 1885.' The illustration superimposed Dumont's face above soldiers attacking Batoche. In 1885, almost all Canadians despised Dumont. At the end of the rebellion he was a hunted fugitive, who faced execution if arrested. No soldier serving in 1885 would ever have believed the Canadian government's distortion of history.

In July 1885 the men returned home tanned, fit, and hardened. Then, after travelling thousands of kilometres, the adventure had suddenly ended. Colonel Amyot had announced to the 9th Voltigeurs that they were released from duty and for their loyal services could keep their uniforms as "en souvenir de la campagne."[42] Walter Stewart remembered being "left alone to change my uniform and get my hair cut."[43] One diary simply reads: "Today we drew our pay, disbanded and set out for home."[44] The campaign was over . . . .

For the young recruits, this adventure on the Canadian plains never came to an end. It was, as Georges Beauregard wrote after his return to Montreal, an "expedition du Nord-Ouest dont nous garderons le souvenir toute notre vie."[45] It was, as one account remembered, "to all ranks . . . a never-to-be-forgotten and much prized adventure."[46] Late in life, looking back, Newton Myer asserted, "my North-West experiences exerted a powerful influence upon the whole of my after life."[47]

Soldier Robert Monro recalled marching northward singing his battalion's favorite song, "Old King Cole." He remembered one thousand men at a church parade singing "Onward Christian Soldiers." The sound had spilled across the vast lone prairie. It was a moving moment "not easily forgotten."[48] Sitting at his home in Ontario, seventy-four-year-old A.O. Wheeler recalled of the rebellion:

Troops and Wagons Crossing the Bridge at Qu'Appelle, 1885

Ottawa was concerned that the rebellion would spread from Riel's base at Batoche. Even with inexperienced troops, General Middleton chose to move quickly against this centre.

> I now have a disabled shoulder, the Saskatchewan Medal and Clasp, an old felt hat with a red flannel band, a pair of spurs, a buffalo powder horn and a rusty bayonet, which I use for a candlestick.[49]

Out of the campaign an esprit de corps developed that became a lasting bond. One soldier wrote of the comradeship:

> It recalls to memory the jovial faces, happy jest, and hearty laughter of the men, a jolly bunch, over their frugal meal, at the campfires, in the dusk of evening, inhaling the sweet scented prairie air, and the fragrant odours of the smudges.[50]

In the Great Lone Land, so appropriately named, the men had awakened to a clear bugle call, encountered Indians, buried comrades, endured the elements, and cursed the food – all for fifty cents a day. Robert Monro recalled that he learned to swim at Fort Pitt. At Fort Pitt Corporal Cook had nearly drowned. Here on the vast prairies they had celebrated birthdays. Richard Webb's diary laments reaching twenty: "My birthday, 3000 miles from home!"[51] While they served in the North-West, some family circumstances had altered dramatically. A telegram had informed Georges Beauregard of his father's death in Quebec City. Unhappily, it was impossible for the young soldier to attend the funeral.

Reunion of Boulton's Scouts

The soldiers associated the North-West Rebellion with their youth. This three-month adventure in the "The Great Lone Land" became a bond that forever united the men. In 1935, on the 50th Anniversary of the campaign, the men reassembled to share their experience once again.

The campaign was an experience that created bonds that lasted as long as the men lived. The great northwest symbolized their youth. For many men the campaign of 1885 remained the highlight of their lives. And, although the years scattered the once-callow recruits across a continent, time, too, reassembled the men to share their adventure, once again.

At a fiftieth anniversary reunion, a Winnipeg newspaper reported a gathering of "white-locked citizen soldiers – some of whom haven't seen each other for forty-nine years." [52] The men sang "Boys of the Old Brigade," had Alick Riel (Louis' brother) introduced, and raised a toast to their dead. Major Reverend C.C. Carruthers told the assembled: "Our comrades died for this land and we are not going to let them down. We will make this country the envy of the white world." [53] W.F. Burnham, a bugler for Middleton, played the last post and, no doubt, stories and drink dominated the remainder of the happy evening.

At these reunions the men recalled battle scenes, debated strategy, and laughed. Over a drink of whiskey, someone would ask the men in the Field Force if they remembered Shorty Niers.

> We had one man in our troop called Shorty Niers, generally called Short and Dirty. Shorty could not hit a freight car at 100 yards with a rifle, but he could talk. . . . One day he was sitting on the grass with a number of fellows of the Midland battalion from Port Hope, listening to his yarns, when a flock of ducks flew over. Shorty said to one of them, "Give me a rifle quick." He fired and brought down a duck. They thought he was a great shot. Shorty ordered one of them to get his duck. On examination he found that he had creased its neck. He said, "That was a poor shot. I aimed for its eye and missed by an inch." [54]

Tom Whitehead remembered one young recruit finally informing his family of his whereabouts. The soldier wrote: "I am in the North-West fighting Half-breeds. Good-bye until I see you again. Yours truly, George Wright."[55] And whatever became of Private T.B. Kiley? On the return home the Halifax soldier had deserted at Rat Portage, but not before thoughtfully leaving a message: "Left. Yours truly, Kiley."[56] And remember Surgeon John McCarthy's treatment for blisters? The doctor would ask which foot was worse. If it were the right, a left hand pill was prescribed; if the left, a right hand pill. All the pills, reminisced G.J. Anderson, were concocted from Plaster of Paris, pepper, and baking soda. One reunion in Toronto finally solved the fifty-year-old mystery of Sergeant Tom World's missing plum pudding, left to cool outside his tent. The culprits proved to be J.A. Forin and J.F. Grierson, now a judge and a crown attorney.

Nor was all the discussion relegated to the past. A report from North Battleford that the Prime Minister, Louis St. Laurent, had referred to the rebellion as an uprising angered Walter Gurney. Hell! St. Laurent was a three-year-old toddler when they marched north. Now he was revising history. At another gathering, in 1943, eighty-three-year-old Sergeant -Major Freemantle – "Rattlesnake Pete" to his friends – told a Vancouver reporter that he wanted to fight Hitler. Hitler! The German dictator was not even born until 1889.

At these reunions each soldier and Mountie proudly wore a memento of the campaign – the North West 1885 Canada medal. Ironically, for a campaign that prided itself on being distinctively Canadian, it was the Imperial government that assumed the responsibility and cost of minting the 5,250 medals.

What incredible events and innovations their lifetimes had witnessed! Certainly one high point was their adventure on the western plains. The men could recount to wide-eyed grandchildren stories of walking across an endless prairie, profuse with wild flowers and strewn with buffalo bones. The old soldiers could relate their adventures on steamwheelers and railcars, relive the incredible prairie weather, and describe the mosquitoes. They could recite captivating Indian names – Yellow Blanket, Fine Day, Little Poplar, Poundmaker, Big Bear, and Wandering Spirit. The veterans of the North-West Rebellion had witnessed sights that were no more, sights forever gone. Yes, it was, in the words of one soldier, "My Great Adventure."[57]

As late as 1949, sixty-four years after the conflict, the thirteen living men of the 270-man 10th Royal Grenadiers reassembled to recount old adventures. Their brochure proudly proclaimed, as always, "Ready, Aye, Ready!"[58] By 1960, of the 5,000 soldiers who participated in the campaign, only seven remained alive. In response to a reporter's question, John Smith, in his ninety-sixth year, attributed his longevity to his abstinence from smoking

Winnipeg Field Battery, North-West Rebellion

The military campaign on the empty plains of Canada molded many of the young soldiers. Newton Myer recalled "my North-West experiences exerted a powerful influence upon the whole of my after life."

and drinking. And what did Mr. Smith think of the present generation? Perhaps quite characteristically Smith observed, "They don't work like we used to. They're pretty lazy."[59] In 1972, eighty-seven years after the campaign, the last veteran of the North-West Rebellion died at the age of 104.

The men who marched north with the Alberta Field Force in the late spring of 1885, or with the other two columns, found military service a release from the drudgery of their ordinary lives. That spring of 1885 the young men had anticipated excitement. They were going to a vast, empty land to deal with Louis Riel and to fight Indians. It didn't concern them that their military skills were rudimentary, that most men had never fired a rifle. The troops had realized the historical significance of their march. They were, as the unnamed young Mountie told his riding companion, "making history, eh?"[60]

Those events one hundred years ago were once the future. On the morning of April 20, 1885, the 400 men departing from the tiny hamlet of Calgary could look at their tall, bearded commander, Thomas Bland Strange, and anticipate "a great adventure." Ahead lay a difficult assignment. The Field Force had to locate Big Bear's band somewhere – they weren't even sure where – in the northern wilderness. In all probability they would attack these rebel Indians and, at the same time, safely rescue the white hostages held in the Indian camp.

Those men on horseback spurred their mounts and headed for the cold crossing of the Bow River. Behind the scouts followed supply wagons and foot soldiers. The marching men wearing green uniforms had already travelled half a continent to be here. For the soldiers present, and the two echelons that would follow, this was the beginning of an incredible march through an empty wilderness.

About ten weeks later the campaign ended. The mounted force returned overland to Calgary while the infantry units of the Field Force moved eastward by boat to Winnipeg. By July 15th the Winnipeg troops were home and the 65th Mount Royal Rifles were awaiting train connections to Montreal. The campaign was over. It was a time to let off steam. To be sure, there were fireworks, speeches, feasts, and dignitaries, but perhaps no one celebrated more effectively that rainy July in 1885 than a nameless trooper, who, amply fortified by alcohol, demonstrated before muddy Winnipeg what life and youth were all about. Captain A. Hamlyn Todd wrote of the incident:

> The soldiers laid themselves out to paint the town red, and I was told that one of them, to mark the effort, painted a horse that colour, and rode about the town.[61]

NOTES – *the* Alberta Field Force *of 1885*

PREFACE

1. D.P. Morton and R.H. Roy, Eds., *Telegrams of the North-West Campaign, 1885* (Toronto: The Champlain Society, 1972), p. 268.
2. David J. Bercuson and J.L. Granatstein, *The Collins Dictionary of Canadian History* (Toronto: Collins Publishers, 1988).
3. Samuel B. Steele, *Forty Years in Canada* (Toronto: McClelland, Goodchild & Stewart Limited, 1915), p. 231.

CHAPTER 1 – *the* North-West Rebellion

1. Allan C. Dunlop, "Willie Goes to War," *The Nova Scotia Historical Quarterly* V (March 1975), p. 4.
2. John H. Archer, ed., "North-West Rebellion 1885: Recollections, Reflections and Items, from the Diary of Captain A. Hamlyn Todd," *Saskatchewan History* XV (Winter 1962), p. 4.
3. Frederick Middleton, *Suppression of the Rebellion in the North West Territories of Canada, 1885*, ed. G.H. Needler (Toronto: Univ. of Toronto Press, 1948), p. 15.
4. Daniel M. Gordon, "Reminiscences of the N.W. Rebellion Campaign of 1885," *Queen's Quarterly* XI, No. 1 (July 1903), p. 9.
5. David H.Breen, "'Timber Tom' and the North-West Rebellion," *Alberta Historical Review* XIX (Summer 1971), p. 4.
6. Glenbow-Alberta Institute Archives [hereinafter GAIA], Scrapbook compiled in New Brunswick, partly from Maritime Provinces' newspapers, 971.204 R 548r.
7. Donald Creighton, *John A. Macdonald: The Old Chieftain* (Toronto: The Macmillan Company of Canada, 1965), p. 418.
8. Middleton, *Suppression of the Rebellion*, p.8. Middleton's directive stated: This column, after over-awing the Indians in the district, would move on to Edmonton, and proceed down the North Saskatchewan to Fort Pitt, where I hoped to met them after having disposed of Poundmaker and his band. We should then together follow up, and dispose of Big Bear, which would pretty well break up the rebellion.
9. *Calgary Herald*, May 7, 1885.

CHAPTER 2 – *the* Indian Danger in Southern Alberta

1. John C. Donkin, *Trooper and Redskin in the Far North-West* (London: Sampson, Low, Marston, Searle and Rivington Limited, 1889), p. 103.
2. Vernon LaChance, ed., *Diary of Francis Dickens* (Kingston, Ontario: Bulletin of the Department of History and Political and Economic Science in Queen's University, 1930), No. 59. p. 12.
3. *Fort Benton River Press*, March 25, 1885.
4. *Saskatchewan Herald*, March 13, 1885.
5. *The Manitoban*, September 16, 1871.
6. James Ernest Nix, *Mission Among the Buffalo* (Toronto: The Ryerson Press, 1960), p. 67.
7. *The Manitoban*, September 16, 1871.
8. William Francis Butler, *The Great Lone Land* (London: Sampson Low, 1872), p. 250.
9. Canada, *Sessional Papers, 1873*, No. 9, p. cxxiii.
10. Cecil E. Denny, *The Law Marches West* (Toronto: J. M. Dent and Sons (Canada) Ltd., 1939), p. 119.
11. GAIA, Father Constantine Scollen, D 970.1 S522.
12. *Winnipeg Daily Times*, July 20, 1885.
13. Hugh A. Dempsey, *Crowfoot – Chief of the Blackfeet* (Edmonton: Hurtig Publishers, 1972), p. 95.
14. Alexander Morris, *The Treaties of Canada with the Indians of Manitoba and the North-West Territories* (Toronto: Belfords, Clarke & Co., Publishers, 1880), p. 248.
15. Dempsey, *Crowfoot*, p. 106.
16. Guillaume Charette, ed., *Vanishing Spaces – Memoirs of Louis Goulet*, trans. Ray Ellenwood (Winnipeg: Editions Bois – Brules, 1980), p. 81.
17. Canada, *Sessional Papers, 1880*, Vol. 13, No. 4, p. 78.
18. J.W. Schultz, *My Life as an Indian* (Greenwich, Conn.: Fawcett Publications, Inc., 1935), p. 185.
19. Dempsey, *Crowfoot*, p. 115.
20. Granville Stuart, *Forty Years on the Frontier* (Cleveland: The Arthur H. Clark Company, 1925), p. 154.
21. Ronald Atkin, *Maintain the Right* (Toronto: The Macmillan Company of Canada Ltd., 1973), p. 148.
22. Dempsey, *Crowfoot*, p. 115.
23. Canada, *Sessional Papers, 1880*, Vol. 14, No. 3, p. 30.
24. Hana Samek, *The Blackfoot Confederacy 1880-*

1920 (Albuquerque: University of New Mexico Press, 1987), p. 40.

25. Frank Fitzpatrick, *Sergeant 331* (New York: Published by Author, 1921), pp. 72-73.

26. Ibid.

27. Denny, *The Law Marches West*, pp. 143-144.

28. ______, *The Riders of the Plains* (Calgary: The Calgary Herald Company, 1905), p. 160.

29. Canada, *Sessional Papers, 1883,* Vol. 4, No. 5; *1884*, Vol. 3, No. 4; *1885,* Vol. 3, No. 3. "Reports of the Department of Indian Affairs."

30. Canada, *Sessional Papers, 1885,* Vol. 3, No. 3, p. xlix.

31. GAIA, St. Joseph's Industrial School, B1.2 .S143.

32. Canada, *Sessional Papers, 1884,* Vol. 3, No. 4, p. lii.

33. *Calgary Herald*, May 21, 1885.

34. Ibid., February 12, 1885.

35. Canada, *Sessional Papers, 1885,* Vol. 3, No. 3, p. 88.

36. Ibid.

37. *Calgary Herald*, February 26, 1885.

38. Mike Mountain Horse, *My People the Bloods* (Calgary: Glenbow-Alberta Institute, 1979), pp. 49-51.

39. Hugh A. Dempsey, *Indian Tribes of Alberta* (Calgary: Glenbow-Alberta Institute, 1978), p. 24.

40. ______, *Red Crow* (Saskatoon: Western Producer Prairie Books, 1980), p. 152.

41. GAIA, Dewdney Papers, File 39, Vol. III, pp. 553-554.

42. *Victoria Colonist*, April 17, 1885.

43. *Fort Benton River Press*, March 12, 1885. In 1884 a report from one American Indian agent stated: "In May and June there were times when the Blackfeet stripped the trees and ate the inner bark to keep their souls and bodies together." Samek, *The Blackfoot Confederacy,* 1880-1920, p. 40.

44. Ibid., April 15, 1885.

45. Ibid., April 22, 1885.

46. *Montreal Daily Star*, May 9, 1885.

47. Morton and Roy, eds., *Telegrams,* p. 157.

48. Canada, *Sessional Papers, 1885,* Vol. 3, No. 3, p. 158.

49. Denny, *The Riders of the Plains*, p. 129.

50. Dempsey, *Crowfoot*, p. 143.

51. Canada, *Sessional Papers, 1883,* Vol. 4, No. 5, p. 168.

52. Louis Cochin, *Reminiscences of Louis Cochin, O.M.I.* (Battleford: Battleford Historical Publications, 1927), p. 26. Cochin observed terrible conditions at Poundmaker's reserve. He wrote: "I saw the gaunt children, dying of hunger, come to my place to be instructed. Although it was thirty to forty degrees below zero their bodies were scarcely covered with torn rags... the hope of having a little morsel of good dry cake was the incentive which drove them to this cruel exposure each day, more, no doubt, than the desire of educating themselves. The privation made many die."

53. Canada, *Sessional Papers, 1883,* Vol. 4, No. 5, p. 163.

54. *Calgary Herald*, Magazine Section, October 25, 1930.

55. Denny, *The Riders of the Plains*, p. 159-160.

56. John Peter Turner, *The North-West Mounted Police, 1873-1983* (Toronto: University of Toronto Press, 1950), I, p. 631.

57. *Calgary Herald*, April 30, 1885.

58. Ibid.

59. Ibid.

60. Desmond Morton, *The Last War Drum* (Toronto: A. M. Hakkert, Ltd., 1972), p. 116.

61. *Calgary Herald*, May 14, 1885.

62. Ibid., May 7, 1885.

63. Ibid., April 16, 1885.

64. John A. Macdonald in the *House of Commons Debates, 1885,* April 13, Vol. II, p. 1038.

65. F.C. Cornish, "The Blackfeet and the Rebellion," *Alberta Historical Review* VI (Spring 1958), p. 21.

66. Morton and Roy, eds., *Telegrams,* p. 95.

67. "Lulu's Diary," *Canadian Golden West XII* (Spring 1976), p. 8.

68. *Montreal Daily Star*, May 13, 1885.

69. *Calgary Herald*, November 18, 1933.

70. *Lethbridge Herald,* July 11, 1935.

71. GAIA, Elizabeth B. Price, A. .P946 f. 6.

72. *Montreal Daily Star*, April 27, 1885.

73. The news travelled with amazing speed. At Gleichen, even with the telegraph, the whites were stunned to discover that the Indians knew of Riel's uprising hours before they did. Cornish, "The Blackfeet and the Rebellion," p. 21.

74. F.W. Howay, "Crowfoot: The Great Chief of the Blackfeet," *Canadian Historical Association, Annual Report,* 1930, pp. 107-112.

75. GAIA, M-260, Department of Indian Affairs, Treaty Day List, 1885.

76. *Fort Macleod Gazette*, October 13, 1885.

77. *Calgary Herald*, January 30, 1886.

78. James G. MacGregor, *Father Lacombe* (Edmonton: Hurtig Publishers, 1975), p. 276.

79. *Calgary Herald*, May 7, 1885.

80. Ibid., April 9, 1885. Many Indians had no knowledge of warfare. In southern Alberta the last Indian battle had occurred in 1870, fifteen years earlier.

81. Canada, *Census of the Three Provisional Districts of the North-West Territories, 1884-5* (Ottawa: Maclean, Roger & Co., 1886), pp. 18-33.

82. *Winnipeg Daily Times*, April 3, 1885.

83. Thomas Bland Strange, *Gunner Jingo's Jubilee.* 2nd ed. (London: Remington and Co. Ltd., 1894), pp. 406-407.

84. Middleton, *Suppression of the Rebellion*, p. 58.

85. *A Cyclopaedia of Canadian Biography being Chiefly Men of the Time* (Toronto: Rose Publishing Company, 1888), p. 790.

CHAPTER 3 – Gunner Jingo

1. *Calgary Herald*, March 26, 1885.
2. Ibid., January 18, 1913.
3. Morton and Roy, eds., *Telegrams*, p. 108.
4. GAIA, Mrs. E. Borgal, A .B732.
5. Joseph Hicks, "With Hatton's Scouts in Pursuit of Big Bear," *Alberta Historical Review* XVIII (Summer 1970), p. 14.
6. Strange, *Gunner Jingo's Jubilee*, p. 408.
7. Ibid.
8. Ibid.
9. Steele, *Forty Years in Canada*, p. 213.
10. E.A. Hayes, "Okotoks Old-Timer," *Calgary Herald*, April 20, 1935.
11. Ibid.
12. *A Cyclopaedia*, p. 785.
13. Strange, *Gunner Jingo's Jubilee*, p. 222.
14. For details see *A Cyclopaedia*, pp. 786-787.
15. Strange, *Gunner Jingo's Jubilee*, p. 181.
16. Ibid., p. 187.
17. Ibid., p. 219.
18. Ibid., p. 348.
19. Ibid.
20. *Toronto Globe*, April 24, 1885.
21. "The Bombardier: The Father of the Canadian Artillery." *Canadian Defence Quarterly* II, No. 1 (October 1924), p. 5.
22. Ibid. For an article by Strange see "Sieges, and the Changes Produced by Modern Weapons," Literary and Historical Society of Quebec, March 1874.
23. *A Cyclopaedia*, p. 788.
24. Strange, *Gunner Jingo's Jubilee*, p. 367.
25. Ibid., p. 348.
26. Morton, *The Last War Drum*, p. 112.
27. Strange, *Gunner Jingo's Jubilee*, p. 420.
28. Ibid., p. 380.
29. The cattle numbered 700. See *Calgary Herald*, February 12, 1885.
30. *Calgary Herald*, October 15, 1884.
31. Ibid., November 30, 1883.
32. Strange, *Gunner Jingo's Jubilee*, p. 387.
33. R.G. MacBeth, "With General Strange in the Big Bear Country," *Maclean's Magazine* XXVII, No. 12 (October 1914), p. 29.
34. *Calgary Herald*, January 23, 1884.
35. Strange, *Gunner Jingo's Jubilee*, p. 391.
36. Ibid., p. 401.
37. Morton and Roy, eds., *Telegrams*, p. 274.
38. Strange, *Gunner Jingo's Jubilee*, p. 401.
39. Ibid., pp. 89-90.
40. Ibid., p. 117.
41. Ibid., p. 141.
42. Ibid., p. 526.
43. Ibid., p. 397.
44. Morton and Roy, eds., *Telegrams*, p. 95.
45. Strange, *Gunner Jingo's Jubilee*, p. 414.
46. "The Bombardier: The Father of the Canadian Artillery", p. 7.
47. *Winnipeg Daily Times*, April 10, 1885.
48. *Toronto Globe*, April 24, 1885.
49. MacBeth, "With General Strange in the Big Bear Country," p. 28.
50. W.A. Griesbach, *I Remember* (Toronto: The Ryerson Press, 1946), pp. 70-71.
51. Ibid., p. 71.
52. Morton, *The Last War Drum*, p. 112.
53. Ibid., p. 116-117.
54. R.G. MacBeth, *The Making of the Canadian West* (Toronto: William Briggs, 1898), p. 165.

55. Iris Allan, ed., "A Riel Rebellion Diary," *Alberta Historical Review* XII (Summer 1964), p. 23.
56. *Manitoba Daily Free Press*, April 20, 1885.
57. Ibid., April 14, 1885.
58. *Macleod Gazette*, April 25, 1885.
59. R.G. MacBeth, "Gen. Strange's Column, '85," *Scarlet and Gold,* Fourteenth Annual, 1932, p. 84.
60. Lachlin McKinnon, *Lachlin McKinnon Pioneer* (Calgary: John S. McAra, n.d.), p. 6.
61. Ibid.

CHAPTER 4 – *the* Canadian Denver

1. Thomas S. Burns and George B. Elliott, comps. and eds., *Calgary, Alberta: Her Industries and Resources* (Calgary: McClelland and Stewart West, Glenbow-Alberta Institute reprint, 1974), pp. 22-23.
2. Ibid., p. 15. Growth was slow. Population by 1901 was only 4,392.
3. Ibid., p. 11.
4. Denny, *The Law Marches West*, p. 187.
5. George Murdoch, a recent arrival from New Brunswick, served as Calgary's first mayor. He proved to be an ardent town promoter. See Burns and Elliott, *Calgary, Alberta: Her Industries and Resources,* p. 58.
6. GAIA, City of Calgary, Official Minutes of Meetings, Box 1, f. 2., 1885, April 29, 1885.
7. Strange, *Gunner Jingo's Jubilee*, p. 423.
8. Canada, *Sessional Papers, 1885,* Vol. 13, No. 153, pp. 118- 121.
9. *Winnipeg Daily Times,* March 27, 1885.
10. MacBeth, *The Making of the Canadian West,* pp. 158-159.
11. *Montreal Daily Star,* May 20, 1885.
12. *Calgary Herald,* March 5, 1885.
13. Ibid., August 13, 1884.
14. Ibid., July 23, 1884.
15. Ibid., January 29, 1885.
16. Ibid., March 6, 1885.
17. Ibid., October 29, 1884.
18. *Toronto Globe,* July 18, 1885.
19. *Calgary Herald,* March 12, 1885.
20. *Winnipeg Daily Times,* April 23, 1885.
21. Canada, *Sessional Papers, 1886,* Vol. XIX, No. 13, pp. 1-60.
22. GAIA, Folder and clippings on Riel Rebellion.
23. Ibid., Strange-Lotbinière Correspondence, M 692, Reel 2, April 19, 3011.
24. Morton and Roy, eds., *Telegrams,* p. 172.
25. Ibid., p. 316.
26. Alex Laidlaw, *From the St. Lawrence to the North Saskatchewan* (Halifax, N.S.: n.p., 1885), p. 21.
27. *Edmonton Bulletin,* June 27, 1885.
28. *Calgary Herald,* September 16, 1885.
29. Ibid., May 7, 1885.
30. Ibid., May 14, 1885.
31. *Edmonton Bulletin,* June 27, 1885.

CHAPTER 5 – Organizing the Field Force

1. Jean B. D. Larmour, "Edgar Dewdney, Commissioner of Indian Affairs and Lieutenant Governor of the North-West Territories," (Master's Thesis, University of Saskatchewan, Regina, 1969), pp. 165-195, chapter VIII.
2. GAIA, Dewdney Papers, "Letters of James Anderson," A.D515, pp. 1523-1536.
3. Strange, *Gunner Jingo's Jubilee,* p. 404.
4. Ibid., p. 412.
5. Ibid.
6. Ibid.
7. Morton and Roy, eds., *Telegrams,* p. 142.
8. Ibid.
9. Strange, *Gunner Jingo's Jubilee,* p. 408.
10. *Calgary Herald,* May 14, 1885.
11. Strange, *Gunner Jingo's Jubilee,* p. 409.
12. Ibid., p. 398.
13. James Woodsworth, *Thirty Years in the Canadian North-West* (Toronto: McClelland, Goodchild & Stewart Publishers, 1917), p. 96.
14. *Le Manitoba,* May 7, 1885.
15. George McKay was one of five well-known brothers, Thomas, member of Territorial Council; Joseph, North-West Mounted Police; James, lawyer; and John, clergyman.
16. George McKay, *Fighting Parson* (Kelowna, B.C.: Privately printed, 1968), p. 211.
17. Ibid., p. 207.
18. Steele, *Forty Years in Canada,* p. 214.
19. For MacKenzie and McDougall, see Canada, *Sessional Papers, 1886,* XIX, No. 13, pp. 12, 42. For Lacombe, see *Calgary Herald,* May 13, 1886.

20. E.A. Hayes, "Okotoks Old-Timer," *Calgary Herald,* April 20, 1935.

21. R.G. MacBeth, "Sir Samuel Benfield Steele," *Canadian Magazine* LII, No. 5 (March 1917), p. 972.

22. GAIA, Strange-Lotbinière correspondence, Reel 2, June 20, 1885, m 692.

23. Middleton, *Suppression of the Rebellion,* p. 65.

24. Charles Daoust, *Cent-Vingt Jours de Service actif* (Montreal: Eusèbe Senécal & Fils, Imprimeurs-Editeurs, 1886), p. 28.

25. *Montreal Daily Star,* April 20, 1885.

26. Ibid.

27. Ibid.

28. *Calgary Herald,* April 16, 1885.

29. See Morton and Roy, eds., *Telegrams,* pp. 186, 200, 287; Strange, *Gunner Jingo's Jubilee,* pp. 419-420.

30. *Illustrated War News,* p. 26.

31. *Toronto News,* April 20, 1885. An angry Ouimet sought damages. In September, 1885, Edmund Sheppard, editor of the Toronto News, was fined $200.

32. *Montreal Daily Star,* April 25, 1885.

33. Strange, *Gunner Jingo's Jubilee,* p. 426.

34. MacBeth, *The Making of the Canadian West,* p. 151.

35. Morton and Roy, eds., *Telegrams,* p. 38.

36. *Manitoba Daily Free Press,* April 16, 1885.

37. Ibid.

38. Ibid.

39. *Qu'Appelle Vidette,* April 23, 1885.

40. Morton and Roy, eds., *Telegrams,* p. 67.

41. Ibid., p. 55.

42. Georges Beauregard, *Le 9me bataillon au Nord-Ouest (Journal d'un Militaire)* (Québec: Imprimerie de Jos. – G.. Gingras & Cie, 1886), p. 12.

43. George F.G. Stanley, ed., "Le journal d'un militaire au nord-ouest canadien," *Revue d'Histoire de l'Amérique française* X, No. 2 (september 1956), p. 266.

44. Beauregard, *Le 9me bataillon,* p. 16.

45. Ibid.

46. Ibid.

47. Ibid., p. 19.

48. Stanley, ed. "Le journal d'un militaire,"p. 272.

49. Ibid.

50. Morton and Roy, eds., *Telegrams,* p. 196.

51. Ibid.

52. Ibid., p. 202.

53. Beauregard, *Le 9me bataillon,* p. 25.

54. Ibid., p. 24.

55. Ibid., p. 29.

56. GAIA, Folder and clippings on Riel Rebellion

57. Beauregard, *Le 9me bataillon,* p. 32.

58. *Calgary Herald,* July 1, 1885. Frederick Ings expresses a negative opinion of the 9th in *Before the Fences* (Calgary: McAra Printing Limited, 1980), p. 32.

59. *Calgary Herald,* May 9, 1885.

60. See Stanley, ed., "Le journal d'un militaire au nord-ouest canadien," pp. 21, 224. Beauregard, *Le 9me bataillon,* p. 35.

61. Beauregard, *Le 9me bataillon,* p. 37.

62. J. Drolet, "A Rebellion Letter," *Alberta History* XXX, No. 3 (Summer 1982), p. 28.

63. Beauregard, *Le 9me bataillon,* p. 37.

64. Ibid., p. 41.

65. GAIA, Folder and clippings on Riel Rebellion.

66. Stanley, ed., "Le journal d'un militaire," p. 277.

67. *Winnipeg Daily News,* May 6, 1885.

68. Ibid.

69. John Stewart held key connections with government officials in Ottawa. In addition, his brother was mayor of that city.

70. John D. Higinbotham, *When the West Was Young* (Toronto: The Ryerson Press, 1933), p. 319.

71. *Fort Macleod Gazette,* April 29, 1885.

72. National Archives of Canada [hereinafter NAC], MG 27 III DII, Vol. 11, WJT to Lady Tupper, May 9, 1885.

73. Steele, *Forty Years in Canada,* p. 231.

74. *Manitoba Daily Free Press,* June 23, 1885.

75. Middleton, *Suppression of the Rebellion,* pp. 70-71.

76. Morton and Roy, eds., *Telegrams,* p. 115. The alleged criminal, Thomas Bell, avoided arrest and later received a North-West medal.

77. Middleton, *Suppression of the Rebellion,* p. 18.

78. J.A.V. Preston, "The Diary of Lieut. J.A.V. Preston," *Saskatchewan History* VIII, No. 3 (Autumn 1955), p. 107.

79. *Calgary Herald,* May 16, 1885.

80. R. Monro, "On the March with 'The Little Black Devils'," *Scarlet and Gold,* Seventeenth Annual, p. 55.

81. Strange, *Gunner Jingo's Jubilee,* p. 417.

82. Middleton, *Suppression of the Rebellion,* p. 16.

83. Strange, *Gunner Jingo's Jubilee,* p. 440.

84. Monro, "On the March," p. 55.

85. Ibid., p. 60.

86. Ibid.

87. Public Archives of British Columbia, Newspaper clippings of the Riel rebellion.

88. Strange, *Gunner Jingo's Jubilee,* p. 417.

89. Ibid., p. 406.

90. Ibid., p. 416.

CHAPTER 6 – *the* March to Edmonton

1. After Strange departed with the first column (April 20), Osborne Smith commanded the Calgary base for one week. With Strange's approval, Smith entertained a plan to march northeastward to Sounding Lake, then north to Frog Lake. However, Middleton overruled Strange's subordinate going "on his own hook." See Strange, *Gunner Jingo's Jubilee,* p. 425.

2. Ibid., p. 434.

3. Jean D'Artique, *Six Years in the Canadian North-West* (Toronto: Hunter, Rose and Company, 1882), p. 88.

4. Strange, *Gunner Jingo's Jubilee,* p. 434.

5. John P. Pennefather, *Thirteen Years on the Prairies* (London: Kegan Paul, Trench, Trubner & Co. Ltd., 1892), p. 26.

6. Ibid., pp. 22-23.

7. Ernest J. Chambers, *65ème Regiment, Carabiniers Mont-Royal* (Montreal: Guerdin, 1906), p. 100.

8. Steele, *Forty Years in Canada,* p. 213.

9. MacBeth, "With General Strange," p. 30.

10. *Calgary Herald,* April 23, 1885.

11. MacBeth, *The Making of the Canadian West,* p. 162.

12. Strange, *Gunner Jingo's Jubilee,* p. 437.

13. Ibid., p. 432.

14. Daoust, *Cent Vingt Jours,* p. 46.

15. C.E. Rivett-Carnac, ed., "Letters from the North-West," *Royal Canadian Mounted Police Quarterly* XVII (April 1952), p. 17.

16. MacBeth, *The Making of the Canadian West,* p. 162-163.

17. Howard Angus Kennedy, "Memories of '85," *Canadian Geographical Journal* LXX (May 1965), p. 154.

18. Daoust, *Cent-Vingt Jours,* p. 46.

19. Strange, *Gunner Jingo's Jubilee,* p. 434.

20. Ibid., p. 439.

21. Daoust, *Cent-Vingt Jours,* p. 61.

22. Pennefather, *Thirteen Years on the Prairies,* p. 22.

23. Ibid., p. 26-27.

24. This region usually experiences a noticeable warming trend between April 20 (Strange's departure from Calgary) and May 10 (the arrival of the third echelon in Edmonton) The daily maximum temperature at Calgary, for example, increases 4.5 °C.

25. *Manitoba Daily Free Press,* May 20, 1885.

26. Strange, *Gunner Jingo's Jubilee,* p. 433.

27. Daoust, *Cent-Vingt Jours,* p. 48.

28. Louis Normandeau, "65th Mount Royal Regiment and the Riel Rebellion," *Alberta Historical Review* IX (Autumn 1961), p. 24.

29. Strange, *Gunner Jingo's Jubilee,* p. 440.

30. GAIA, Folder: Riel Rebellion clippings.

31. Ibid., Leonard Gaetz, D 921.23, .G129.

32. Pennefather, *Thirteen Years on the Prairies,* p. 25.

33. *Manitoba Daily Free Press,* June 2, 1885.

34. GAIA, Edward Barnett, D920, .B261.

35. Strange, *Gunner Jingo's Jubilee,* p. 352.

36. Ibid., p. 440.

37. Ibid., p. 443.

38. *Toronto World,* May 23, 1885.

39. Strange, *Gunner Jingo's Jubilee,* p. 441.

40. Canada, *Sessional Papers, 1885,* XVIII, No. 3, p. 206.

Band	Tribe	No. on Reserve
Sharphead	Assiniboine	164
Bobtail	Cree	114
Ermineskin	Cree	118
Muddy Bull	Cree	88
Samson	Cree	294

41. W.H. Williams, *Manitoba and the North-West* (Toronto: Hunter, Rose & Company, 1882), p. 177.

42. The father of Bobtail and Ermineskin was Jean-Baptiste Piche, described as a "wild" French-Canadian from Quebec.

43. *Toronto Daily Mail,* June 13, 1885.

44. Ibid.
45. *Toronto Globe,* July 1, 1885.
46. Ibid.
47. See *Edmonton Bulletin* and *Toronto Daily Mail,* June 13, 1885.
48. *Toronto Daily Mail,* June 13, 1885.
49. GAIA, Constantine Scollen, D 970.1 .S522.
50. *Edmonton Bulletin,* April 18, 1885.
51. GAIA, Constantine Scollen.
52. Ibid.
53. Ibid.
54. Strange, *Gunner Jingo's Jubilee,* p. 444.
55. Steele, *Forty Years in Canada,* p. 215.
56. Strange, *Gunner Jingo's Jubilee,* p. 444.
57. MacBeth, *The Making of the Canadian West,* p. 163.
58. *Manitoba Daily Free Press,* May 20, 1885.
59. Pennefather, *Thirteen Years on the Prairies,* p. 27.
60. *Manitoba Daily Free Press,* May 20, 1885.
61. Daoust, *Cent-Vingt Jours,* p. 62.
62. GAIA, Edward Barnett.
63. Normandeau, "65th Mount Royal Regiment," p. 24.
64. *Edmonton Bulletin,* July 4, 1885.
65. Daoust, *Cent-Vingt Jours,* p. 178.
66. W.A. Griesbach, *I Remember* (Toronto: The Ryerson Press, 1946), p. 79.
67. Hicks, "With Hatton's Scouts," p. 14.
68. *Manitoba Daily Free Press,* May 20, 1885.
69. GAIA, Newspaper file on Riel Rebellion clippings.

CHAPTER 7 – Holding Northern Alberta

1. Canada, *Census of the Three Provisional Districts of the North-West Territories, 1884-5,* pp. 6-7. The census records:

Roman Catholics	2978
Methodists	692
Church of England	480
Presbyterians	291

2. GAIA, Letters of Thomas Anderson, PAC #636.081 .P976.
3. Hugh McKellar, *Presbyterian Pioneer Missionaries in Manitoba, Saskatchewan, Alberta, and British Columbia* (Toronto: Murray Printing Co., Ltd., 1924), p. 137.
4. GAIA, Letters of Thomas Anderson.
5. Peter T. Ream, *The Fort on the Saskatchewan,* 2nd ed. (Edmonton: Metropolitan Printing, 1974), p. 79.
6. Morton and Roy, eds., *Telegrams,* p. 311.
7. Frank Oliver, "The Indian Drum," *Queen's Quarterly* XXXVI (Winter 1929), p. 21.
8. Ibid., p. 25.
9. Ibid., p. 29.
10. GAIA, Letters of Thomas Anderson.
11. *Manitoba Daily Free Press,* May 6, 1885.
12. Ibid.
13. Ibid.
14. *Edmonton Bulletin,* April 4, 1885.
15. Ibid.
16. William Newton, *Twenty Years on the Saskatchewan* (London: Elliot Stock, 1897), p. 91.
17. GAIA, Letters of Thomas Anderson.
18. GAIA, Folder: Riel Rebellion clippings.
19. James G. MacGregor, *Edmonton Trader* (Toronto: McClelland and Stewart Limited, 1963), p. 177.
20. GAIA, Letters of Thomas Anderson.
21. Provincial Archives of Alberta [hereinafter PAA], Memories of Anna Laura Robertson Harrison, 70.207.
22. Newton, *Twenty Years on the Saskatchewan,* p. 89.
23. *Edmonton Bulletin,* April 18, 1885.
24. Ibid., April 25, 1885.
25. Ibid.
26. Oliver, "The Indian Drum," p. 30.
27. *Manitoba Daily Free Press,* May 4, 1885.
28. MacBeth, *The Making of the Canadian West,* p. 165.
29. GAIA, Raymond Gaetz.
30. Daoust, *Cent-Vingt Jours,* p. 133.
31. *Winnipeg Daily Times,* June 2, 1885.
32. PAA, Box 88, D-IV-122, "The St. Albert Mounted Rifles - Being the Personal Remembrances of an Old Timer, Miss Kate Maloney."
33. William Pierce, a well-known surveyor, claimed that some Edmonton Métis outfitted to assist Riel. See *Alberta Historical Review* XVI (Autumn 1968), pp. 23-24.

34. Strange, *Gunner Jingo's Jubilee,* p. 458.

35. Canada, *Sessional Papers, 1885,* Vol. 13, No. 153, p. 76.

36. House of Commons, *Debates, 1885,* IV, pp. 2998-2999.

37. T. Arnold Haultain, *The Souvenir Number of the Canadian Pictorial and Illustrated News* (Toronto: 1885), p. 115.

CHAPTER 8 – Downstream to Frog Lake

1. GAIA, Henry Brock, A .B864.

2. Ibid.

3. Canada, *Sessional Papers, 1885,* Vol. 5, No. 6a, p. 55.

4. *Manitoba Daily Free Press,* May 20, 1885.

5. Strange, *Gunner Jingo's Jubilee,* p. 447.

6. Canada, *Report upon the Suppression of the Rebellion,* p. 55.

7. Strange, *Gunner Jingo's Jubilee,* p. 455.

8. *Manitoba Daily Free Press,* May 20, 1885.

9. Strange, *Gunner Jingo's Jubilee,* p. 456.

10. Ibid.

11. *Manitoba Daily Free Press,* June 2, 1885.

12. Strange, *Gunner Jingo's Jubilee,* p. 461.

13. The arrested men, Garneaux and St. Germaine, later sought damages of $5000 from Strange for false imprisonment. The results of the case are not clear. See Strange, *Gunner Jingo's Jubilee,* p. 461.

14. McKay, *Fighting Parson,* p. 216.

15. Annie L. Gaetz, "Reminiscences of the North-West Rebellion, 1885," *Canadian Cattlemen* XVI, No. 14 (October 1953), p. 42.

16. The Indians returned some of the goods, but these were, in trader Pruden's words, "so cut up and torn or otherwise damaged as to be worthless." See George F.G. Stanley, "Indian Raid at Lac La Biche," *Alberta History* XXIV, No. 3 (Summer 1976), p. 27.

17. At Whitefish Lake (today Atikameg), 100 kilometres north of Victoria, Louis Way-chu-kun, a delegate from Big Bear, arrived and conducted a stormy war council. Chief Seenam, however, rejected the boasting and offers of booty and won the support of the assembled.

18. Peter Erasmus, *Buffalo Days and Nights* (Calgary: Glenbow-Alberta Institute, 1976), p. 270.

19. Two dates for the dream are given: 1880 and 1884. The dream was related to Peter Erasmus.

20. Joseph F. Dion, *My Tribe the Crees* (Calgary: Glenbow- Alberta Institute, 1979), p. 103.

21. GAIA, B. West and P. Nash, BG. 3 .W516.

22. Sam Bull, *100 Years at Whitefish: 1855-1955,* Canadiana Room, Calgary Public Library, p. 6.

23. Ibid., pp.8-9.

24. Strange, *Gunner Jingo's Jubilee,* p. 465.

25. Ibid.

26. *Manitoba Daily Free Press,* June 2, 1885.

27. John Maclean, *McDougall of Alberta* (Toronto: The Ryerson Press, 1927), p. 187.

28. *Winnipeg Daily Sun,* Rebellion Number, July 3, 1885.

29. MacBeth, *The Making of the Canadian West,* p. 170.

30. Ibid., p. 171.

31. *Manitoba Daily Free Press,* June 8, 1885.

32. R.G. MacBeth, "On the Fighting Line in Riel's Day," *Maclean's Magazine* XXVII, No. 4 (February 1915), p. 46.

33. MacBeth, *The Making of the Canadian West,* p. 172.

34. Milton Williams, "Twice Disappointed," *Alberta Historical Review* XI, No. 4 (Autumn 1963), p. 16.

35. Ibid.

36. Steele, *Forty Years in Canada,* p. 216.

37. Williams, "Twice Disappointed," p. 18.

38. Strange, *Gunner Jingo's Jubilee,* p. 452.

39. Hicks, "With Hatton's Scouts," p. 16.

40. Ibid., p. 15.

CHAPTER 9 – Prisoners in the Indian Camp

1. Canada, *Sessional Papers, 1885,* Vol. 3, No. 3, p. 206.

2. *Le Manitoba,* December 3, 1885.

3. Theresa Gowanlock and Theresa Delaney, *Two Months in the Camp of Big Bear,* (Parkdale, Ontario: Parkdale Times, 1885), p. 33.

4. William Bleasdell Cameron, *Blood Red the Sun,* (Calgary: Kenway Publishing Company, 1926), p. 100.

5. Guillaume Charette, *Vanishing Spaces,* p. 130.

6. *Toronto Daily Mail,* July 9, 1885.

7. Dorcas Alma Hewitt, compiler, *The Fort Pitt Trail* (Winnipeg: Inter-Collegiate Press of Canada, Ltd., 1968), p. 5.

8. *Manitoba Daily Free Press,* June 23, 1885.

9. Hugh Dempsey, in *Big Bear* (Vancouver: Douglas & McIntyre Ltd., 1984), suggests that Little Poplar may have had ulterior motives : "They (Little Poplar's followers) professed friendship, but likely were keeping the occupants of the fort under surveillance until others came." p. 168.

10. Gowanlock and Delaney, *Two Months in the Camp,* p. 37.

11. Ibid., p. 31.

12. Charette, *Vanishing Spaces,* p. 127.

13. Elizabeth M. McLean, "Prisoners of the Indians," *The Beaver,* Outfit 278 (June 1947), p. 14.

14. W.J. McLean, "Tragic Events at Frog Lake and Fort Pitt during the North-West Rebellion," *Manitoba Pageant,* Whole No. 48, p. 24.

15. GAIA, Robert Hougham, A. .H38 f. 6.

16. Canada, Department of Secretary of State, *Epitome of Parliamentary Documents in Connection with the North-West Rebellion, 1885* (Ottawa: Maclean, Roger & Co., 1886), p. 370.

17. Charette, *Vanishing Spaces,* p. 138.

18. Ibid.

19. Maclean, "Tragic Events at Frog Lake," Whole No. 48, p. 24.

20. *Toronto Globe,* June 23, 1885.

21. GAIA, Robert Hougham.

22. *Toronto Globe,* June 23, 1885.

23. *Toronto Daily Mail,* June 9, 1885.

24. Ibid., June 27, 1885.

25. Ibid.

26. *Toronto Daily Mail,* July 9, 1885.

27. Gowanlock and Delaney, *Two Months in the Camp,* p. 31.

28. Canada, *Sessional Papers, 1886,* Vol. 13, No. 52, p. 197.

29. Ibid.

30. Ibid.

31. McLean, "Tragic Events at Frog Lake," Whole No. 47, p. 9.

32. *Toronto Daily Mail,* July 9, 1885.

33. Gowanlock and Delaney, *Two Months in the Camp,* p. 20.

34. Ibid., p. 35.

35. *Toronto Globe,* June 29, 1885.

36. *Toronto Daily Mail,* July 9, 1885.

37. Ibid. Upon her release, Mrs. Quinney informed the Saskatchewan Herald (June 8, 1885) that the prisoners were not so badly treated as was first represented due to the influence of other bands and some of the Half-breeds in camp.

38. McLean, "Tragic Events at Frog Lake," Whole No. 47, p. 8.

39. Cameron, *Blood Red the Sun,* p. 55.

40. Examples include: Lone Man's wife was Big Bear's daughter, Kahneepotaytayo, who led the dancing performances, was married to the daughter of Wandering Spirit.

41. GAIA, Robert Hougham.

42. Cameron, *Blood Red the Sun,* p. 151.

43. Ibid., p. 150.

44. *Le Manitoba,* December 3, 1885.

45. McLean, "Prisoners of the Indians," p. 17.

46. Charette, *Vanishing Spaces,* p. 131.

47. Duncan McLean, "The Last Hostage," *The Albertan Weekend Magazine,* August 17, 1968, p. 6.

48. Cameron, *Blood Red the Sun,* p. 139. In 1886 Hodson was appointed hangman for the Dominion of Canada.

49. *Toronto Globe,* July 17, 1885.

50. *Toronto Daily Mail,* July 9, 1885.

51. McLean, "The Last Hostage," p. 3.

52. *Montreal Daily Star,* June 14, 1885.

53. McLean, "Prisoners of the Indians," p. 15.

54. GAIA, Glenbow File Clippings.

55. Elizabeth McLean, "Our Captivity Ended," *The Beaver,* Outfit 278 (September 1947), p. 38.

56. Gowanlock and Delaney, *Two Months in the Camp,* p. 118.

57. *Toronto Daily Mail,* July 9, 1885.

58. McLean, "Tragic Events at Frog Lake," Whole No. 47, p. 7.

59. Canada, *Census of Manitoba, 1885-6* (Ottawa: Maclean, Roger & Co., 1887).

60. Cameron, *Blood Red the Sun,* p. 113.

61. Ibid., p. 133.

62. Ibid., p. 84.

63. Ibid., p. 140.

64. McLean,"Our Captivity Ended," p. 17.

65. Cameron, *Blood Red the Sun,* p. 142.

66. McLean, "Tragic Events at Frog Lake," Whole No. 48, p. 19.

67. *Toronto Globe,* July 17, 1885.

68. McLean, "Tragic Events at Frog Lake," Whole No. 49, p. 22.

69. *Toronto Daily Mail,* July 9, 1885.

70. Stuart Hughes, ed., *The Frog Lake "Massacre"* (Toronto: McClelland and Stewart Limited, 1976), p. 320.

71. McLean, "Prisoners of the Indians," p. 17.

72. Amelia M. Paget, *The People of the Plains* (Toronto: Ryerson Press, 1903), p. 41.

73. Cameron, *Blood Red the Sun,* p. 154.

74. Ibid.

75. Ibid.

CHAPTER 10 – Contact with the Indians

1. Joseph Hicks,"With Hatton's Scouts," p. 15.

2. Hayes, "Okotoks Old-Timer."

3. Pennefather, *Thirteen Years on the Prairies,* p. 35.

4. Ibid.

5. Ibid., p. 35.

6. Hicks, "With Hatton's Scouts," p. 15.

7. GAIA, McDougall Papers, A .M137B f. 4.40.

8. Pennefather, *Thirteen Years on the Prairies,* p. 21.

9. Ibid., p. 51.

10. *Winnipeg Daily Times,* June 20, 1885.

11. Charette, *Vanishing Spaces,* p. 133.

12. MacBeth, *The Making of the Canadian West,* p. 175.

13. Daoust, *Cent-Vingt Jours,* p. 85.

14. McKay, *Fighting Parson,* p. 224.

15. Hicks, "With Hatton's Scouts," p. 16.

16. Strange, *Gunner Jingo's Jubilee,* p. 476.

17. *Manitoba Daily Free Press,* June 8, 1885.

18. Strange, *Gunner Jingo's Jubilee,* p. 476.

19. Ibid., p. 478.

20. *Manitoba Daily Free Press,* June 8, 1885.

21. *Manitoba Free Press,* August 25, 1885.

22. *Calgary Herald,* July 22, 1885.

23. Steele, *Forty Years in Canada,* p. 221.

24. Ibid.

25. Cameron, *Blood Red the Sun,* p. 159.

26. Strange, *Gunner Jingo's Jubilee,* p. 481.

27. Pennefather, *Thirteen Years on the Prairies,* p. 38.

28. Saskatchewan Archives, Saskatoon, Campbell Innes Papers – Angus McKay Memoirs.

29. Hayes, "Okotoks Old-Timer."

30. MacBeth, *The Making of the Canadian West,* p. 176.

31. Steele, *Forty Years in Canada,* p. 221.

32. Ibid.

33. Hicks, "With Hatton's Scouts," p. 17.

34. Strange, *Gunner Jingo's Jubilee,* p. 482.

35. Steele, *Forty Years in Canada,* p. 222.

36. GAIA, Strange-Lotbinière correspondence.

37. Ibid.

38. *Winnipeg Daily Sun,* Rebellion Number, July 3, 1885.

39. Strange, *Gunner Jingo's Jubilee,* p. 484.

40. GAIA, Strange-Lotbinière correspondence.

41. MacBeth, *The Making of the Canadian West,* p. 178.

CHAPTER 11 – Frenchman's Butte

1. *Toronto Daily Mail,* May 4, 1885.

2. Cameron, *Blood Red the Sun,* p. 141.

3. *Montreal Daily Star,* July 14, 1885.

4. *Le Manitoba,* December 10, 1885.

5. *Toronto Daily Mail,* July 9, 1885.

6. Rivett-Carnac, ed., "Letters from the North-West," p. 17.

7. Hicks, "With Hatton's Scouts," p. 17.

8. GAIA, Stange-Lotbinière correspondence.

9. MacBeth, *The Making of the Canadian West,* p. 178.

10. *Winnipeg Daily Sun,* Rebellion Number, July 3, 1885.

11. Strange, *Gunner Jingo's Jubilee,* p. 486.

12. Ibid.

13. Hugh A. Dempsey, ed., *William Parker: Mounted Policeman* (Edmonton: Hurtig Publishers, 1973), p. 70.

14. *Winnipeg Daily Sun,* Rebellion Number, July 3, 1885.

15. *Illustrated War News,* p. 34.

16. *Toronto Daily Mail*, June 25, 1885.
17. Hughes, ed., *The Frog Lake "Massacre,"* p. 323.
18. *Toronto Globe*, July 17, 1885.
19. *Winnipeg Daily Sun*, Rebellion Number, July 3, 1885.
20. *Calgary Herald*, July 22, 1885. See also Hicks, "With Hatton's Scouts," p. 18.
21. Chambers, *65éme Regiment*, p. 112.
22. Dempsey, *William Parker*, p. 71.
23. *Winnipeg Daily Sun*, Rebellion Number, July 3, 1885.
24. MacBeth, *The Making of the Canadian West*, p. 179.
25. *Winnipeg Daily Times*, June 20, 1885.
26. Hicks, "With Hatton's Scouts," pp. 18-19.
27. Cameron, *Blood Red the Sun*, p. 160.
28. Hughes, ed., *The Frog Lake "Massacre,"* p. 323.
29. *Montreal Daily Star*, July 14, 1885.
30. Canada, *Sessional Papers, 1886*, Vol. 13, No. 52, p. 195.
31. Cameron, *Blood Red the Sun*, p. 165.
32. *Montreal Daily Star*, July 14, 1885.
33. Hicks, "With Hatton's Scouts," p. 18.
34. *Montreal Daily Star*, July 14, 1885.
35. *Toronto Daily Mail*, July 9, 1885.
36. *Le Manitoba*, December 10, 1885.
37. George Mann, *The Fort Pitt Trail*, comp. Dorcas Alma Hewitt (n.p., 1968), p. 7.
38. Cameron, *Blood Red the Sun*, p. 161.
39. *Toronto Daily Mail*, June 27, 1885.
40. Ibid., July 9, 1885.
41. Gowanlock and Delaney, *Two Months in the Camp*, p. 44.
42. Cameron, *Blood Red the Sun*, p. 161.
43. Strange, *Gunner Jingo's Jubilee*, p. 488.
44. Ibid., p. 491.
45. Ibid., p. 492.
46. Ibid.
47. Ibid.
48. Hicks, "With Hatton's Scouts," p. 18.
49. *Calgary Herald*, July 22, 1885.
50. *Toronto Globe*, July 17, 1885.
51. *Calgary Herald*, July 22, 1885.
52. Rivett-Carnac, ed., "Letters from the North-West," p. 17.
53. GAIA, Strange-Lotbinière correspondence.
54. *Toronto Globe*, June 1, 1885.
55. *Winnipeg Free Press*, June 4, 1885.
56. MacBeth, *The Making of the Canadian West*, p. 179.
57. *Winnipeg Free Press*, June 23, 1885.
58. *Manitoba Free Press*, June 10, 1910.
59. Anon., "With General Strange's Column in the Riel Rebellion," *Scarlet and Gold*, Seventeenth Edition, 1935, p. 28.
60. *Fort Macleod Gazette*, July 7, 1885.
61. Canada, *Sessional Papers, 1885*, Vol. 5, No. 6a, p. 44.
62. Middleton, *Suppression of the Rebellion*, p. 62. Middleton adhered to Continental (European) military strategy whereby a decisive battle destroyed an enemy.
63. GAIA, Strange-Lotbinière correspondence.
64. Ibid.
65. Ibid.
66. McLean, "The Last Hostage," p. 8.
67. Hughes, ed., *The Frog Lake "Massacre,"* p. 319.
68. Ibid., p. 323.
69. It was a timely release for Mrs. Quinney. Within three weeks she gave birth to a baby boy.
70. *Winnipeg Daily Sun*, Rebellion Number, July 3, 1885.

Chapter 12 – Skirmish at Loon Lake

1. *Toronto Mail*, June 25, 1885.
2. C.A. Boulton, *Reminiscences of the North-West Rebellions* (Toronto: Grip Printing, 1886), p. 364.
3. Dempsey, *William Parker*, p. 72.
4. MacBeth, *Making of the Canadian West*, p. 181.
5. Hicks, "With Hatton's Scouts," p. 19.
6. Steele, *Forty Years in Canada*, p. 224.
7. Hicks, "With Hatton's Scouts," p. 19.
8. Ibid.
9. Ibid., p. 29.
10. McKay, *Fighting Parson*, pp. 226-227.
11. Ibid., p. 227.
12. Steele, *Forty Years in Canada*, p. 224.

13. Ibid.

14. F.C. Jamieson, *The Alberta Field Force of 1885* (Battleford: Canadian North-West Historical Society Publications, 1931), p. 46.

15. Steele, *Forty Years in Canada,* p. 225.

16. Haultain, *The Souvenir Number,* p. 118.

17. Details of the battle vary as to sequence. This account follows that given by Steele, *Illustrated War News,* p. 118.

18. McKay, *Fighting Parson,* p. 227.

19. McLean, "Tragic Events at Frog Lake," Whole No. 50, p. 6.

20. Ibid.

21. J.R. Henry, "Sergeant Fury," *Royal Canadian Mounted Police Quarterly* XVIII (July 1973). p. 45.

22. GAIA, Strange-Lotbinière correspondence.

23. Hayes, "Okotoks Old-Timer."

24. Hicks, "With Hatton's Scouts," p. 22.

25. Thomas E. Wilson, *Trail Blazer of the Canadian Rockies* (Calgary: Glenbow-Alberta Institute, 1972), p. 51.

26. Steele, *Forty Years in Canada,* p. 224.

27. The Indians killed were Kah-min-na-kos, Pawce-Mocees, Big Snake, Seekakootch, and one unidentified.

28. Hewitt, comp., *The Fort Pitt Trail* , p. 6.; McLean, "Our Captivity Ended," p. 38.; *Toronto Globe,* July 17, 1885.

CHAPTER 13 – After Big Bear

1. *Manitoba Free Press,* June 10, 1910.

2. GAIA, James H. Johnson, A .J72C.

3. For example, at Fort Saskatchewan Inspector Griesbach was promoted to Major Griesbach.

4 . Morton and Roy, eds., *Telegrams,* p. 238.

5. Ibid., p. 318.

6. GAIA, Strange-Lotbinière correspondence.

7. Ibid.

8. Dempsey, *William Parker,* p. 73.

9. *Calgary Herald,* April 20, 1935.

10. Middleton, *Suppression of the Rebellion,* p. 62.

11. Ibid.

12. MacBeth, *The Making of the Canadian West,* p. 185.

13. Strange, *Gunner Jingo's Jubilee,* p. 468.

14. Ibid.

15. GAIA, John F. McInnes, A .M152. Many written accounts criticize Middleton. See R.C. Laurie, *Reminiscences of Early Days in Battleford and with Middleton's Column* (Battleford: Sask.: Privately printed, 1935); Lewis Redman Ord, *Reminiscences of a Bungle, by One of the Bunglers* (Toronto: Grip Printing and Publishing Co., 1887); John Macoun, *Autobiography of John Macoun* (Ottawa: The Ottawa Field Naturalists' Club, 1922).

16. Strange, *Gunner Jingo's Jubilee,* p. 468.

17. GAIA, James H. Johnson.

18. Middleton, *Suppression of the Rebellion,* p. 64.

19. Ord, *Reminiscences of a Bungle,* p. 71.

20. Arthur O. Wheeler, "The D.L.S. Intelligent Corps in the Riel Rebellion," *The Canadian Surveyor* IV, No. 12 (April 1934), p. 7.

21. Boulton, *Reminiscences of the North-West Rebellions,* p. 369.

22. Ord, *Reminiscences of a Bungle,* p. 51.

23. Ibid., p. 46.

24. Middleton, *Suppression of the Rebellion,* p. 65.

25. Laurie, *Reminiscences of Early Days in Battleford,* p. 121.

26. Angus Howard Kennedy, "A War Correspondent in the '85'," *The Cree Rebellion of 1884* (Battleford, Sask.: Saskatchewan Herald, 1926), p. 153.

27. Middleton, *Suppression of the Rebellion,* p. 64.

28. Ibid., p. 66.

29. Boulton, *Reminiscences of the North-West Rebellions,* p. 370.

30. Steele, *Forty Years in Canada,* p. 228.

31. Middleton, *Suppression of the Rebellion,* p. 68.

32. Boulton, *Reminiscences of the North-West Rebellions,* p. 371.

33. Ibid.

34. Ord, *Reminiscences of a Bungle,* p. 56.

35. Wheeler, "The D.L.S. Intelligent Corps in the Riel Rebellion," p. 7.

36. Allen, "A Riel Rebellion Diary," p. 22.

37. R.H. Roy, ed., "Rifleman Forin in the Riel Rebellion," *Saskatchewan History* XXI, No. 3 (Autumn 1968), p. 106.

38. GAIA, Diary of R.W. Rutherford, M 4843 Box 44.

39. R. Lyndhurst Wadmore, Diary, June 7, 1885.

40. Roy, ed., "Rifleman Forin in the Riel Rebellion," p. 107.

41. GAIA, Diary of R.G. Cassels, BG. 3. Q.3.
42. Canada, *Sessional Papers, 1886,* Vol. 5, No. 6a, p. 50.
43. *Toronto Daily Mail,* July 9, 1885.
44. GAIA, Diary of R.G. Cassels.
45. Ibid.
46. Ibid.
47. Roy, ed., "Rifleman Forin in the Riel Rebellion," p. 109.
48. GAIA, Henry Brock.
49. GAIA, Col. G.E. Saunders, .5215 f. 11, 30.
50. William Laurie, "What I Saw of the North-West Rebellion," *Scarlet and Gold,* Seventh Annual (1925), p. 29.
51. Donkin, *Trooper and Redskin,* p. 157.
52. Ibid.
53. Preston, "The Diary of Lieut. J.A.V. Preston," p. 102.
54. R.C. Macleod, ed., *Reminiscences of a Bungle, by One of the Bunglers and Two Other Northwest Rebellion Diaries* (Edmonton: University of Alberta Press, 1983), p. 85.
55. *Manitoba Free Press,* July 1, 1910.
56. Metropolitan Toronto Library, Diary of Staff-Sergeant Walter Stewart.

Chapter 14 – Strange to the Beaver River

1. Morton and Roy, eds., *Telegrams,* p. 342-343.
2. Ibid., p. 347.
3. Donkin, *Trooper and Redskin,* p. 89.
4. Kennedy, "Memories of '85," p. 155.
5. Strange, *Gunner Jingo's Jubilee,* pp. 500-501.
6. Ibid., p. 501.
7. Jamieson, *The Alberta Field Force of 1885,* p. 43.
8. Morton, *The Last War Drum,* p. 133.
9. GAIA, Strange-Lotbinière correspondence.
10. *Toronto Mail,* June 25, 1885.
11. *Le Manitoba,* July 9, 1885.
12. *Calgary Herald,* July 21, 1885.
13. Canada, *Sessional Papers, 1886,* Vol. 5, No. 6a, p. 60.
14. *Toronto Daily Mail,* June 27, 1885.
15. MacBeth, *The Making of the Canadian West,* p. 190.
16. *Toronto Daily Mail,* June 25, 1885.
17. *Manitoba Free Press,* June 24, 1910.
18. Ibid., July 8, 1910.
19. Ibid., July 1, 1910.
20. Pennefather, *Thirteen Years on the Prairies,* p. 46.
21. *Manitoba Free Press,* June 24, 1910.
22. Ibid.
23. *Toronto Daily Mail,* June 27, 1885.
24. *Manitoba Free Press,* August 5, 1910.
25. Strange, *Gunner Jingo's Jubilee,* p. 501.
26. *Manitoba Free Press,* August 5, 1910.
27. British Columbia Archives, Riel Rebellion Newspaper File.
28. Strange, *Gunner Jingo's Jubilee,* p. 501.
29. J.O.M. Williams, "With General Strange's Column, 1885," *Canadian Sagas,* I, No. 1, pp. 34-35.
30. *Manitoba Free Press,* July 8, 1910.
31. Ibid.
32. Strange, *Gunner Jingo's Jubilee,* p. 503.
33. Hughes, ed., *The Frog Lake "Massacre,"* p. 324.
34. Pennefather, *Thirteen Years on the Prairies,* p. 48.
35. G.B. Brooks, "A Chapter from the North-West Rebellion," *Canadian Magazine,* Vol. 1, No. 6 (1893), pp. 473-474.
36. *Toronto Daily Mail,* July 9, 1885.
37. Pennefather, *Thirteen Years on the Prairies,* p. 48.
38. MacBeth, *The Making of the Canadian West,* p. 194.
39. Steele, *Forty Years in Canada,* p. 229.
40. Pennefather, *Thirteen Years on the Prairies,* p. 48.
41. Strange, *Gunner Jingo's Jubilee,* p. 504.
42. Ibid., p. 503.
43. Brooks, "A Chapter from the North-West Rebellion," p. 471.
44. Hughes, ed., *The Frog Lake "Massacre",* p. 303.
45. Ibid., p. 311.
46. Brooks, "A Chapter from the North-West Rebellion," p. 472.
47. *Toronto Daily Mail,* July 9, 1885.
48. Middleton, *Suppression of the Rebellion,* p. 69.

49. Laurent Legoff died, aged 92, at St. Albert in 1932.

50. Irresponsible looting by the soldiers was common. At Batoche Scout Rusden recorded (Macleod, *Reminiscences of a Bungle*), p. 291 : The fight was no sooner over than looting began and the houses were very soon stripped... the discipline seemed to have suddenly got very lax. Everyone did pretty much as he liked.

51. Cameron, *Blood Red the Sun*, p. 181.

52. Ibid., p. 180.

53. Hayes, "Okotoks Old-Timer."

54. Hughes, ed., *The Frog Lake "Massacre"*, p. 326.

55. Ibid.

56. Ibid.

57. Canada, *Sessional Papers, 1887*, Vol. 13, No. 3, Rebellion Losses Claim #126, p. 524. Legoff was awarded $595.

58. GAIA, Strange-Lotbinière correspondence.

59. McKay, *Fighting Parson*, p. 207.

60. Kennedy, "A War Correspondent in 'The 85'," pp. 93-94.

61. *Manitoba Daily Free Press*, June 23, 1885.

62. George Ham, *Reminiscences of a Raconteur* (Toronto: The Musson Book Company, 1921), pp. 90-91.

63. *Manitoba Daily Free Press*, June 23, 1885.

64. GAIA, Strange-Lotbinière correspondence.

65. Brooks, "A Chapter from the North-West Rebellion," p. 474.

66. MacBeth, *The Making of the Canadian West*, p. 198.

67. Pennefather, *Thirteen Years on the Prairies*, p. 52.

68. *Toronto Daily Mail*, July 9, 1885.

69. Ibid.

70. Middleton, *Suppression of the Rebellion*, p. 68.

71. Morton and Roy, eds., *Telegrams*, pp. 349-350.

72. See C.A. Boulton, *Reminiscences of the North-West Rebellion*, p. 374.; Macleod, *Reminiscences of a Bungle*, p. 87.; and A.O. Wheeler, diary, Wednesday, June 17.

73. W.A. Waiser, "Surveyors at War: A.O. Wheeler's Diary of the North-West Rebellion," *Saskatchewan History* XXXVII, No. 2 (Spring 1985), p. 50.

74. GAIA, Strange-Lotbinière correspondence.

75. Iris Allan, ed., "A Riel Rebellion Diary," p. 23.

Chapter 15 – Freedom for the Prisoners

1. Hewitt, *The Fort Pitt Trail*, p. 6.
2. McLean, "Tragic Events," Whole No. 50, p. 5.
3. *Toronto Daily Mail*, July 9, 1885.
4. Ibid.
5. McLean, "Tragic Events," Whole No. 50, p. 7.
6. Canada, *Sessional Papers, 1886*, Vol. 13, No. 52, p. 212.
7. Goulet, *Vanishing Spaces*, p. 141.
8. *Toronto Daily Mail*, July 9, 1885.
9. Hewitt, *The Fort Pitt Trail*, p. 6.
10. McLean, "The Last Hostage," p. 8.
11. McLean, "Tragic Events," Whole No. 50, p. 7.
12. Goulet, *Vanishing Spaces*, p. 141.
13. *Montreal Daily Star*, July 14, 1885.
14. *Toronto Daily Mail*, July 9, 1885.
15. *Montreal Daily Star*, July 14, 1885.
16. Hewitt, *The Fort Pitt Trail*, p. 6.
17. McLean, "Our Captivity Ended," pp. 38-39.
18. McLean, "Tragic Events," Whole No. 50, p. 6.
19. Ibid.
20. *Toronto Globe*, July 17, 1885.
21. *Toronto Daily Mail*, July 9, 1885.
22. GAIA, Robert Hougham.
23. McLean, "Our Captivity Ended," p. 38.
24. GAIA, Robert Hougham.
25. McLean, "Tragic Events," Whole No. 50, p. 7.
26. McLean, "Our Captivity Ended," p. 39.
27. Dressy Man was released from prison in 1890.
28. *Toronto Globe*, July 17, 1885.
29. McLean, "Our Captivity Ended," p. 40.
30. McLean, "Tragic Events," Whole No. 50, p. 7.
31. McLean, "Tragic Events," Whole No. 51, pp. 11-12.
32. Ibid., p. 12.
33. Ibid., p. 13.
34. Ibid.
35. Ibid.
36. McLean, "Our Captivity Ended," p. 40.
37. Ibid.

38. GAIA, Robert Hougham.
39. McLean, "Tragic Events," Whole No. 51, p. 15.
40. *Toronto Daily Mail,* July 9, 1885.
41. Macleod, ed., *Reminiscences of a Bungle,* p. 308.
42. McLean, "Tragic Events," Whole No. 51, p. 16.
43. Morton and Roy, eds., *Telegrams,* p. 344.
44. Middleton, *Suppression of the Rebellion,* p. 70.
45. Strange, *Gunner Jingo's Jubilee,* p. 506.

CHAPTER 16 – Heading Home

1. These included: mounted – French's Scouts, Boulton's Scouts, Dominion Land Surveyors' Corps, Herchmer's Mounted Police; infantry – 90th Winnipeg Rifles, 10th Grenadiers, Midland Regiment ("C" Company); artillery – "A" Battery, Winnipeg Field Battery.
2. Gordon, "Reminiscences of the North-West Rebellion," p. 17.
3. Ibid.
4. Archie Ballantine, "Steamboating on the Saskatchewan," *Saskatchewan History* XVIII, No. 3 (Autumn 1965), p. 102.
5. Gordon, "Reminiscences of the North-West Rebellion," p. 17.
6. George Stirling Ryerson, *Looking Backwards* (Toronto: Ryerson Press, 1924), p. 83.
7. *Montreal Daily Star,* July 6, 1885.
8. Ibid.
9. Ibid.
10. Monro, "On the March," p. 63.
11. *Montreal Daily Star,* July 4, 1885.
12. Ibid., July 6, 1885.
13. GAIA, C. Rannie, A R211.
14. GAIA, Robert Kellock Allan, M12.
15. Ibid.
16. NAC, Tupper Correspondence, MG 27 III DII, Vols. 1 and 2.
17. GAIA, Robert Kellock Allan.
18. PAA, 80. 43 F. Hubert Wood Letter, June 8, 1885.
19. *Debates of the Senate, 1885,* Vol. 2, p. 937.
20. Macleod, *Reminiscences of a Bungle,* p. 310.
21. D.G. Goodspeed, *Battle Royal* (Toronto: Charters Publishing Co. Ltd., 1962), p. 15.
22. Macleod, *Reminiscences of a Bungle,* p. 310.
23. Ibid.
24. NAC, *Reminiscences of Joseph Crowe,* M 29, E 80.
25. Ibid.
26. Daoust, *Cent-Vingt Jours,* p. 189.
27. *Manitoba Daily Free Press,* July 16, 1885.
28. Macleod, *Reminiscences of a Bungle,* p. 311.
29. Ibid.
30. Ibid., pp. 98-99.
31. *Edmonton Bulletin,* June 20, 1885.
32. Daoust, *Cent-Vingt Jours,* p. 194.
33. Ibid., p. 197.
34. Roy, ed., "Rifleman Forin in the Riel Rebellion," p. 110.
35. Ibid.
36. GAIA, Diary of R.S. Cassels.
37. Donkin, *Trooper and Redskin,* p. 156.
38. Haultain, *The Souvenir Number,* p. 78.
39. Donkin, *Trooper and Redskin,* p. 159.
40. G.H. Needler, *Louis Riel – The Rebellion of 1885* (Toronto: Burns & MacEachern, 1957), p. 68.
41. *Manitoba Free Press,* August 5, 1910.
42. This speed, based on Forin's diary, appears excessive. They average daily distance was approximately 120 kilometres.
43. *Manitoba Daily Free Press,* July 16, 1885.
44. Daoust, *Cent-Vingt Jours,* p. 203.
45. Monro, "On the March," p. 70.
46. Preston, "The Diary of J.A.V. Preston," p. 105.
47. Kennedy, "A War Correspondent in 'The 85'," p. 95.
48. GAIA, Charles Longman, A .L856.
49. R.G. MacBeth, "On the Fighting Line in Riel's Day," *Maclean's Magazine* XXVII, No. 12 (October 1914), p. 30.
50. G.H. Needler, The Battleford Column (Montreal: Provincial Publishing Co. Ltd., 1957), p. 68.
51. NAC, Diary of Lawrence Miller, MG 29, E 42.
52. *Manitoba Free Press,* August 5, 1910.
53. Preston, "The Diary of J.A.V. Preston," p. 106.
54. *Manitoba Daily Free Press,* July 16, 1885.
55. Public Archives of Manitoba, Diary of A.N. Mowat, 90th Winnipeg Rifles, 1885.
56. MacBeth, *The Making of the Canadian West,* p. 207.

57. George T. Denison, *Soldiering in Canada* (Toronto: George N. Morang and Company (Limited), 1901), pp. 326-328.

58. Roy, ed., "Rifleman Forin in the Riel Rebellion," p. 110.

59. A.O. Wheeler, Diary, July 16, 1885.

60. NAC, Diary of Lawrence Miller, MG 29, E 42.

61. Daoust, *Cent-Vingt Jours,* p. 210.

62. Robert A. Sherlock, *Experiences of the Halifax Battalion in the North-West* (Halifax: Jas. A. Doley, 1885), p. 18.

63. Canadian Meteorological Service, *Daily Climatological Data* (Toronto: 1971).

64. Roy, ed., "Rifleman Forin in the Riel Rebellion," p. 110.

65. Haultain, *The Souvenir Number,* p. 142.

66. Ibid.

67. *Montreal Star,* July 20, 1885.

68. Daoust, *Cent-Vingt Jours,* p. 213.

69. Ibid., p. 225.

70. Ibid., p. 214.

71. Haultain, *The Souvenir Number,* p. 142.

72. Beauregard, *Le 9me Bataillon,* p. 86.

73. *Calgary Herald,* July 15, 1885.

74. Stanley, "Le journal d'un militaire," p. 425.

75. *Calgary Herald,* July 15, 1885.

76. Beauregard, *Le 9me Bataillon,* p. 90.

77. Haultain, *The Souvenir Number,* p. 134.

78. Ibid.

79. Ibid.

80. Stanley, "Le journal d'un militaire," p. 429.

81. Beauregard, *Le 9me Bataillon,* p. 93.

82. In 1886, in the bitter aftermath of Riel's hanging, Colonel Amyot spoke in Parliament of his unit's reception in Ontario "where we were received like brothers, wherein we felt we were all citizens of a large and intelligent country, forming one people under one flag." See *Ottawa Free Press,* March 12, 1886.

83. *Calgary Herald,* July 22, 1885.

84. Ibid.

85. Ibid.

86. Ibid.

87. Ibid., July 29, 1885.

88. *Fort Macleod Gazette,* August 4, 1885.

89. Higinbotham, *When the West Was Young,* p. 321.

90. Canada, *Sessional Papers, 1885,* Vol. 13, No. 153, p. 73.

91. W. Bleasdell Cameron, "Rebellion's End," *The Beaver,* Outfit 283 (September 1952), p. 4.

CHAPTER 17 – Epilogue

1. *New York Times,* April 3, 1885.

2. Canada, *Census of the Three Provisional Districts,* 1886.

3. Canada, *Census of Manitoba 1885-6.*

4. Strange, *Gunner Jingo's Jubilee,* pp. 463-464.

5. *A Cyclopaedia,* p. 790.

6. Ibid.

7. GAIA, Strange-Lotbinière correspondence.

8. GAIA, Sir Alexander Campbell, A .C187 B.

9. GAIA, Strange-Lotbinière correspondence.

10. *Calgary Herald,* February 11, 1887.

11. GAIA, Strange-Lotbinière correspondence.

12. Ibid.

13. Ibid.

14. Ibid.

15. MacBeth,"Gen. Strange's Column, '85," p. 84.

16. *A Cyclopaedia,* p. 784.

17. Bercuson and Granatstein, *The Collins Dictionary of Canadian History.* The Dictionary has references for Big Bear and Poundmaker.

18. Canada, *Sessional Papers, 1885,* Vol. 13, No. 153, p. 13.

19. GAIA, West and Nash - collectors.

20. Robert Jefferson, *Fifty Years on the Saskatchewan* (Battleford, Saskatchewan: Canadian North-West Society Publications, 1929), p. 159.

21. T.E. Champion, *History of the 10th Royals and Royal Grenadiers* (Toronto: The Hunter, Rose Company, Ltd., 1896), p. 109.

22. John Hawkes, *The Story of Saskatchewan and Its People,* Vol. I (Chicago-Regina: The S.J. Clarke Publishing Company, 1924), p. 143.

23. Ibid.

24. Canada, *Sessional Papers, 1886,* XIX, No. 13, p. 231.

25. *Saskatchewan Herald,* April 23, 1885.

26. C. Whitehead, "A Day in Battleford," *Scarlet and Gold,* Fifth Annual, p. 91.

27. Norman Fergus Black, *History of Saskatchewan and the North-West Territories* (Regina: Saskatchewan Historical Company, 1913), p. 997.

28. *Canada Year Book 1918*, J. deLabroquerie Tache, Ottawa, 1919.

29. NAC, W.D. Mills collection. See Richard Webbe.

30. Archer, "North-West Rebellion 1885, p. 18.

31. GAIA, Robert Hougham.

32. G.H. Needler, *Louis Riel-The Rebellion of 1885* (Toronto: Burns and MacEachern, 1957), p. 70.

33. Laidlaw, *From the St. Lawrence*, p. 15.

34. Goodspeed, *Battle Royal*, p. 54.

35. Daoust, *Cent-Vingt Jours*, p. 38.

36. Preston, "The Diary of Lieut. J.A.V. Preston," p. 107.

37. *Victoria Colonist*, March 31, 1885.

38. Roy, ed., "Rifleman Forin in the Riel Rebellion," p. 111.

39. Denison, *Soldiering in Canada*, p. 329.

40. Daoust, *Cent-Vingt Jours*, p. 34.

41. Preston, "The Diary of Lieut. J.A.V. Preston," p. 106.

42. Beauregard, *Le 9me bataillon*, p. 99.

43. Metropolitan Toronto Library, Diary of Staff-Sergeant Walter F. Stewart.

44. Preston, "The Diary of Lieut. J.A.V. Preston," p. 107.

45. Beauregard, *Le 9me bataillon*, p. 100.

46. D.S.C. MacKay, ed., "The North-West Rebellion, 1885. A Memoir by Colour Sergeant C.F. Winters," *Saskatchewan History* XXXV, No. 1 (Winter 1982), p. 15.

47. NAC, W.D. Mills collection.

48. Monro, "On the March," p. 64.

49. Wheeler, "The D.L.S. Intelligent Corps," p. 8.

50. Archer, "North-West Rebellion 1885," p. 16.

51. NAC, W.D. Mills collection.

52. *Winnipeg Free Press*, June 1, 1935.

53. Ibid.

54. Hayes, "Okotoks Old-Timer."

55. NAC, W.D. Mills collection.

56. Sherlock, *Experiences of the Halifax Battalion*, p. 19.

57. Monro, "On the March," p. 70.

58. GAIA, S.H. Dye, BC .D995.

59. *Peterboro Review*, January 26, 1961.

60. Kennedy, "Memories of '85," p. 154.

61. Archer, "North-West Rebellion 1885," p. 18.

PHOTOS – *the Alberta Field Force of 1885*

British Columbia Archives

222	6516	Mann Children, 1887

Canadian Pacific Railway

65	8997	Troops travelling West
246	M1282	Winnipeg Victory Arch

Geological Survey of Canada

128	199537	Big Bear's camp, 1883

Glenbow-Alberta Institute

18	NA 395-8	Sarcee Indians
23	NA 3432-1	Blackfoot Chiefs
26	NA 1654-1	Father Lacombe & Blackfoot
35	NA 354-23	Blood Indians, Fort Calgary
38	NA 1847-2	General Strange
48	NA 670-53	Calgary, 1885
50	NA 1728-1	Murdoch at his log shack
51	NA 1075-14	Stephen Avenue, Calgary
52	NA 660-1	Stephen Avenue, Calgary
54	NA 967-12	Train Station
60	NA 4035-143	Lieut.- Gov. Dewdney
63	NA 294-1	Sam Steele and detachment
67	NA 1353-5	Lieut.- Col. Ouimet
73	NA 619-2	Rocky Mountain Rangers
84	NA 3205-2	Transport team
87	NA 3203-1	Samson, Cree Chief
91	NA 1099-1	Father Constantine Scollen
94	NA 936-1	View of Edmonton
114	NA 1817-3	Barricaded Transport Scow
119	NA 642-15	McDougall/Indian Chiefs
130	NA 1323-4	Crees and Traders at Fort Pitt
133	NA 4216-1	Imasees
135	NA 2483-5	Wandering Spirit
137	NA 119-1	W.B. Cameron /Horse Child
142	R 133.9	Cree Thirst Dance
148	R 133.44	Sketches of Frog Lake
154	NA 1193-9	Mounties at Fort Pitt
161	NA 1353-16	Big Bear and General Strange
164	R 133.30	On the Trail after Big Bear
177	R 133.2	Loon Lake Crossing
181	1353-33	Skirmish at Loon Lake
188	NA 1036-1	Steamer Northwest, 1885
190	R 133.55	Scouts Clearing the Trail
192	363-66	First Ford, Loon Lake
193	363-68	Second Ford, Loon Lake
196	NA 1480-25	General Middleton on Horse
198	R 133.27	Artillery Mess on Trail
207	R 133.28	Burning Smudges
208	R 133.21	At the Chipewyan Mission
210	R 133.24	Swimming Horses
214	R 133.51	Camp at Cold Lake
226	NA-3173-16	Bugle Band
238	NA 1480-37	Fort Pitt, N.W.T.
258	NA 1542-1	Indian Chiefs,Ottawa, 1886

Manitoba Archives

69	–	Lt.-Col. Osborne Smith
242	–	Welcome Arch in Winnipeg

National Archives Canada

4	PA12197	Frederick Dobson Middleton
40	C-59042	Thomas Bland Strange
71	C-1763OA	Militia leaving Winnipeg
205	C86563	"The Alligators"
228	C17491	Surrender of Big Bear
236	C18949	Steamer Northcote
260	C1876	Marching to Humboldt
263	C-17635C	Crossing Bridge, Qu'Appelle
264	C22525	Reunion of Boulton's Scouts
266	C79108	Winnipeg Field Battery

Provincial Archives Alberta

88	P131	Bobtail, Cree Chief
93	B.1675	Fort Ethier
102	A. 1370	Edmonton Scouts
116	B2406	Fort Victoria
150	B 1680	Key Persons, Fort Pitt, 1884
166	A 1461	Winnipeg Light Infantry

Saskatchewan Archives

152	–	Fort Pitt

Western Canada Pictoral Index

224	248-7924	McLean Children, 1895

R.C.M.P. Museum, Regina

105	–	Buildings, Fort Saskatchewan
107	–	Fort Edmonton
176	–	Steele's Police Scouts, 1885

Illustrations – Maps

6	–	North-West Rebellion, 1885
21	–	Indian Reservations, 1885
179	–	Skirmish at Loon Lake
194	–	The Pursuit of Big Bear

INDEX – the Alberta Field Force of 1885

Military Units, Abbreviations – Midland Battalion (*M.B.*), Mount Royal Rifles (*M.R.R.*), North-West Mounted Police (*N.W.M.P.*), Queen's Own Rifles (*Q.O.R.*), Quebec Voltigeurs (*Q.V.*), Steele's Scouts (*S.S.*), Winnipeg Light Infantry (*W.L.I.*)

D

E

F

G

H

I

K

L

M

Military Units, Abbreviations – Midland Battalion (*M.B.*), Mount Royal Rifles (*M.R.R.*), North-West Mounted Police (*N.W.M.P.*), Queen's Own Rifles (*Q.O.R.*), Quebec Voltigeurs (*Q.V.*), Steele's Scouts (*S.S.*), Winnipeg Light Infantry (*W.L.I.*)

N

O

P

Q

R

S

Military Units, Abbreviations – Midland Battalion (*M.B.*), Mount Royal Rifles (*M.R.R.*), North-West Mounted Police (*N.W.M.P.*), Queen's Own Rifles (*Q.O.R.*), Quebec Voltigeurs (*Q.V.*), Steele's Scouts (*S.S.*), Winnipeg Light Infantry (*W.L.I.*)

T

U

V

W

Y

Military Units, Abbreviations – Midland Battalion (*M.B.*), Mount Royal Rifles (*M.R.R.*), North-West Mounted Police (*N.W.M.P.*), Queen's Own Rifles (*Q.O.R.*), Quebec Voltigeurs (*Q.V.*), Steele's Scouts (*S.S.*), Winnipeg Light Infantry (*W.L.I.*)

the ALBERTA FIELD FORCE *of* 1885

Jack Dunn